Foreign Assistance: A View from the Private Sector. Kenneth W. Thompson.

Hispanismo, 1898–1936: Spanish Conservatives and Liberals and Their Relations with Spanish America. Fredrick B. Pike.

Democracy in Crisis: New Challenges to Constitutional Democracy in the Atlantic Area. E. A. Goerner, ed.

The Task of Universities in a Changing World. Stephen D. Kertesz, ed.

The Church and Social Change in Latin America. Henry A. Landsberger, ed.

Revolution and Church: The Early History of Christian Democracy, 1789–1901. Hans Maier.

The Overall Development of Chile. Mario Zañartu, S.J., and John J. Kennedy, eds.

The Catholic Church Today: Western Europe. M. A. Fitzsimons, ed.

Contemporary Catholicism in the United States. Philip Gleason, ed.

The Major Works of Peter Chaadaev. Raymond T. McNally.

A Russian European: Paul Miliukov in Russian Politics. Thomas Riha.

A Search for Stability: U. S. Diplomacy Toward Nicaragua, 1925–1933. William Kamman.

Freedom and Authority in the West. George N. Shuster, ed.

Theory and Practice: History of a Concept from Aristotle to Marx. Nicholas Lobkowicz.

Coexistence: Communism and Its Practice in Bologna, 1945–1965. Robert H. Evans.

Marx and the Western World. Nicholas Lobkowicz, ed.

Argentina's Foreign Policy 1930–1962. Alberto A. Conil Paz and Gustavo E. Ferrari.

Italy after Fascism, A Political History, 1943–1965. Giuseppe Mammarella.

The Volunteer Army and Allied Intervention in South Russia, 1917–1921. George A. Brinkley.

Peru and the United States, 1900–19.. .. C. Carey.

WITHDRAWN

INTERNATIONAL STUDIES OF THE

COMMITTEE ON INTERNATIONAL RELATIONS

UNIVERSITY OF NOTRE DAME

Empire by Treaty: Britain and the Middle East in the Twentieth Century. M. A. Fitzsimons.

The USSR and the UN's Economic and Social Activities. Harold Karan Jacobson.

Death in the Forest: The Story of the Katyn Forest Massacre. J. K. Zawodny.

Chile and the United States: 1880–1962. Fredrick B. Pike.

Bolshevism: An Introduction to Soviet Communism, 2nd ed. Waldemar Gurian.

East Central Europe and the World: Developments in the Post-Stalin Era. Stephen D. Kertesz, ed.

Soviet Policy Toward International Control of Atomic Energy. Joseph L. Nogee.

The Russian Revolution and Religion, 1917–1925. Edited and translated by Bolesław Szcześniak.

Soviet Policy Toward the Baltic States, 1918–1940. Albert N. Tarulis.

Introduction to Modern Politics. Ferdinand Hermens.

Freedom and Reform in Latin America. Fredrick B. Pike, ed.

What America Stands For. Stephen D. Kertesz and M. A. Fitzsimons, eds.

Theoretical Aspects of International Relations. William T. R. Fox, ed.

Catholicism, Nationalism and Democracy in Argentina. John J. Kennedy.

Why Democracies Fail. Norman L. Stamps.

The Fate of East Central Europe. Stephen D. Kertesz, ed.

German Protestants Face the Social Question. William O. Shanahan.

The Catholic Church in World Affairs. Waldemar Gurian and M. A. Fitzsimons, eds.

Soviet Imperialism: Its Origins and Tactics. Waldemar Gurian, ed.

The Foreign Policy of the British Labour Government, 1945–1951. M. A. Fitzsimons.

Social Change in the Soviet Union

Social Change in the Soviet Union

Russia's Path toward an Industrial Society

Edited by BORIS MEISSNER

Translated by DONALD P. KOMMERS

UNIVERSITY OF NOTRE DAME PRESS
Notre Dame   London

Copyright © 1972 by
University of Notre Dame Press
Notre Dame, Indiana 46556

Published as *Sowjetgesellschaft im Wandel.*
Russlands Weg zur Industriegesellschaft. © 1966 by
W. Kohlhammer, Stuttgart, Berlin, Cologne, Mainz

Library of Congress Catalog Card Number: 74-185408
Manufactured in the United States of America by
NAPCO Graphic Arts, Inc., Milwaukee, Wisconsin

CONTENTS

FOREWORD TO THE ENGLISH EDITION xi

PREFACE TO THE GERMAN EDITION xiii

KARL-HEINZ RUFFMANN
SOCIAL CHANGE IN RUSSIA PRIOR TO THE
OCTOBER REVOLUTION 1

BORIS MEISSNER
SOCIAL CHANGE IN BOLSHEVIK RUSSIA 23
  I. The Evolution of Soviet Society 23
    1. Revolution and War Communism (1917–1921)
    2. The New Economic Policy (1921–1928) 3.
    Stalin's "Revolution from Above" (1928–29 to
    1938–39) 4. War and Late Stalinism (1939–1953)
    5. The "New Course" and Khrushchevism (1953–
    1964)
  II. The Social Structure of Soviet Society 72
    1. Formal Class Structure in the Soviet Union 2.
    The New Working Class 3. The Kolkhoz Peasants
    4. White-Collar Employees and the Intelligentsia
    5. Social Stratification in the Soviet Union 6. The
    Real Class Structure of the Soviet Union
  III. Summary and Outlook 141

OSKAR ANWEILER
EDUCATIONAL POLICY AND SOCIAL STRUCTURE
IN THE SOVIET UNION 173
    1. A Sociological Analysis of Soviet Education 2.
    Soviet Education after 1917: Its Egalitarian-Demo-

cratic and Proletarian-Revolutionary Phase 3. Social
Differentiation under Stalin's Cadre Policy 4. The
Educational Level and Social Structure of the
Soviet Population 5. Sociological Aspects of
Khrushchev's Educational Reforms 6. Education
in Modern Society: The Soviet Variant

KARL C. THALHEIM

THE SOCIOLOGICAL IMPACT OF SOVIET
    ECONOMIC POLICY   211

BORIS MEISSNER

SOVIET SOCIETY UNDER KHRUSHCHEV'S
    SUCCESSORS   233

CONTRIBUTORS   241

INDEX   243

FOREWORD TO THE ENGLISH EDITION

American specialists in Soviet affairs have frequently lamented the paucity of studies of Soviet society, particularly broad studies which trace the evolution and development of the Soviet system and which test the models of social analysis offered inside the Soviet Union and in the West. The reasons for this gap in the literature were to be found partly in the absence of sufficient data upon which to base a thorough study and partly in the dearth of scholars trained in sociological analysis who were also willing to turn their efforts to what appeared to be unpromising tasks.

However, in more recent years much new material has appeared in connection with the revival of sociology in the Soviet Union, tenuous as it may be, and the disinclination noted above has had much less effect among European scholars, whose approach traditionally combined social, economic, and political aspects. There is indeed today a rich storehouse of scholarship on Soviet affairs in German, much of which has not been translated and hence has remained unknown to wider circles of scholars and the reading public. Boris Meissner, one of the best know and most respected of the German scholars in this field, has long been a leader in making use of all available data to achieve penetrating insights into the many facets of Soviet policy.

In this volume Professor Meissner and his able colleagues provide a rare overview of Soviet society, its evolution and change from its prerevolutionary origins to recent times. Although these essays were written before the results of the 1970 Soviet census had been published, they anticipate many of the developments revealed by the latest information and provide both the background essential for interpreting current materials and a model for future studies. For this edition Professor Meissner has also added a discussion of recent developments, particularly since the twenty-third Party Congress. The analyses contained in these studies are of major importance for understanding the nature of the Soviet system and comparing the claims made on its behalf with the reality of its achievements.

George Brinkley
Notre Dame

PREFACE TO THE GERMAN EDITION

Many aspects of the Soviet system have been subject to scholarly analysis. But comprehensive studies of social change in the Soviet Union as well as studies that seek to link the development of Russian society to conditions which existed prior to the Revolution are sorely lacking. This book, which includes data drawn from Soviet sources made available in recent years and from the results of limited sociological field studies, is a collective attempt to describe the deep-seated social changes that have taken place in twentieth-century Russia.

Individual contributions to this book are based on reports delivered at the first sociological conference held by the German Society for East European Affairs (4–6 June 1963) on the theme, "Social Change in Russia." These papers were later revised and brought up-to-date in the light of the conference discussion.

Given the research results of neighboring disciplines these essays represent a new field of inquiry. The main task of sociologists specializing in Eastern affairs, however, is to cultivate this field and to evaluate the findings of studies included here in the light of further investigation.

This book describes the distance that Russia has traveled in going from a society overwhelmingly agrarian to one that is largely industrial but has yet to reach its potential in this respect. It also deals with the social composition and differentiation that is to be found in contemporary Soviet society, the class character of which is regarded especially as a product of a totalitarian ruling system.

The evolution of Soviet society shows also that it is indeed possible to use the power of the state to develop an economy along predetermined lines, but that it is not possible in this manner wholly to do away with other forms of social backwardness. At a certain stage in the evolution of Soviet society totalitarian rule and the omnipotent state proved actually to be a hindrance in furthering economic and social development.

Social stress, which has not diminished very much since the downfall of Khrushchev, is conditioned by the stagnation that is clearly manifest in so many areas of Soviet life today, a situation that has encouraged an opposition group within the Soviet intelligentsia which maintains that Russia's only hope of entering the modern world is by loosening the grip of totalitarianism.

Prof. Dr. Boris Meissner
Cologne

SOCIAL CHANGE IN RUSSIA PRIOR TO THE OCTOBER REVOLUTION[1]

KARL-HEINZ RUFFMANN

The relationship between continuity and change is a central problem for historians as well as sociologists. The problem is most important but also highly troublesome in the analysis of revolutionary epochs. This is the case with the French Revolution of 1789 (when it is considered alongside the first industrial revolution that originated in England around 1760), as it is most certainly the case with the Russian Revolution of 1917. Undoubtedly the latter, in many obvious respects, marks a sharp break between the old and the new. But was it as total a break as is often maintained by Marxist and non-Marxist scholars? Western historical research on East European affairs has been preoccupied with the following questions: To what extent does Soviet foreign policy represent a continuation of earlier Russian policy? To what extent does it contain entirely new, i.e., Bolshevik, ingredients? In view of the close linkage today between foreign policy and social structure this is far more than a question merely of academic interest. It is of critical importance for us, politically, to know whether and in what measure social evolution in tsarist Russia has influenced developments in the Bolshevik era. To what extent can one really speak of an entirely new Russian social structure since 1917 and 1928?

1

And we cannot avoid asking how social change in both the tsarist and Soviet periods relates to developments which were simultaneously taking place in the West.

The first major attempt (if I am right) to examine this question more closely, though at the time it was not possible to give a complete or even a satisfactory answer to it, was a collection of writings by American sociologists, economists, jurists, and historians that appeared in Cyril E. Black's *The Transformation of Russian Society: Aspects of Social Change Since 1861*,[2] published in 1960. Black's book, like the present volume, focuses largely on events that have occurred since 1917 and 1928. However, my own contribution here will describe the historical background of these events. Hopefully, it will shed some light on the relationship between continuity and change as well as on some of the particular and general aspects of social evolution in Russia and the Soviet Union. First, I shall attempt to describe the social changes which occurred under the tsarist empire from the outset of the eighteenth century to the eve of the October Revolution, with comparative glances at the social history of old Europe. Second, I shall attempt to identify those crucial forces which have conditioned the course and direction of social change in Russia.

The treatment and interpretation of social change in Russia begins with 1861, as is evident from the subtitle of the American volume just mentioned. Our emphasis upon this particular year in Russian history, arbitrary and fortuitous as it is, corresponds exactly to the historical dividing line that Marxism-Leninism regards as the decisive break between the feudal and capitalistic eras; this was the year when the tsar abolished peasant serfdom.

In order to completely understand and evaluate the course of stability and change in Russian social development up to 1917 three fundamental factors, all of which deeply affected the whole course of Russian history, must be kept in mind. First was the subordinate condition of the estates, i.e., their special relationship of dependence upon the tsarist autocracy. Second was the so-called era of "social sorrow," a period which saw a steadily widening and deepening rift between two social classes, leading to the ominous dualism between a small ruling class of noble landlords—wholly unlimited in its power, at least since the time of Catherine II—and a large class of peasants owned by the nobility and unjustly relegated to a condition of abject serfdom. Third was the absence of an urban middle class in the old western European sense. For Russian cities in the Kievan Empire did not evolve like the early European cities, first, because of Mongolian domination and, second, because of the destruction of all regional and local forces by the central authority of the tsar. As a result they lacked the organically rooted and firmly anchored legal status that produced the principle that the "city makes men free." Thus a bourgeoisie with a firmly interwoven class tradition and pronounced corporate consciousness could not develop.

The following observation will help us to appreciate the significance of this situation: While European absolutism brought an end to the old rights of the estates and stripped them of their political power, the organization and pattern of a class-ordered society was nevertheless consciously preserved; in contrast, the Petrine and post-Petrine autocracy did not have to battle the legitimate claims of the estates. It was not confronted with a social system comparable to the old European class system, but with a basic feeling of dependence on the part of all social classes and groups. In 1764 Ivan Bezkov, a top advisor to Catherine II, declared: "In Russia there are only two classes of men, namely noblemen and serfs."[3] To this we can add that not only was the mass of peasants actually and legally subject to the unlimited control and power of the nobility and the state, but at the same time—since the days of Ivan Grosnyi at the latest, and hence since the middle of the sixteenth century—the nature of the whole Russian nobility was conditioned by its absolute dependence upon the tsar. In other words, the organization of the nobility was based on the principle of service and profit

in the interest of the tsar and the state. Peter the Great's famous
law of 24 January 1722 concerning service ranks, which sought
(without completely succeeding) to order and arrange offices
and honors in every conceivable area of public life into fourteen classes, marked the end of this more than a century of
internal development in Russia. The Petrine table of ranks
remained in force until 1917. It constituted the cornerstone of
the Russian social order until the end of the tsarist empire and,
as a Petersburg state lawyer pointed out in 1870 in his excellent
study of the nobility, "established the predominance of the
chin, i.e., the service rank, over the *porada*, i.e., inherited rank,
in the social structure of Russia."[4] Thus, when the nobility was
liberated from its obligation to perform state service in 1762
the basic idea behind the Petrine rank orders did not lose its
vitality, and "the nobility justified itself by engaging in public
functions graded and recorded under state service."[5]

Since the law of 1722 which required the nobility to perform
state service also enabled people from the lower ranks of the
Russian population, along with many foreigners, to rise high
in the society (occasionally into the top aristocracy), the size
of the Russian aristocracy grew considerably, but one could
hardly describe this as unusual if compared to the experience
of the rest of Europe. At the beginning of the eighteenth century in Europe, nearly one out of every hundred residents of
a state belonged to this estate; in France it was one out of every
one hundred and forty, in Hungary and Great Britain one out
of every twenty-four, in Poland—where the ideas of nation and
nobility were virtually identical—almost one out of every twelve.
In the Russian Empire around 1796, on the other hand, only
one out of every three hundred male subjects of the tsar, at the
very most, belonged to the nobility. Yet we need to remind ourselves that while at the end of the seventeenth century the Russian landed nobility consisted of 3,000 families, there were an
estimated 120,000 noblemen (with family members they numbered around 500,000) under Catherine II. They constituted—

and this figure remained almost constant until 1917—some 1.4 percent of the entire population, which in 1796 was estimated about 36 million. Only 4.1 percent of the total population lived in cities. It consisted primarily of traders, peasant craftsmen, working people, and humble servants, groups among whom, socially speaking, there were no sharp differences; this figure included a small part of the nobility (particularly the high aristocracy living in Petersburg and Moscow) in addition to some merchants and commercial contractors who either already belonged to the nobility or sought and secured admission into it. The rest of the population, well over 90 percent, was rural. These people—aside from the majority of the nobility and the clergy—consisted of masses of peasants who were owned partly by the crown and partly by the nobility.

How did this thoroughly agrarian basis of Russian society change in the course of the nineteenth and up to the end of the tsarist empire in the twentieth century? Let us first briefly consider the population as a whole. Although almost no new territory was added to the Russian Empire in Europe, the population soared from 45 million in 1815 to no less than 174.1 million in 1913. The average yearly increase amounted to 11.3 persons per thousand, as compared to 8.9 in Germany, somewhat more in England, and only 3.4 in France. During this period the urban population in European Russia grew from about 6 percent in 1815 to over 8 percent in 1870, 12.8 percent in 1897, and 17.6 percent in 1913, while as early as 1800 urban dwellers in middle and western Europe averaged about 25 percent of the entire population. (It was 50 percent in Great Britain, and in 1897 33 percent of U.S., 54 percent of German, and 77 percent of English residents lived in cities.)[6] The social structure of Russia had, characteristically enough, therefore—in any case when compared to western Europe—retained as a constant feature its agrarian character. That such a view, which is certainly valid, is nevertheless too one-sided is borne out when one considers the following five very closely interlocking factors that have influenced the development of Russia's social structure during the period under consideration. These are: (1) the total failure of serfdom as an institution, owing to the rapid population increase and the beginning of industrialization in the second quarter of the nineteenth century; (2) changes in the legal as well as the economic and social status—the latter particularly—of the Russian peasant, owing on the one hand, to the abolition of serfdom, and, on the other, to Stolypin's agrarian reforms; (3) the emergence of an intelligentsia after the middle of the nineteenth century; (4) the rise of an industrial proletariat since the end of the nineteenth century; and (5) the beginnings of a bourgeoisie toward the end of the nineteenth and at the start of the twentieth century.

Although all five factors, as already noted, are obviously interrelated, it will be more convenient to keep them analytically separate in the ensuing discussion.

Peasant serfdom, which originated principally as a means of giving economic security to aristocrats in state service and was intensified more and more in the course of time, largely lost its essential purpose and justification when state service on the part of the nobility was formally abolished in 1762. Since the second and third decade of the nineteenth century, at the very latest, serfdom hindered, even crippled, the economic and social progress that was so much needed. It was "the evil of evils, the misfortune of our misfortune"—as the jurist and philosopher of history, Konstantine Kavelin, put it in 1855[7]—occasioning even deeper misery on the part of the peasant masses while adding to the indebtedness and poverty of small and medium landed proprietors.

It should be mentioned, in particular, that between 1815 and 1835 alone the peasant population increased by no less than 1.5 million farm workers, whose incorporation into the economy rendered serfdom an impossibility. The *mir*, organized in the sixteenth century, was not a legal expression of the peasants' sense of independence, but rather an administrative device invented by the government. The mir was collectively responsible for raising taxes and conscripting men for service; peasants were prohibited from leaving the community. The excess population that was forced to remain in the agricultural economy became a heavy economic burden mainly, but no longer exclusively, for aristocratic landowners, since the nobility's land monopoly had already been abolished in 1801. And on the whole these landowners could no longer cope with the situation either financially or morally. Even when the landowner took seriously his legal duty to provide goods and services, the ever-increasing demands, which could be met only by more severe forced labor (barshchina) and higher taxes in the form of money or goods (obrok), left him no lasting and practical way out. Because of frequent arid years, causing bad harvests, because of the general backwardness of the country from a technical and industrial point of view and, last but not least, because of the irresponsible laziness and wasteful life style of no small portion of the nobility, such a critical situation prevailed that after 1840 at least 50 percent of all landed property was burdened by debt, while serfs were put up for sale (despite an official ban on such sales) for a loss, as though they were mere commodities.

Conditions in the nonagricultural sector of the economy were hardly less alarming. Since the landed proprietors, to say nothing of the serfs, had, for reasons already discussed, no real buying power, there was no domestic market for industrial products. Except for the rural home industry which provided for necessary daily needs, there were only individual factories, such as distilleries and brickworks, together with state mills and manufacturing establishments designed mainly for supplying the needs of the military. The manufacturing establishments constructed in Russia during the eighteenth century, under Catherine II especially, were operated primarily with serf labor. In the first half of the nineteenth century these laborers, including those engaged in the traditional home industry trades, along with dependent and quasi-dependent craftsmen, made up less than

1 percent of the entire population. In 1830 they numbered approximately 250,000 out of 50 million inhabitants, in 1860 approximately 860,000 out of 70 million.[8] The source of the economy's stagnation was not hard to find. In western Europe, as a consequence of the first great wave of industrialization, the economy was transformed. No such development took place in the empire of the tsar. As already mentioned, this was due partly to the shortage of capital in the country. But it was due mainly to the fact that factories operating with serf labor were simply too unprofitable to entice nonaristocratic and foreign speculators to make the necessary capital investments in support of domestic industry.

The result of all this was clear. Serfdom impeded modernization of the Russian economy and the social order. But men of discernment in the tsarist government came to realize, even before and still more after the Crimean War, that modernization of the socioeconomic system was inevitable if the power of the Russian state was to be maintained internally and externally. With this in mind the serfs were finally emancipated—though humanitarian considerations were important they were not decisive—by the act of 3 March 1861.[9]

A related question that leads us into a consideration of the second of the five factors mentioned above is: To what extent was the Emancipation Act of 1861 responsible for initiating or even accelerating social change in Russia? Anyone who seeks to answer this question must consider, at the outset, that while the peasants (among whom 22.5 million were privately owned serfs) were legally guaranteed their personal freedom in the sense of being permitted to act in a legal capacity, their economic and social situation remained unchanged; thus, whatever improvement did occur was of no real consequence. Their land, or the land they worked, remained in the hands of landowning proprietors; the peasants merely retained a limited right to the enjoyment of their small farms and the agricultural land on which they had lived up to that time, with the right eventually to acquire both. Their chances of acquiring property at this time was very poor because they were unable to command the financial resources necessary for doing so. The peasant's link to the village community was still strong. It provided him with a measure of security and, in comparison to the period before 1861, his relationship to the mir was much more firmly anchored in law. Two governing principles were operative in the mir. One was that all property was owned in common by those living on it, the land to be distributed equally or otherwise among them. The other was the mir's responsibility to collect taxes from all of its individual members; in the performance of this function the mir acted as an executive organ of the government treasury with far-reaching authority over its members. These regulations virtually forced the peasant, despite the personal freedom which he had gained, to remain within the village community. He simply could not raise the redemption money necessary to pay off his obligation to the mir, although this was a legal possibility. Because of his family, moreover, he was really not able to redeem himself and thus escape, for the amount of land each family received was determined by the number of its taxable members, i.e., male members, and naturally the community did not want to lose any taxpayers.

Viewed as a whole this comprehensive and complicated set of agrarian laws, together with the official proclamation of emancipation in early 1861, created a whole new system of economic and social dependence. It gave to the Russian masses no real freedom of movement and, as a result, restricted their mobility within the larger society, now as before, to extremely narrow boundaries. The effect was that the demand for industrial personnel, in view of scarce capital resources in the economy as a whole, was not very strong and did not emerge very quickly; moreover, this system remained intact for more than four decades without undergoing any really decisive changes.

In the meantime, Russian peasants fought "a desperate battle in a desperate situation."[10] This was a direct result of agrarian reforms during and after 1861, which gave to former serfs too little land of their own and subjected them, moreover, to a charge that was to be paid later by redemption (vykup), i.e., by paying the purchase price originally established by the state. As a result, from the very outset a healthy and self-sufficient peasantry failed to develop. Even in the large grain-export centers of the fertile black-earth region, the peasant was for the most part unable to provide his family with the minimum necessities of life. He simply could not liquidate his financial burdens, levied very unfairly on his land when in comparison to that of the large landed proprietor; as a result, he sank deeper and deeper into debt.

In order to shed more light on this development the following factors should be noted:[11] While the peasant population more than doubled between 1861 and 1905, the agricultural land which belonged to the peasants increased by only a tenth. In 1905 it amounted to scarcely 160 million hectares, somewhat over 38 percent of all owned land in the central area of Russia (excluding Poland, the eastern sea provinces, and Finland). Through the continuous apportionment and division of peasant land the average size of the Russian farm unit declined from 14.43 hectares in 1877 to 11.47 in 1905. The area of community-owned land was not sufficient, as indicated by the official statistics of 1897, to cover the personal needs of 71 percent of the peasants or to support the livestock of 20 percent of them. The need and desire for land, the unbearable tax burden, the inability to leave the mir, and many frightful incidents of famine owing to bad harvests (especially between 1891 and 1901) combined to engender a social upsurge that caused peasant unrest in an increasing number of localities and regions, culminating finally in the revolutionary explosion of 1905.

Until 1905 the landowning nobility and the bureaucracy regarded the mir as a secure institution and as the best instrument for the maintenance of the agrarian order that was established in 1861. This first revolution, however, brought about a change in the organization of the mir. Now socially conservative circles saw everywhere in the dissolution of the mir an excellent means for deflecting the peasant's hunger for land, insofar as possible, away from their own large landholdings. In addition to this P. S. Stolypin, Minister of the Interior since 1906 and later Minister President, introduced a new agrarian policy with the clear purpose of "creating a society based economically on ownership of property by individual peasants."[12] Stolypin's first agrarian law of November 1906 finally granted a peasant the freedom to leave the mir with the right to keep the land that was previously assigned to him and to work it as his own personal property. The uneconomical layout of land could be avoided by the proposal to consolidate landholdings. In this way a really viable and profitable farm economy based on private enterprise—a singular event in recent Russian social history—was established, actually on the initiative of the state. To be sure, these economic units were confined to a total of 13 million hectares in 1913, only 10 percent of the land occupied by the peasants; moreover this land served the needs of only two million farmsteads.

So much depended on whether and in what form the additional procurement and consolidation of agricultural land would be introduced. Actually Stolypin's agrarian reforms got at the problem in two ways. One approach was for the state farm bank, which was established at the beginning of the 1880s, to help peasants meet their financial obligations to the landowners and to transfer large areas of royal dependencies and state-owned property, as well as certain properties of private landowners, to peasants on relatively easy credit terms. In this way over 98,000 square meters of land—an area greater than the entire German Reich at the time—were put into peasant hands between 1906 and 1910 alone. It is worth noting, in addition, that in 1906 only 18.7 percent of those who borrowed from the farm bank were individual peasants; six years later the figure was 82.9 percent. About the same time the peasants proceeded to systematize and modernize their methods of operation and to form agricultural associations. It is also worth mentioning that from 1905 until the outbreak of World War I the number of these associations grew from 5,000 to 32,000 while their membership increased from one to ten million.

A second Stolypin reform to redistribute the land was designed to encourage peasants to settle and acquire new land in the Asiatic parts of the Russian Empire, mainly Siberia, the Altaic region, central Asia, and Caucasia. Since the 1880s an erratically growing stream of poor, land-hungry peasants (74,000 of them in 1881 and as many as 280,000 in 1900) had poured over the Urals toward the East in a totally unplanned and uncontrolled migration. Stolypin and his agrarian reforms are to be credited with giving direction to this movement by the construction of a new railroad network which accelerated the eastward flow of peasants. By 1914, despite many setbacks and losses, 3.5 million peasants (2.15 million since Stolypin's settlement policy was introduced in 1906) had permanently settled in Siberia and middle Asia.

The most interesting and important result of Stolypin's reform policies is that they were responsible for bringing about and hastening far-reaching differentiation within the peasant population of Russia. This is of utmost importance because the Russian village—despite much wishful thinking to the contrary—was no longer an absolutely homogeneous social structure. With regard to the extent and depth of this slowly evolving change the following two points should be stressed: On the one hand, Stolypin's policies resulted in the rise of the kulaks, a class of independent peasants who were very well-off, but not, as a rule, really wealthy, by Western standards at least. On the other hand, the deep poverty of the village, inhabited by a large peasant proletarian population, stood out in very sharp contrast to the kulaks; these peasants, owing to lack of opportunity or weakness of will, did not succeed in liberating themselves from the mir and, as a result, they and members of their families had to hire themselves out to large landowners or kulaks. And so there was virtually no chance to found and consolidate a farm economy based on individual enterprise which would keep pace with the extraordinary growth of the peasant population. Until 1917, immediately after the outbreak of the revolution, only some 30 percent of the peasants really owned their own land. The need and hunger for property on the part of the peasant masses who remained in the mir became more and more pressing; together with some 15 million peasants who served in the war they constituted a broad and easy target for radical propaganda and revolutionary activity; the depth and dynamism of the 1917 Revolution owed much to this group.

Probably the greatest and most ominous problem that afflicted agriculture, rendering any solution to the problem absolutely impossible during the course of the nineteenth century, was the fact that a fundamentally long-term reconstruction and healthy stabilization of the social order by satisfying the peasants with a timely yet radical expropriation of large landholdings was not feasible. This was so because the nobility constituted the only independent class whose support could be counted upon and because Russia lacked an influential middle class during the entire nineteenth century. Such a class might possibly have constituted a new basis for the tsarist regime; in addition, as an independent group of shop assistants and as the engine responsible for powering a newly emerging industrial society, it could have absorbed the landless peasant masses into the industrial proletariat.

Russian cities, measured in terms of their population and size (ignoring for the moment the principal cities of Petersburg and Moscow), were not very important, as already mentioned; fundamentally they were burdened by a century-long absence of an autonomous economic and cultural life. Thus, it is of little wonder that the newly passed ordinances of 1846 and 1870 were not able to establish genuine self-government any more than were the documents of grace issued by Catherine II for the cities in 1785. In the words of Werner Philipp, what was lacking at the beginning of the new era in western Europe was "that important conjunction of the professional organization of crafts and specialized labor with the religious justification of secular vocations and personal responsibility, together with an open-minded, humanistically grounded culture."

This leads us to inquire—and thus we come to the third factor—into the origin and sociological classification of the Russian intelligentsia of the nineteenth century.

The term *intelligentsia*, which denotes a given attitude in both an intellectual-cultural and sociopolitical sense, first appeared in the Russian language around 1860 and then became a matter of common usage.[14] Yet this group can doubtless trace its origin back to 1830–1840 when the Russian educated class, under the influence of German idealism, brought about a basic change in attitudes. By the Russian intelligentsia one understands generally a middle class which has emerged gradually since that decade and stands midway between the nobility and the bureaucracy, on the one hand, and the peasant masses, on the other; in terms of its political radicalism, at least, it quickly surpassed that of contemporary thought in Germany. Actually the Russian intelligentsia, which was marked by the predominance of ideologists, was not in any real sense a middle class, but rather an intellectual movement which at first (up to about 1860) was comprised almost exclusively of deposed aristocrats, while afterwards it was constituted mainly but not entirely of people in the liberal professions: publicists, literati, doctors, lawyers, students, teachers, sons of priests, etc.—in short, a radical intellectual elite, something quite beyond the traditional classes and categories to which we are accustomed. The intelligentsia was chiefly characterized by three things: (1) its advanced education, particularly in philosophy and natural science, (2) its concern for social justice and opposition to the tsar, and (3) its characteristic fanatical-messianic feeling of moral solidarity, so much so that one could occasionally regard it as a kind of order. This meant that the intelligentsia was less a sociological phenomenon than a mental attitude.

The members of the intelligentsia were clearly "alienated" and frequently "declassed" intellectuals, whether they were revolutionary or not: alienated insofar as they fell outside of the existing class structure, having consciously removed themselves from it; declassed insofar as they disassociated themselves from their earlier social status. One of the main characteristics of the Russian intelligentsia was that it no longer fit into the system of officially existing and recognized classes and groups. Hence the intelligentsia could hardly be regarded as a social class. Also numerically the intelligentsia did not constitute a social class, but it did represent a very real political threat which for decades gave more trouble to the autocracy than did the nobility or—as is true after 1905—the emerging bourgeoisie. Its influence upon the course of internal Russian history in the last decade of the tsarist empire was substantial, for the intelligentsia prepared the way for almost all progressive and radical endeavors. The intelligentsia sprouted Narodniki, anarchists, Socialist Revolutionaries, and Marxists, on the one hand, and Russian liberals, on the other hand. As is well known, the spirit of the radical intelligentsia had penetrated the leadership of no party as much as it did the Bolsheviks; such Russian intellectuals became the prototypes of a new leadership class (in contrast to Western social democratic parties whose membership includes the broad working masses and where union leaders are usually in positions of party leadership).

In his contribution to the multi-authored volume edited by Richard Pipes, *The Russian Intelligentsia*, Martin Malia says: "Paradoxically, it was the disintegration of the social system which had brought the intelligentsia into being that at last gave it a chance to act. So long as Russian society remained simple, the intelligentsia failed to make contact with the masses because the very brutality of social relationships made it easy for the autocracy to keep the peasants in hand. In the 1890s, however, under the impact of rapid industrialization, Russian society began to develop the diversity of modern social classes common to the West. . . . From 1906 on there was even a parliament, and politics became legal for the first time in modern Russian history."[15] Consequently, continues Malia, it "became possible for the less alienated intellectuals to adapt to the real world," while "bands of die-hard intelligentsia exiles, such as that grouped around Lenin, were becoming increasingly anachronistic."

Rather than continuing with this line of thought, let us consider further Malia's reference to "the diversity of modern social classes." This obviously involves looking into the origin of the industrial proletariat and the bourgeoisie after the time of the tsar (corresponding to our fourth and fifth considerations). Both factors were a natural consequence of Russia's industrialization, which, together with the agrarian law of 1861, created the first important condition for the rise of a socio-economic order rooted in capitalism. Indeed it is almost impossible to speak of such an order existing in the 1860s, let alone being firmly established.

Agreeing at least in part with some Soviet historians, Roger Portal has characterized the 1870s as the decisive "onset phase" of the so-called "industrial revolution" or, better still, of the "industrial upswing" in Russia, "because at that time . . . technical progress accelerated very quickly while the labor market (because of the peasant law of 1861) opened up, resulting in deep-seated changes in the social structure."[16] On the other hand, the noted French authority denied that the "general upheaval in Russian society" was a direct consequence of an "uncompleted" industrial revolution at the very end of the nineteenth century.

Thus, it appears opportune, first of all, to mention certain dates and facts relating to technical and industrial developments in Russia for which the state was almost exclusively responsible.[17] As is well-known the steam engine was the classical sign of technical progress in the nineteenth century. Beginning in the

1840s, and particularly the 1860s, it started to play a certain role but one that was not yet really decisive. This was not true, however, with respect to the textile industry in the area of Moscow and the metallurgical enterprises in the Urals, both of which at that time were the most important branches of industry. Production in the Ural industries—to add a marginal notation to Portal's observation about the opening of the labor market—lagged considerably in the 1860s because factories, following the liberation of the peasants, lost part of their working force; up to that time they employed only serf labor. Far more important than this transitional, and certainly not unsymptomatic, phenomenon was clearly the construction and expansion of an extensive railway network during the last quarter of the century. Since 1870, and especially since 1890, there has also been a major upswing in the development of heavy industry, followed by the rise of numerous other branches of industry. The yearly rate of industrial growth soared to 8 percent in the 1890s, reaching a level that was then unmatched by any other industrial nation in the West.

This development in the economic life of Russia, sketched here only in very rough outline, was quickly and inexorably followed by the rapid growth of an industrial proletariat. From 1830 to 1860, as already mentioned, the total number of factory workers—most of whom were serf laborers (for example, in the mining industry), although some were already wage earners (in Moscow textile factories)—was less than 1 percent of the entire population. Between 1860 and 1900 this figure doubled. In 1897, out of a population of 129 million, at least 2.5 million were factory workers, possibly even more; after 1900 the figure climbed very quickly to over 3 million, amounting to 2.3 percent of the entire population, which when compared to western Europe was an extraordinary low figure. It is therefore all the more noteworthy and astonishing that this small and recent social class, whose living and working conditions—very much like those in the early days of Western capitalism—improved only very slowly because of the almost total lack of protective social and labor legislation, should emerge as the most powerful dynamic force during the first Russian revolution in 1905. The situation could hardly have been otherwise at a time when there were still so very few central industrial areas with high concentrations of population; only in such areas was the reconstruction of the social order possible. It did occur, for example, in the highly populated centers of Petersburg and Moscow, where in 1897 the population already totaled 1.26 and 1.03 million inhabitants respectively.

Also important is the fact that—in contrast to most industrialized Western countries where the working class traces its origin partly to craftsmen and the petty bourgeoisie—the first generation of Russian factory workers consisted exclusively of proletarianized peasants who, insofar as they had not before worked for wages in factories connected with the estates or in domestic home trades, remained chained to their old village community by their tax obligations and by their claim to a share of the family land. Not by chance then did the Narodniki (and later the Socialist Revolutionaries) represent the view that the Russian worker was in reality a peasant employed temporarily in the factory and hence could not be regarded as a proletarian in the ordinary sense of the word. Actually this traditional view had already lost its validity in the 1890s when the worker's link to the village community was severed by the Stolypin reforms of 1906–1910. Yet, toward the end of this period and especially with respect to the situation in 1917, the year of the revolution, one has to ascribe considerable importance to the reality of peasant social-revolutionary thought and action among Russian workers, whose makeup had changed considerably during the World War. No less important was the fact that many of them had been drafted into military service; their places were taken by untrained laborers who were recruited from the villages. Approximately 400,000 industrial workers were recruited also from the same source; they were needed to build the war industries. The importance of this event is indicated by Gunther Stokls brief comment: ". . . as a consequence the opportunities for agitation mounted, resembling the rising of Pugachev, while signs of a socialist consciousness could be seen on the horizon."[18]

Here, once again, in contrast to old Europe, a clear and extremely momentous event appears in Russian society at the beginning of the twentieth century; we are able to note likewise that the development of the Russian bourgeoisie—the "forgotten class" as one author put it[19]—was held up for an extremely long period of time. The industrial boom of the 1890s produced not only (as was the case with the early period of German development) greedy speculators and newly rich parvenus, whose sharp rise ended just as quickly; for the first time, also, there now emerged an independent and self-conscious upper bourgeoisie, which was economically tied to the business upswing and distinguished itself, moreover, by liberally patronizing the arts. In 1897 the upper bourgeoisie constituted about 1 percent of the entire population, while the middle and lower bourgeoisie amounted to around 4 percent. The bourgeoisie then grew erratically (among other things this resulted in an increase in the urban population of over 5 percent), rapidly gained in economic strength, and as a consequence represented a new and important factor in the political system. Politically it was oriented largely toward the liberal center of the political spectrum. Its cultural influence, because it lacked a tradition of its own, was spotty and still quite negligible. The original non-Russian element within the bourgeoisie is also worth noting here; it included numerous Germans and Jews who played a particularly important role in finance and industry, which "for them was the best way of climbing the social ladder and getting out of those narrow confines of West Russia where they had settled."[20] In 1913 the upper and middle social classes, including the trading sector and the kulaks, constituted 15.9 percent of the entire population. Workers and white-collar employees totaled 16.7

percent of the population, while 65.1 percent was made up of individual peasants and homeworkers.

From all this we may set forth the following propositions: On the eve of the revolutionary events of 1917, Russia found herself, despite the dominance of the agricultural economy, moving toward social change of the most basic kind—nothing less really than deep-seated social reconstruction and modernization. The backwardness of Russia, in contrast to the socioeconomic order in contemporary West Europe, was rooted mainly in the century-long absence of a bourgeoisie, in the equally long continuance of peasant serfdom, and in the lack of any dialogue between state and society.

NOTES

1. This article merely sketches events in the Russian heartland and does not treat the question of social change involving the non-Russian nationalities inside the tsarist empire.

2. Cambridge, Massachusetts. Regarding this subject see, above all, the articles by Gerschenkron, Eason, Von Laue, Feldmesser, Fischer, Volin, and Gliksman which appear in this book.

3. *Polnoe sobranie zakonov Rossiiskoi imperii s 1649 goda* (St. Petersburg, 1830) vol. XVI, no. 12103. For subsequent descriptions of social relations in Russia during the eighteenth century see K. H. Ruffmann, "Russischer Adel als Sondertypus der europäischen Adelswelt" in *Jahrbücher f. Geschichte Osteuropas* 9, n. s. (1961), p. 161 ff.

4. A. Romanovich-Slavatinskii, *Dvorianstvo v Rossii ot nachala XVIII v. do otmeny krepostnogo prava* (St. Petersburg, 1870), 2nd ed. (Kiev, 1912), p. 16.

5. R. Wittram, *Peter der Grosse: Der Eintritt Russlands in die Neuzeit* (Berlin-Göttingen-Heidelberg, 1954), p. 124.

6. The figures were taken from C. E. Black, ed., *The Transformation of Russian Society*, p. 72 ff.; W. Philipp, *Russlands Aufstieg zur Weltmacht 1815–1917; Historia Mundi*, vol. X; *19. und 20. Jahrhundert* (Bern and Munich, 1961), p. 185 ff.; and W. Treue, "Das wirtschaftliche und soziale Gefuge" in *ibid.*, p. 546 ff.

7. Quoted from K. Stahlin, *Geschichte Russlands von den Anfängen bis zur Gegenwart*, vol. IV, part 1 (Graz, 1961), p. 50. Concerning the social and economic situation in Russia before 1861 see J. Blum, *Lord and Peasant in Russia from the Ninth to the Nineteenth Century* (New York, 1961), esp. p. 277 ff.; R. Stupperich, *Die Anfänge der Bauernbefreiung in Russland* (Berlin, 1939); P. I. Liashchenko, *Istoriia narodnogo khoziaistva SSSR*, vol. I (Moscow, 1952), p. 453 ff.; *Ocherki ekonomicheskoi istorii Rossii pervoi polovini XIX veka. Sbornik statei*, M. K. Rozkova, ed. (Moscow, 1959). See, moreover, the short overview by W. Philipp, *Russlands Aufstieg*, p. 187 ff. and G. Stokl, *Russische Geschichte von den Anfängen bis zur Gegenwart* (Stuttgart, 1962), pp. 485–487.

8. R. Portal, "Das Problem einer industriellen Revolution in Russland im 19. Jahrhundert" in *Forschungen zur osteuropäischen Geschichte* 1 (Berlin, 1954), p. 211.

9. For the text of the liberation proclamation and law see *Polnoe sobranie zakonov*, 2nd ser., vol. XXXVI, no. 35657. Other major sources are: *Krest'ianskaia reforma v Rossii 1861 goda. Sbornik zakonodatel'nikh aktov* (Moscow, 1954); *Otmena krepostnogo prava. Doklady ministrov vnutrennikh del o provedenii krest'ianskoi reformy 1861–1862* (Moscow, 1952);

A. S. Nifontov, B. V. Zlatustovskii, eds., *Krest'ianskoe dvizhenie v Rossii v 1881–1889 gg. Sbornik dokumentov*, (Moscow, 1960). The rich literature on the liberation of the peasants includes the following prominent works: G. T. Robinson, *Rural Russia under the Old Regime*, 3rd ed. (New York, 1961); A. A. Kornilov, *Krest'ianskaia reforma*, (St. Petersburg, 1905); Dzhivelegov, Mel'gunov, Picheta, eds., *Velikaia reforma. Russkoe obshchestvo i krest'ianskii vopros v proshlom i nastoiaschem*, 6 vols. (Moscow, 1911); P. A. Zaionchkovskii, *Otmeny krepostnogo prava v Rossii* (Moscow, 1954).

10. G. T. Robinson, *Rural Russia*, p. 94.

11. In this connection see especially the data and figures from W. Philipp, *Russlands Aufstieg*, pp. 208 and 211; G. T. Robinson, *Rural Russia*, p. 94 ff., and E. Amburger, "Staat und Gesellschaft in Russland am Vorabend der Oktober-revolution" in *Sowjetunion, Werden und Gestalt einer Weltmacht*, (von H. Ludat, ed. Giessen, 1962), p. 53 ff.

12. G. Stokl, *Russische Geschichte*, pp. 605–608; See also P. A. Kriwoshein and P. A. Stolypin, *Die Kolonisation Sibiriens* (Berlin, 1912); C. v. Dietze, *Die Stolypinsche Agrarreform und Feldgmeinschaft* (Breslau, 1920); from the Soviet side see S. M. Dubrovskii, *Stolypinskaia zemel'naia reforma. Iz istorii sel'skogo khoziaistva i krest'ianstva Rossii v nachale XX veka* (Moscow, 1963).

13. *Russlands Aufstieg*, p. 189.

14. M. Malia, "What Is the Intelligentsia?" in R. Pipes, ed., *The Russian Intelligentsia* (New York, 1961), p. 1. See also the following: G. Fischer, *Russian Liberalism: From Gentry to Intelligentsia* (Cambridge, Mass., 1958) and also the intelligentsia essay of the same author in C. E. Black, ed., *The Transformation of Russian Society*, p. 253 ff., and P. Scheibert, *Von Bakunin zu Lenin*, vol. I, *Die Formung des radikalen Denkens in der Auseinandersetzung mit deutschem Idealismus und französischem Bürgertum* (Leiden, 1956); see also D. N. Ovsianko-Kulikovskii, *Istoriia russkoi intelligencii* (St. Petersburg, 1910–1911).

15. Pipes, *op. cit.*, pp. 16–17.

16. Portal, *op. cit.*, pp. 211 and 214.

17. In addition to Portal (who has examined the recent Soviet literature) and M. J. Tugan-Baranowski, *Geschichte der russischen Fabrik* (Berlin, 1900), see particularly C. E. Black, ed., *The Transformation of Russian Society*, p. 42 ff., p. 209 ff., and p. 311 ff., and T. H. von Laue, *Sergei Witte and the Industrialization of Russia* (New York-London, 1963) and J. Notzold, *Wirtschafts-politische Alternativen der Entwicklung Russlands in der Ära Witte und Stolypin* (Berlin, 1966).

18. *Russische Geschichte*, p. 629.

19. V. T. Bill, *The Forgotten Class: The Russian Bourgeoisie From the Earliest Beginnings to 1900* (New York, 1959).

20. E. Amburger, "Staat und Gesellschaft in Russland" p. 49.

SOCIAL CHANGE IN BOLSHEVIK RUSSIA

BORIS MEISSNER

I. THE EVOLUTION OF SOVIET SOCIETY

1. *Revolution and War Communism (1917–1921)*

The Russian Revolution was rooted largely in the weakness of the old Russian social and political structure.[1] This weakness —apart from war conditions—was the main reason why Russian liberals were unable to achieve their aims and consolidate their victory subsequent to the successful revolution in February of 1917. The Mensheviks and the Right Socialist-Revolutionaries, all advocates of a democratic socialism, were unable to block the ultimate triumph of the Bolsheviks, who were strategically allied at the time with the Left Socialist-Revolutionaries.

Lenin and Trotsky's insistence upon a radical social revolution was in correspondence actually with the wishes and expectations of the radicalized masses. By exploiting and manipulating the elementary social forces released by the revolution, they were able to outmaneuver opponents whose principal objective it was to reshape Russian social and political structures along Western democratic lines.

The Bolshevik minority's seizure of power during the October Revolution was nurtured in the soil of Soviet legality.[2] But the new regime was shaped mainly by professional revolutionaries among the Bolsheviks, most of whom belonged to the radical wing of the old Russian intelligentsia, and not by those who could genuinely have been regarded as spokesmen for workers and peasants. The organizational principles of the Bolshevik Party were used as the basis for the creation of the Soviet state and society.[3]

Indeed, sweeping social changes have occurred in Russia since the October Revolution of 1917. These changes took place in several periods or stages of development pursuant to decisions dictated both by economic considerations and power politics.[4]

In the first phase of development marked by revolution and War Communism the ideological objective, which was based on Marxist class theory and the philosophy of historical material-ism,[5] was particularly significant. Marx saw in the private owner-ship of the means of production the ultimate source of man's alienation and exploitation. For him the abolition of private property was the *sine qua non* of a rulerless and, hence, classless society; such a society would make possible the development of the human personality under optimal conditions of freedom and equality.[6]

Lenin was himself guided by these basic notions of Marx when he placed the most important sectors of the economy under the direct control of the state and abandoned a market economy.[7] He viewed this as the best way of achieving the mature socialism required by Marx in the event of a "proletarian revolution" and thus as a means to reducing the gap between Russia and the developed industrial societies of the West. To reach the first goal the upper social classes who were in the sad-dle prior to the October Revolution had to be destroyed. Among these so-called "exploiting classes" were large sectors of the urban population (industrial personnel, merchants, home-owners, civil servants, etc.) together with landowners and well-to-do peasants (kulaks). These "capitalist" classes, constituting 15.9 percent of the population in 1913, were shorn of their property as the country moved toward a nationalized economy; thus, these people were deprived of the very basis of their livelihood. In 1918 and 1919 all industrial, financial, trade, and transportation enterprises along with all private property in homes and land were nationalized, while the estates of landlords and most large farmers were divided among the peasant proletariat. The legal right to inherit private property was abolished, and in 1920 small commercial enterprises were also nationalized.

By the end of War Communism, as a result of this first attempt at leveling the socially higher strata of the prerevolutionary period, the only members of these strata who remained were those who preferred the lowering of their status to emigration. In the summer of 1918 the systematic nationalization of industry took place along with the step-by-step limitation of the rights of labor. By January 1, 1921 most heavy industry, involving 5,834 factories, had been nationalized,[8] providing the Bolshevik Party with its first genuine opportunity since the summer of 1918 to institute a vigorous egalitarian social policy (uravnilovka). Lenin wanted to give ordinary workers a fixed income that would equal the salary of a government employee. Economic catastrophe, resulting from the civil war and the blockade of the Western allies, helped to level the country socially. A general condition of equality was finally achieved but at a minimal level of existence.

During War Communism, however, countervailing tendencies, important for an understanding of later developments in the Soviet Union, began to emerge. The number of industrial workers dropped by one-half (1.5 million in 1920–21, compared to 3 million in 1917) because of the food situation in the cities, while white-collar employees increased by more than 60 percent (2.4 million in 1920, compared to 1.5 million in 1913).[9]

White-collar employees were largely drawn from those former members of the upper social strata whose civil rights had been curtailed. Next to Lenin, Trotsky above all had favored the employment of bourgeois "specialists."[10] As early as 28 March 1918 Trotsky observed:

> These technicians, engineers, physicians, teachers, and former officers constitute, like our idle machines, the national resources of our people. We must press them into service if we are to master the fundamental problems which beset us. . . .[11]

In 1921, as a result of this policy, 33.7 percent of the commanding officers in the Red Army, in whose creation Trotsky played a leading role, consisted of former tsarist officers and military officials.[12]

In the country the agricultural revolution, based on an alliance of the labor and peasant proletariat (Smychka),[13] was carried out in two stages. To begin with, a great part of the expropriated agricultural land was given to individual peasants for their use.

It is frequently asserted that the revolution yielded an increase of more than 150 million hectares of usable agricultural land and that ordinary peasants had received 97 percent of previously cultivated land.[14] This assertion is not supported by Soviet figures. According to statements of the Central Statistical Office of the USSR, agricultural land in tsarist Russia (as measured by USSR boundaries on 17 September 1939) totaled 367.2 million hectares.[15] Of this land area 214.7 million hectares (58 percent) were already being tilled by ordinary peasants.[16] Of this amount more than 80 million hectares were in the hands of well-to-do peasants, the kulaks.[17] There remained 152.2 million hectares (42 percent),[18] 61 million of which were in the hands largely of aristocratic landowners,[19] while 91 million were in the possession of the state, the crown, or the church.[20] This property was for the most part annexed by the state,[21] while property in the possession of large landowners was given mainly to peasants to use for as long as they lived. Since individual peasants were working 265 million hectares of land subsequent to the revolution,[22] the arable agricultural land that was actually transferred to them amounted to only 50 million hectares (23.2 percent).[23]

This increase was not sufficient to satisfy the intensified craving for land that resulted from the mass migration of eight million people from city to country.[24] The average land increase per peasant was less than half a desyatin (1 desyatin equals 1.09 hectares or 2.7 acres).[25] The second stage of the agrarian revolution took place in the summer and autumn of 1918, when the Bolshevik regime expropriated 50 million hectares of land owned by the kulaks and distributed them to peasants.[26] At the same time the old village commune, the *mir*, was also expropriated and the land redistributed. The redistribution of mir property enlarged the number of small peasant farmsteads, each now with about four desyatins of land and one horse, from 57.6 to 72.1 percent, while large farm enterprises of more than sixteen desyatins and four or more horses virtually disappeared.[27]

The dictatorial policies of the Bolsheviks—forced requisitions of farm products together with initial efforts toward the collectivization of agriculture through the introduction of producers' cooperatives or collective farms (*kolkhozes*) and state farms (*sovkhozes*)[28]—were bitterly opposed by the peasants. Agricultural output declined substantially because of peasant opposition to these reforms and resulted, actually, in a critical food shortage in 1921.[29] Between 1917 and 1920 the population declined from 143.5 to 134.2 million; the urban population plummeted from 25.8 to 20.8 million, while the rural population dropped from 117.7 to 113.4 million people.[30] Relative to the urban population, however, the percentage of the rural population actually increased from 82 to 85 percent of the country's inhabitants. The distinctive character of Russia as a still developing and overwhelmingly agrarian nation hit home more forcefully now than before the revolution. The agrarian social structure had undergone far-reaching and radical change yet many old familiar features of village life lingered on. Only in the industrialized sectors of the nation did the Bolsheviks take stern and forceful measures to replace the old social structure with a totally new model of social organization. The principles that had been set forth at the time by Lenin and his comrades were revised later only in limited spheres of action.

The socio-structural changes in the period of War Communism had been conditioned on the one hand by internal causes and, on the other, by the application of an ideology which, while indeed containing elements of typically Russian revolutionary thought, had its origin in a completely different cultural milieu. With the further development of Soviet society, however, much greater significance has to be attached to Russian national elements for the failure of War Communism. The first signs of such a change, which was accompanied by a change in the function of ideology, were already evident at the time of the Russian-Polish War of 1920.[31]

2. The New Economic Policy (1921–1928)

The felt-need to preserve the social achievements of the revolution prompted a large segment of the population to support the Bolsheviks in their confrontation with certain forces of restoration.[32] The Bolsheviks interpreted their victory in the civil war as an expression of popular support for a one-party state. But the Kronstadt revolt of March 1921, with its rebellious cry for "soviets without Bolsheviks," together with a rapidly mounting peasant insurrection, rendered this a doubtful proposition.[33] The crisis brought on by these events forced Lenin into a profound change of policy in order to deal more realistically with the imperatives of social change. Lenin viewed small independent farmers, a peasant petty bourgeoisie which he characterized as a vacillating force,[34] as the principal threat to the "dictatorship of the proletariat." At this stage of the game the only way that the Bolsheviks could consolidate their power was to yield to some of the economic demands of the middle peasantry. The New Economic Policy (NEP) announced at the Tenth Party Congress of the Russian Communist Party in March 1921 served this purpose;[35] it was aimed primarily at the agricultural sector and sought to placate the peasantry by the restoration of a limited market economy based on individual initiative. All other major sectors of the economy, such as heavy industry, which was organized into trusts, remained under the absolute control of the Bolshevik regime.

Lenin himself characterized the new economic policy instituted by the NEP as "state capitalism." His belief that the bourgeois and anarchist character of the peasant masses endangered the regime only stiffened his resolve to resist the plans of the "workers opposition" to subordinate the economy to the policies and regulations of labor unions.[36] Lenin regarded such plans as an anarcho-syndicalist deviation replete with petty bourgeois elements. For NEP to succeed it was critically important, of course, to check inflation; the currency reform of 1924 helped in this regard. In 1927, ten years after the revolution, industrial production had reached the level of 1913, although productive output varied considerably from one branch of industry to the next. Finally, with better provisions, resistance to Bolshevik rule on the part of the masses seemed to diminish.

When the economic reconstruction of Russia began in the spring of 1921, the Bolshevik Party was forced to back off from its original attempt completely to level society along socialist lines. The drab egalitarianism of War Communism very soon transformed itself into a society marked by social diversity.[37]

At first the peasants, who were allowed to sell their surplus products in the free market, made larger profits. Large gaps developed between the salaries of state employees and ordinary workers. To further resuscitate the economy Bolshevik leaders reintroduced private enterprises at the level of small business, handicrafts, and smaller industrial factories. The economic condition of the petty bourgeoisie improved as a result, while those who belonged to the old upper and middle strata of society sought to exploit the market economy in their own interests. The bourgeois tendency of the party was in fact so conspicuous that it became the subject of Mayakovsky's well-known satirical play, *The Bedbug*.

Ten years after the revolution, when the NEP was nearing its end with the introduction of economic planning, the social structure of the population did not seem, on the surface at least, to have changed very much from that of the prewar period.[38] In 1928 urban workers and white-collar employees made up 17.3 percent of the population, compared to 16.7 percent in 1913; during this time the total number of peasants and unorganized domestic workers jumped from 65.1 in 1913 to 72.9 percent of the population in 1928. Only the "capitalist" class experienced a substantial reduction in membership, going from 15.9 to 4.5 percent of the entire population. A relatively small number of them disappeared as a result of the civil war, revolution and emigration. But by 1928 the mass of urban "capitalists" had become white-collar employees.[39] It is of some interest to note here that their children took greater advantage of improved educational opportunities provided during the NEP period than did the children of laboring men.[40]

Descendants of the old capitalists were also increasingly to be found among the growing cadres of technicians and engineers, who were actually classified as "workers." What is more, the new working-class generation was being recruited mainly from the peasantry and not from the urban proletariat.[41]

The change in the social structure, however, actually ran much deeper than these data would indicate. Prior to the revolution those people whom the Bolsheviks classified as "capitalists" held the leading positions in society. Both workers and white-collar employees were largely dependent upon them. By 1928 this situation had changed substantially; both groups (workers and white-collar employees) were now employed mainly by government agencies or state-managed enterprises which in the last resort were subject to party control. The leadership of the party not only had the commanding positions in industry, banking, finance, transportation, along with a monopoly of such posts in foreign trade; the party also tightened the reins even more by (1) eliminating the last independent social organizations, (2) expanding the "dictatorship of the proletariat" through mass organizations, and (3) seeking to prevent the development of factions within the party itself.

These policies implied nothing less than the creation of a "total state" as well as a turning away from Marx and Engel's teaching that the state would wither away.[42] The Soviet regime, justified as a transitory stage en route to communism, increasingly assumed the characteristics of a permanent dictatorship.

During the NEP period agriculture was dominated largely by the individual peasant who tilled his own plot of ground. By 1928 these peasants made up 72.9 percent of the entire population, substantially higher than in 1913. The number of farmsteads alone increased from 16 million in 1916 to 25.3 million in 1927.[43] In the village social stratification was beginning to occur as a result of substantial increases in the size of industrial operations.

In 1928 the rural population (119.4 million) consisted of the following:[44]

Rural proletarians	3.4 million
Small farmers	34.0 million
Medium farmers	52.0 million
Well-to-do farmers	11.0 million
Rich farmers	5.0 million
Others	14.0 million

Well-to-do farmers possessed cultivated land consisting of around six to ten desyatins, they were also in a position to lease land other than their own, to employ hired hands, to rent surplus livestock and equipment, and to engage in agricultural commerce. Thirty percent of all farm machinery was owned by only 6 percent of the village population in 1927–29.

These data show that medium and small farmers predominated, numerically, as before. The percentage of "kulaks," that is, the rich and very well-to-do peasants, and the peasant proletariat had increased considerably in the course of social differentiation.

Rural proletarians and small farmers were unable independently to cultivate their land. Some medium farmers were in the same boat; as a consequence they had to rely on kulaks for assistance in overcoming their difficulties. The party regarded this dependence of the great mass of farmers on the kulaks as a threat to its hegemony in the villages.[45]

During the NEP period the Soviet population increased from 136.8 million in 1920 to 153.4 million in 1929, with a faster rate of population growth in cities than in rural areas; the urban population rose from 20.9 million (15 percent) to 28.7 million (19 percent), the rural population from 115.9 million (85 percent) to 124.7 million (81 percent).[46] This rapid increase in population intensified the problem of supplying the cities and magnified the population pressure in the country.

The step-by-step restrictions imposed by the party on the private sector of the economy, together with the expansion of agriculture *artels* (producers' cooperatives),[47] exacerbated the tension between city and country. The peasants, preferring to provide for their own individual needs, neglected measures designed to augment agricultural production, for they believed that any increase in their value to the economy would merely invite repressive measures on the part of the regime.[48] The resistance of the peasants was responsible for a sharp decline in the amount of grain available for market.[49] Bolshevik forces seeking to accelerate the industrialization process used their behavior as an excuse for speeding up the collectivization of agriculture.

After Lenin's death Stalin gained acceptance of the "general line" that provided for the transformation of the Soviet Union from an agricultural country into an industrialized nation with a planned economy based on a complete socialist foundation.[50] Beginning in 1926 concessions originally made to the private sector of the economy were gradually abolished. Table 1 illustrates this development.[51]

TABLE 1   Percentage of the Private Economy's Contribution to Gross Production
in Industry, Agriculture, and Trade Turnover

| | Industry | | | Trade | | | |
	Large Industry	Small Industry	Total	Wholesale Trade	Retail Trade	Total	Agriculture
1922-23	--	--	--	--	75.3	55.9	--
1923-24	4.4	87.3	33.3	18.1	66.5	44.9	--
1924-25	3.9	84.4	28.0	8.5	48.5	27.8	--
1925-26	4.0	81.9	27.1	7.9	44.4	24.8	98.6
1926-27	2.3	82.1	20.8	4.8	37.0	18.5	98.8
1927-28	1.4	70.6	14.7	1.9	25.4	10.2	98.6
1928-29	0.9	43.8	12.7	0.9	14.3	5.1	98.3

The adoption of the First Five-Year Plan in 1928 marked the end of the NEP period.[52] The guided economy, which restored elements of the old Russian social structure, particularly in the country, was replaced by a totally planned economy which was supposed to affect all areas of social life.

3. Stalin's "Revolution from Above" (1928–29 to 1938–39)

The substance and character of Soviet society was decisively marked by the deep-seated socio-structural changes of 1928–29 to 1938–39; the initiator of these changes had himself described them as a "revolution from above."[53] The revolutionary change that was brought about by Stalin in these ten fateful years had the scale and deep-going effects of a great social revolution, although it proceeded from the rulers and not the ruled. In 1926 Stalin had already justified the necessity of such a revolution under the conditions of Bolshevik Russia by perceiving a qualitative difference between a bourgeois and a proletarian revolution:

> The principal task of a bourgeois revolution is to obtain power and then to exercise it in accordance with the existing economic values of the middle class; the main task of a proletarian revolution is to build a new socialist economy subsequent to the seizure of power. A bourgeois revolution customarily ends when power is seized; in a proletarian revolution the seizure of power is only the beginning, since power is used for the purpose of destroying the old economy and organizing the new.[54]

With these words Stalin had turned Marx upside down, as it were.[55] In Marx's view a new state and social order emerges out of a dominant social conflict. The politico-ideological superstructure, the nucleus of which is the state, has to be adjusted to the emerging socioeconomic substructure. In Stalin's view the legitimacy of a small power elite is based on its possession of the true principles by which the new society, with the help of the state, would be created. In actuality this meant that the ruling group exchanged one social base for another. This continuous revolutionary process, which lasted about ten years, was carried out in two stages, with 1934 serving as the dividing line between them.[56] The planned economic "revolution from above" was at the center of the first stage; the second stage, characterized as the "Great Purge," was a related struggle for absolute political control.

In the first stage of the "revolution from above" Stalin was motivated mainly by considerations of power politics in favoring revolutionary actions over reform. Beginning in 1929 "Soviet patriotism" was invoked more and more to justify his policy. The motives upon which this ideological fork in the road was based were revealed in Stalin's programmatic speech before Soviet economic managers on 4 February 1931:

> In the past we had no fatherland and could have none. But now that we have overthrown the capitalists and placed power in the hands of workers we do have a fatherland and will defend its independence. Do you want to see our socialist fatherland defeated and its independence lost? If you do not then you must eliminate its backwardness in the shortest time possible and beat a real Bolshevik tempo toward the establishment of a socialist economy. There is no other way. In this connection Lenin himself said that either we perish or we overcome the advanced capitalist countries (*dognat' i peregnat'*). We are behind the capitalist countries by fifty to a hundred years. But we must catch up with them in ten years. Either we bring this about or we are finished.[57]

Malenkov, who at this time was Stalin's private secretary, declared many years later, at the founding of the Cominform in September 1947, that without the long years of "active" defense preparations assisted by the five-year economic plans the Soviet Union would not have been victorious in World War II.[58] It was because of this that he described 1928, the beginning of the First Five-Year Plan, as the year of the great revolution.

An immediate by-product of this revolution was mainly the renewal of an attempt socioeconomically to level the society. The gap between the classes was narrowed. Social differentiations which had developed during the NEP period were largely done away with.[59]

The new regime underlined the absolute primacy of heavy industry. There followed a policy of enforced industrialization that was linked to the Soviet effort totally to socialize the economy; in the country this took the form of collectivization.[60] Afterwards the collectivization of agriculture had been (since 1927) ruthlessly enforced, and at the start of January 1930 the elimination of the kulaks as a class was ordered.[61] The social consequences of this second agrarian revolution were far more destructive and violent than the expropriation of farm property during War Communism.

Millions of kulaks—the estimates run from two to three million—were exiled to northern Siberia and the far eastern regions of the Soviet Union, where a great number of them died.[62] Those left behind were largely deprived of their homes and property. Most of them wandered into the cities where they swelled the number of workers and employees or were absorbed by new industries. Millions of additional human lives were lost by the mass starvation which followed these hurried and repressive measures.[63] Stalin, who was responsible for this inhuman policy, later told Churchill that the elimination of the kulaks was the most difficult decision of his life.[64]

Nearly all small and medium-sized agricultural operations were consolidated into collective enterprises.[65] The percentage of collective farms rose from 4.1 percent in October 1929 to 21 percent by January 1930, then suddenly shot up to 58 percent by March 1930; in 1937 the figure reached 93 percent. In 1939 independent peasants and unorganized domestic workers constituted only 2.6 percent of the entire population.

With the elimination of private business and industry, which had experienced some revival in the NEP era, the propertied middle class that was beginning to emerge from the petty bourgeoisie was also destroyed root and branch. In 1923–24 private sales still made up 57.7 percent of the retail trade; in 1926–27 they were around 39.9 percent; by 1930 they dropped to 5.6 percent, and were eliminated altogether in 1931.[66] The same was true of industry. Gross industrial production in the private sector amounted to 18.7 percent of output in 1924–25, dropped to 14.1 percent in 1926–27, and went all the way down to 0.6 percent in 1929 and to 0.03 percent in 1938.[67]

The possibility of engaging in independent activity was open to the urban petty bourgeoisie only in the cooperative home industry. In 1924–25 industrial production cooperatives (artels) were responsible for 9.1 percent of gross industrial production; this dropped to 8.8 percent in 1930 and then leveled off to around 7 percent. Although production cooperatives accounted for only 8.8 percent of the gross industrial product in 1930, they comprised 43.5 percent of industrial firms.[68] Accordingly, the cooperative industry still embraced the largest part of small industrial and business concerns.

While the petty bourgeoisie enjoyed a measure of free enterprise in the cooperative home industry, all other workers and white-collar employees were wholly absorbed into the socialist system. Since at that time it was still fashionable to include both workers and the petty bourgeoisie within the general notion of "proletariat," the latter were, in the Soviet view, gradually proletarianized. In 1927, when the urban population was around 29.7 million, nonproletarians and their families constituted 31.5 percent of the population as against 68.5 percent who were regarded as part of the proletariat. In 1931 the relationship was 12.6 vis-á-vis 87.4 percent.[69]

The Bolshevik regime blandly ignored the fact that manual laborers comprised only a part of the proletariat and that white-collar employees were not much different in social consciousness and life-style than the petty bourgeoisie, insofar as they had not been members of the old upper and middle social strata. A person of bourgeois background was proletarianized only when he became a manual laborer. But it actually took longer to proletarianize the bourgeoisie than the peasants. For one thing a person was not proletarianized if he was simply forced to give up his former private job in order to become a white-collar employee or enter the engineering-technical field; by the same token a new career in public administration or in a producer's cooperative was as much a social climb for some members of the petty bourgeoisie as it was for those workers whose responsibilities involved the application of what was called "practical intelligence."

The general decline in the standard of living that resulted from people swelling the cities and industrial centers, together with the critical shortage of living quarters, food, consumer goods, and public welfare, had more to do with the levelling of Soviet society than the formal efforts and half measures taken to proletarianize the petty bourgeoisie and members of the former upper strata who were professionally active in the NEP period. This perilous situation was aggravated even further by the rapid urbanization that was generated by forced industrialization and collectivization. In 1929 the Soviet population was 153.4 million; by 1939 it rose to 170.6 million. During this time the urban population increased from 28.7 million (19 percent) to 56.1 million (33 percent), while the rural population declined from 124.7 million (81 percent) to 114.5 million (67 percent).[70] Between the census of 1926 and that of 1939, a period of thirteen years, the urban population had increased by 112.5 percent or by about 29.6 million. It took the United States thirty years, from 1900 to 1930, and Great Britain sixty years, from 1871 to 1931, to achieve the same rate of growth. The total number of cities climbed from 709 in 1926 to 922 in 1939, while the number of urban housing developments skyrocketed from 125 to 1,448.[71] In addition to the nonblack-earth zones of the European part of the Soviet Union, urban growth occurred mainly in West Siberia, Kazakstan, and East Siberia. The process of urbanization was measured principally by the growth of cities. From 1926 to 1939 the number of large cities (over 100,000 inhabitants) increased from 31 to 82. Their inhabitants constituted in 1939

16.1 percent of the entire population in contrast to 6.5 percent in 1926. Between 1926 and 1939 Moscow's population grew from 2 to 4.1 million, Leningrad's from 1.7 to 3.2 million, the industrial center of Swerdlowsk in the Urals from 140,000 to 426,000. Large cities sprung from villages, while others, such as Magnitagorsk or Komsomolsk on the Amur, rose up out of nowhere. This extraordinary growth in urban population was attributable, mainly, to migration from rural areas and, secondarily, to the administrative conversion of villages into cities. Because of cramped living conditions, natural growth of the urban population was small. Out of an urban population increase, from 1926 to 1939, of 29.6 million inhabitants, 18.5 million (62.5 percent) were migrants from the country, 5.8 million (19.6 percent) were former village residents, while 5.3 million (17.9 percent) were the product of natural increase.[72]

Housing conditions were particularly bad in these overcrowded cities. Nine square meters of living space per person is regarded as minimal in the Soviet Union; 6 square meters per person is regarded as being critically deficient.[73] But in 1927–28 living space for each urban resident barely reached this critical level; and between 1932 and 1937 living space per person actually decreased from 5.2 to 4.2, falling to a low of 4 square meters in 1939.[74]

Prior to the revolution only 3 percent of the workers lived within the second ring of the city of Moscow; by 1931–32 40 to 50 percent resided there.[75] Because of livestock losses caused by forced collectivization of agriculture the food shortage among the urban population was not satisfactorily resolved, despite increased grain production. This situation was compounded by a substantial drop, in the wake of rapid socialization, in the real wages of workers and lower-level white-collar employees. Not until 1926–27 was the salary level of the prewar period reached. By 1929–30 salaries exceeded those of the prewar period by 15 percent; however, in 1935 they dipped once again to a mere

50 percent of the prewar period, the low point prior to World War II.

A Moscow worker who earned 24.3 rubles a month in 1913 could buy 3.7 baskets of food along with paying maintenance costs of 6.57 rubles; in 1928, with a salary of 70.2 rubles a month and with maintenance costs of 11.95 rubles he could buy only 5.6 baskets of food supplies. Contrast this to 1935 when, with maintenance costs of 96.42 rubles, a salary of 185.3 rubles would buy no more than 1.9 baskets of food. Thus, by the time the Soviet economy was totally socialized the ordinary worker's living standard was far below that which prevailed in the prewar period.[76]

From 1935 on, real wages began to rise, attaining their highest levels in 1938 and 1939; salaries averaged 270 to 287 rubles per month, corresponding to 2.6 baskets of food. Nevertheless, this was only 75 percent of the living standard achieved in 1913 and 50 percent of the 1929–30 standard. In 1940 real wages plummeted and, though salaries averaged about 323 rubles per month, their actual value sank to the 1935 level.[77] This occurred on the eve of World War II and at a time when the differences between minimum and maximum salaries had already become very substantial and were systematically widened even further. This circumstance had to contribute to quickening the pace of proletarianizing the overwhelming majority of workers and lower-level white-collar employees. On their heads fell the principal burden of an indirect consumer tax—a differentiated sales tax on goods—that was introduced in 1930;[78] the severity of this measure was deepened by the scarcity of consumer goods caused by the nationalization of trade. The working masses in the cities thus bore the burden of financing the new forced economy that was based on a completely socialistic foundation no less than did the kolkhoz peasants, whose social position was still oppressive.

The immediate result of these conditions, as indicated by the decreasing size of working-class families, was a drop in the birthrate of the urban population. In 1927 the average family comprised 4.10 persons, 1.28 of whom were employed while 2.82 were out of work; in 1935 the average family contained 3.80 persons with 1.47 working members and 2.33 nonworking members. In other words, for every working member of the family there were 2.20 nonworking members in 1927 and 1.59 in 1935.[79]

The urban population increase, as already indicated, was primarily the result of migrations from the country. The rural influence that accompanied this influx was not without its impact on the city. The kulaks actually strengthened petty bourgeois elements within the working class. It is of interest to note in this regard that from 1926 to 1939 some 24.4 million peasants moved into the cities. At the same time the number of farmsteads dropped from 25.5 to 20.3 million, i.e., about 20.4 percent down. At the same time the population dropped from 122.4 million to 78.6 million, i.e., about 43.8 million or 35.8 percent.[80] A good half of these peasants moved directly into the city. The other half settled in the immediate vicinity of the city, ended up on collective farms, or were employed by state farms (sovkhozes) or machine-tractor stations (MTS). This meant generally a proletarianization of the peasantry not only in the city, but also in the country. White-collar employees in the country were recruited in large measure from the petty bourgeois elements in the village, so that here also a contrary tendency could be observed.

The makeup of the rural population had changed substantially as a result of these developments. According to Prokopovich[81] there were 122.4 million peasants in 1929. There were also 4.3 million rural people working at other occupations; this added up to a rural population of 126.7 million. In 1938, with a rural population of 114.6 million, farm peasants accounted for only 78.6 million inhabitants, while remaining occupational groups embraced 36 million people. The latter included 28.4 million workers and white-collar employees, along with 5.3 million home-workers and artisans. Forced collectivization, despite its many negative effects, was beneficial in one respect; by reducing the number of farmsteads it relieved the population pressure in the village.

Despite the heavy burden of the state procurement system and the negligible increase in work productivity, collective farm organization did manage to produce larger quantities of arable land and an increased per capita production of grain. The well-being of the average peasant had also improved relative to his condition in prerevolutionary times, although the same could not be said of the average worker or white-collar employee. It should be kept in mind, however, that the salaries of the latter were not the only measure of living standards, for the social expenditures of the state helped mainly to benefit the worker and white-collar employee, not the peasant. These benefits are regarded especially as the product of trade union membership.

The leveling of Soviet society, furthered as it was by the blending of social groups and the pauperization of the toiling masses, was offset very soon by a countervailing tendency toward greater differentiation among white-collar employees and, to a lesser extent, among the workers themselves. This was partially a result of the very nature of an industrial society and partially also the consequence of the political "revolution from above."

The Bolshevik regime could attain its far-reaching economic goals only by the total seizure and control of all available means of production and labor forces, along with the training of qualified specialists to manage the technical processes of production and administration. But this required a rise in the general level of education, one that involved particularly the expansion of general secondary schools and higher education.[82]

Improvements along these lines did substantially increase the number of state employees and engineering-technical leadership personnel. Most state employees, who in the 1920s were known as *apparatchiki* (men of the apparatus), were soon to enjoy advantages denied to manual laborers. This social group actually originated during the years of War Communism, when the number of state employees shot up to 2.4 million, almost double the strength of the tsarist civil service.[83] During the NEP period the number of apparatchiki doubled again, with some 4.6 million men involved administratively in the process of production; they turned out to be technicians and administrators drawn mainly from the old intelligentsia and former upper and middle strata and proletarian members of the party apparatus. Growing numbers of university and advanced technical institute graduates, most of whom were from proletarian families, combined with the petty bourgeoisie to push the number of white-collar employees up to 9.6 million people in the course of the first two five-year plans.[84] Between 1926 and 1937 this group increased much more rapidly than ordinary workers. After 1931 these white-collar employees came to be characterized variously as the "new intelligentsia," the "working intelligentsia," or the "socialist people's intelligentsia."[85] The turning point of this development, which was associated with placing a higher value on members of the "old intelligentsia," who were recruited into the new group on an equal basis, was Stalin's second programmatic speech before Soviet economic functionaries on 23 June 1931.[86] Stalin declared that no "ruling class" could remain in power for long without its own intelligentsia. Thus the working class "would have to create its own technically trained intelligentsia" while at the same time behaving with consideration toward the old intelligentsia. In the same speech Stalin demanded an end to fluctuations of and egalitarianism within the labor force. For salaries were now to be based on achievement. Personal responsibility in the organization of production was to be strengthened. These directives were critically important for the "uniform directory power" (*edinonachalie*)—that is, one-man management —which in 1929 was adopted in industry and other sectors of the economy.[87] The planned economy gave rise to a leadership heirarchy that constituted the basis of the social stratification which developed within the "new intelligentsia."

The upward mobility of large numbers of white-collar employees, and thus of the intelligentsia, was rooted both in the

division between manual and intellectual labor and in the social
stratification that emerged out of a society rapidly industrializ-
ing under the impact of a planned economy. This was a phenomenon that Bolshevik leaders actually encouraged in 1935
when they abolished the 1928 policy of including a "core of
workers"—at first 65 and then 70 percent—among students
admitted to universities and advanced technical schools.[88]

The percentage of workers and workers' children among students, which had climbed between 1928 and 1932 from 24.4
percent to 58.0 percent, dropped to 33.9 percent by 1938. The
number of those from the nonproletarian strata, all of whom
were now becoming white-collar employees or members of the
"intelligentsia" dropped from 50.7 to 27.9 percent between 1928
and 1932, but increased to 44.5 percent in 1938.[89] A similar trend
could be observed in ordinary technical schools.[90] Since then the
Soviet Union has not produced any statistics on the social origin
of students, because they would have made all too clear the
disproportionate influence of the "intelligentsia" vis-à-vis workers
and peasants. Bolshevik leaders, from the beginning, had certain
reservations about the new intelligentsia. This attitude changed
only after the second generation arrived on the scene and after
Stalin's 4 June 1935 address to the graduates of the War Academy, which included his frequently quoted observation that the
"cadres settle everything."[91] For ideological reasons, however, he
was not prepared to recognize the intelligentsia as an independent social class. In his report of 25 November 1936,[92] which
dealt with the draft of the new federal constitution, Stalin
defined the Soviet Union as a socialist state made up of workers
and peasants, and described the "working intelligentsia" as a
detached intermediate social stratum. They had no more rights
than did workers or kolkhoz peasants, although they performed
functions very critical to the success of the socialist system. But
Stalin did not regard the intelligentsia as a class:

> The intelligentsia has never been a class and cannot become
> one. It has been and remains an intermediate stratum whose

members are recruited from all classes of society. In the past the intelligentsia was recruited from the nobility, the bourgeoisie, in part from the peasantry, and only to a small extent from the working class. Today, the intelligentsia is recuited mainly from the ranks of workers and peasants. Still, the intelligentsia is an intermediate stratum and not a class, no matter how it is recruited or what its characteristics are.[93]

Stalin's argument was unconvincing, for in 1937 this group, together with family members, already constituted 14 percent of the Soviet population, almost matching the "capitalist" class in 1913 that was later "liquidated." Bolshevik leaders identified the new intelligentsia with white-collar employees, who in large measure were drawn from the petty bourgeoisie. In terms neither of their social function nor of their social consciousness could they be compared to the old intelligentsia, which evidenced much deeper intellectual traits and considered itself as an order dedicated to revolution and reform.[94]

It is possible that Stalin was himself aware of these differences, but the time was not yet ripe to define the intelligentsia in the state constitution as an independent social group. The Great Purge of 1936–38 produced a complete change in the social composition of the Bolshevik Party, to the advantage of the intelligentsia.[95]

The liquidation of most of Lenin's intellectual comrades was accompanied by a massive repression of proletarian elements in the party as a whole, whose 3.5 million members, as a result, had dwindled to 2 million, although in 1940 party membership shot back up to 3.4 million. In 1939 the intelligentsia constituted 20 percent of 2.3 million party members. After the war this number approached the 50 percent mark, while workers, who represented 65.3 percent of party membership in 1930, declined by more than half in the same period. Of the delegates who attended the Eighteenth Party Congress of the CPSU in March 1939, nearly 54 percent, measured by their education, belonged to the intelligentsia.[96] A similar change took place in

the social structure of the party's Central Committee and its
executive organs. Stalin took this fact into account when he
put the intelligentsia on an equal footing with the other two
classes and abolished all previous restrictions on party membership; these measures were approved in the party statute adopted
by the Eighteenth Party Congress.[97] Thus, in effect, the social
leadership of the intelligentsia, at this time still identified with
white-collar employees, was given constitutional recognition over
that of workers and kolkhoz peasants. The term *working class*
was used instead of *proletariate*, while the party declared that it
represented the "Soviet people as a whole" and not merely the
"working masses." Besides these three classes there existed in the
Soviet Union yet a fourth group, not mentioned in the party
constitution, which stood at the very bottom of the social order.
These were the forced laborers incarcerated in concentration
camps—in 1930 they were renamed "labor correction camps"—
whom Stalin described, for the benefit of intellectuals, as an
"intermediate class."[98] Until 1930 only the northern camps were
subordinate to the jurisdiction of the Soviet secret police, then
known as the OGPU. The total number of prisoners at this time
was probably less than a million.[99] But enforced collectivization
and the Great Purge increased the number of concentration-
camp prisoners substantially. An order issued on 27 October 1934
(GS USSR 1934, no. 56, art. 481) placed the entire prison
system, and thus all forced-labor camps, under the jurisdiction
of the newly created People's Commissariat of Internal Affairs
(NKVD). Under the direction of the Central Administration
of Camps—GULAG—forced-labor camps became a characteristic feature of the Stalinist system. These camps—organized
mainly to develop the Upper North and for military and economic purposes—contained, according to the estimates of Russian experts, from two to fifteen million people.[100]

The State Economic Plan of 1941 disclosed that in NKVD
enterprises alone some 2.3 million persons, nearly all of whom
were prisoners, were pressed into service.[101] The total number of

forced laborers may actually have been higher than these estimates. Forced industrialization, accompanied by urbanization, forced collectivization, the total socialization of all important sectors of society, and the Great Purge changed the sociopolitical structure of Russia more profoundly than the October Revolution itself. One of the most important consequences of these events was a rapid rise in social mobility; other results were an extensive bureaucracy and an end to overpopulation in rural areas, a problem that troubles all developing nations. The "revolution from above" concluded the social transformation of the urban-industrial sector of the Soviet Union that had been initiated after the October Revolution. In the rural-agrarian sectors of the economy collective farms (kolkhozes) replaced traditional forms of farm organization.

But the most important result of all may have been the social upgrading of the intelligentsia. The upper stratum of the new intelligentsia blended more and more into the leadership of the party bureaucracy, which in the course of the Great Purge had gained its independence as an autocratic ruling group. Out of an endogenetic social change that was carried out by the state—not by society—a new class society emerged within the framework of an autocratic ruling system that increasingly, in our time, is marked by totalitarian methods.

4. War and Late Stalinism (1939–1953)

A fourth phase in the social development of Bolshevik Russia began in 1939, extending from the Soviet military intervention in Poland and the Baltic area to the time of Stalin's death. World War II and the postwar era can be regarded as related episodes; they constitute the period of transition from war to peace that is known as the late Stalin era. The transition period is characterized by a stabilization of the new social structure, together with a growing differentiation within the new intelligentsia. The new order survived the test of World War II, but this was attributable more to the appeals made in behalf of Russian nationalism and Soviet patriotism, and to the conscious support of these appeals on the part of the "intelligentsia" and above all on the part of the people, than to any Stalinist type socialism.[102] It must be remembered also that the Germans entered the Soviet Union not as liberators but as oppressors. Thus the wide fissures which rent Soviet society in the beginning were now sealed. Nationalism was the bridge to Russia's prerevolutionary past and the stone from which a new social structure was hewn.[103] With traditional forms the new social group adopted an antiquated life-style, petty bourgeoisie in appearance, which has largely persisted to this day.[104] After the war Stalin's despotism turned into a vicious kind of autocratic-totalitarian rule marked by a Stalin-cult, excessive terror, and a pronounced tendency toward a society sharply split along group lines. No Thermidorean stage occurred in the evolution of the Soviet system; but just as Bolshevism constituted in an economic sense an ersatz capitalism so too did Stalinism manifest an ersatz Bonapartism.[105] The adjustment of individuals and groups to the new social order was facilitated by a totalitarian regime that wedded communism to nationalism and made it appear that what was happening in the Soviet Union was the product of historical continuity.

Social stratification was furthered by a whole series of measures implemented by the Bolshevik regime. Most important among these measures were the policy of basing wages and salaries on individual achievement (a capitalist work ethic), the Stakhanovite movement, bonus payments, and income-tax law revisions.[106]

The reintroduction of interest payments on bank savings also deserves to be mentioned in this regard.[107] These changes in wage and finance policy raised the income of the upper strata of the intelligentsia as well as leading groups within the working class itself, the effect of which was to convert foremen and supervisors, for example, into a "working-class aristocracy."

The weakening of class consciousness among workers that was connected with this development constituted the basic assumption for the stabilization of the new class society in the Soviet Union.

In 1928, at the outset of the First Five-Year Plan, the highest paid workers were making nearly three times (1:2.8) as much as the lowest paid workers. In 1940 the top salary of an employee was 10,600 rubles; the official average monthly wage consisted of only 339 rubles. Thus, a ratio of 1:31.3 was now the measure of the difference between the lowest and highest paid workers.[108]

With reference to the Soviet standard of living in 1948 a Norwegian trade union delegation reported:

> The whole wage system is . . . based on the principle of individual ability to the extent that it is compatible with work procedures and the industry's productive capabilities. In addition there is the bonus system; for example, if a worker exceeds his assigned quota by 100 percent he receives a 150 percent increase in basic salary. The bonus system is very well developed and has led to large salary differentials. In a factory which pays an average monthly salary of 800 rubles it is possible to find workers with monthly salaries ranging from 2,000 to 3,000 rubles, and even salaries ranging from 10,000 to 14,000 rubles.[109]

Dallin estimates that prior to World War II families of the intelligentsia, consisting of some 12 to 14 percent of the employed population, received 30 to 35 percent of the national income, apart from capital accumulation, while workers, peasants, and forced laborers, representing respectively 20 to 25 percent, 53 percent, and 8 to 11 percent of the population, received 33 percent, 29 percent, and 2 to 3 percent of all income.[110]

The upper strata of the Soviet intelligentsia were particularly well-off. In addition to high incomes they received numerous other satisfactions; for example, free official quarters, staff assistance paid by the state, rent-free country houses (*dacha*), free medical care by doctors in first-rate hospitals, luxury villas on the Black Sea, buying privileges in special shops, etc.[111]

The objection that the high salaries, privileges, and bonuses of top-level bureaucrats, prominent writers, scientists, and artists[112] would make it possible to live well under the socialist system operative in the Soviet system but would not allow them to invest capital in greater measure and to secure the profits of the same to their descendants was true only to a limited extent even in the prewar period.

Another policy change of significance was the 1945 reform in the right of inheritance[113] and the law of 26 August 1948 that secured to every Soviet citizen the right to own a dwelling house, either through the purchase or building of a house in or out of the city.[114] To be sure, these had to be one- or two-story houses with no more than five rooms. The state would cede the property, for an unstipulated period of time, on which such homes could be built; as a rule city plots were between 300 and 600 square meters, country plots between 700 and 1,200 square meters. Under this law Soviet citizens could buy or build only one house. The law, however, did not expressly forbid anyone to inherit more than one house. It was because of this that inheritance law reform was so important, for it substantially expanded the legal right of inheritance and, with the reintroduction of testamentary succession, virtually all previous restrictions on the right of inheritance were abolished. A testator could bequeath his property to any person, even if he were not related to the beneficiary. Only in special cases did the state treasury benefit from this reform policy. Back in 1918, as is well known, the state was still the sole heir of all property.

In regard to inheritance law reform, which preceded the abolition of the inheritance tax in 1943,[115] the possibility of acquiring a home was of particular importance. As a practical matter the only people who could afford to buy property were members of the top bureaucracy and the upper stratum of the intelligentsia. For them the possibility of owning individual inheritable property was an enormous breakthrough.

It was also possible for them to acquire such luxury items as automobiles, which were in scarce supply, and to put their savings into other valuables. In any case, due to these privileges the social gap between the upper class, the upper-middle class and the top stratum of the "working aristocracy," on the one hand, and the masses, on the other, was widened and solidified. Differences in income and property were no less significant in furthering social differentiation than measures adopted in the field of education.[116] One clear sign of the independent status of a social group is the capacity of that group to perpetuate itself over time. We saw that this was already happening with the upper social classes during the prewar period, owing mainly to the fact that the number of workers and children of workers represented in the intelligentsia had declined since 1932. This tendency had increased noticeably since 1940. The free schooling that in 1936 had been constitutionally guaranteed for the three upper classes of general secondary schools as well as for the universities and secondary technical schools was abolished in 1940, while the granting of scholarships was severely limited. Children of the propertied classes stood a much better chance of receiving an education and entering the professions than did the children of the broad masses. The special training they acquired in the universities and advanced technical institutes secured for them high social status, together with above-average incomes and many privileges associated with such status.

Social development under Stalin was of such a nature that leading functionaries were being recruited in ever increasing numbers from among university students and graduates of intermediate technical schools. The officer corps was no exception to this rule, since high commanding officers demanded that their recruits be drawn from corresponding military academies. In the Soviet Union every student who qualified for admission to the university was automatically an officer candidate. But university graduates and the sons of officers were favored insofar as the officer corps was concerned.

Suvorov and Nakhimov cadet institutes were established during World War II especially to train these prospective officers. Similar institutions were built to train candidates for administrative positions in the party apparatus and state bureaucracy. The Academy of Social Science and the Higher Party School established by the Central Committee of the CPSU in 1946 were designed for training top party and state officials. Top recruits for the foreign service were trained in the Higher Diplomatic School and the Moscow State Institute for International Relations (IMO). A special institute for internal security existed for those going into police service.

These occupational and educational privileges contributed enormously to the development of a Soviet class society. An unmistakable tendency toward a society of ranks was already manifest in Stalin's time and was generated by Draconian labor measures adopted in 1938–1940[117] which gave the state a total monopoly over the distribution of human labor. It was furthered by the organization, spurred by the war, of a working force for military purposes. The gradations in social rank that all this produced still prevails today in a number of areas. The vertical stratification that this rank ordering brought about, particularly when combined with the natural horizontal stratification of Soviet society, accentuated the differences between various social groups, tending to solidify the walls between them, largely in terms of occupational affiliation. Thus, the gap between individual classes widened, resulting in the further removal of social and political leaders from the masses. This rank order or social hierarchy actually restored many of the gradations in rank characteristic of tsarist Russia.[118] To be sure, these gradations did not take the form of the elaborate and thorough-going scale of ranks that had been introduced by Peter the Great. Nevertheless, the introduction of service ranks, with corresponding insignia, uniforms, and privileges, which had been eliminated by the October Revolution, was a noteworthy return to the forms and style of the prerevolutionary era.[119]

Service ranks, along with their accompanying emblems, had

already been introduced into the Red Army, Secret Service, and Worker-Peasant Militia of the NKVD by regulations adopted on 22 September 1935, 16 October 1935, and 26 April 1936 respectively; since 1940 successive laws have been passed introducing service ranks, rank insignia, and corresponding uniforms. The following dates clearly mark the steps toward the restoration of these old practices:[120]

7 May 1940:	Service ranks and insignia for generals, marshalls, and admirals of the Red Army and Red Navy
9 May 1941:	Service ranks for diplomatic representatives in foreign countries
21 May 1942:	Service ranks and insignia for national guard troops
6 January 1943:	Service ranks and insignia for the entire Red Army (golden shoulder emblems for the officers)
9 February 1943:	Service ranks and insignia for the leading personnel of the Police Service (NKVD)
15 February 1943:	Service ranks and insignia for the entire Red Navy
28 May 1943:	Service ranks and insignia for all diplomats
4 September 1943:	Service ranks and insignia for the railroad service
16 September 1943:	Service ranks and insignia for the public prosecutor service (state attorneys and examining magistrates)
26 June 1945:	Generalissimo of the USSR—highest military rank
6 July 1945:	Military service ranks and insignia for higher police officers in the NKVD-NKGB (including reserve troops)

1 September 1947:   Service ranks and insignia for inland
                        navigation personnel
10 September 1947:*   Service ranks and insignia for managers
                        and technicians in the coal and mine-
                        shaft construction industry
14 October 1947:*   Service ranks and insignia for managers
                        and technicians in the geological service
10 December 1947:*   Service ranks and insignia for directors
                        and technicians in the mining industry
                        and mine construction for the ferrous
                        metal industry
20 March 1948:*   Service ranks and insignia for directors
                        and technicians in the mining industry
                        and in mine construction for the non-
                        ferrous metal industry (Ministry of Non-
                        ferrous Metal Industry and MVD)
3 July 1948:   Service ranks and insignia for directors
                        and technicians in merchant shipping
10 July 1948:*   Service ranks and insignia for directors
                        and other responsible officials in finance
                        and banking
8 November 1948:*   Service ranks and insignia for directors
                        and technicians in the mining industry
                        and mine construction for the chemical
                        industry
13 December 1948:   Service ranks and insignia for the com-
                        munications service (mail and telegraph)
28 January 1949:   Service ranks and insignia for directors
                        and technicians in the Central Office of
                        State Mining Inspection
6 April 1949:   Service ranks and insignia for adminis-
                        trative officials in the Central Office of
                        the Northern Sea Route
18 May 1949:*   Service ranks and insignia for adminis-

	trators and other responsible officials in the state inspection service
10 June 1949:**	Service ranks and insignia for administrators and technicians in the Central Office for Geodesy and Cartography of the MVD
17 June 1949:**	Service ranks and insignia for administrators and responsible officials in the field of procurement
25 June 1949:	Service ranks and insignia for the guards of the Ministry of Transport
3 July 1949:	Service ranks and insignia for the administrative staff of the fishing fleet
11 January 1950:*	Service ranks and insignia for managers and technicians in the oil and gas industry
25 February 1950:	Service ranks and insignia for the leading personnel of civil aviation
28 December 1950:	Service ranks and insignia for administrators and technicians in the hydrotechnical service and in ship repair stations
24 May 1951:*	Service ranks and insignia for directors and technicians in the electrical industry
13 October 1953:*	Service ranks and insignia for managers and technicians in the wood and paper industry

In the nonferrous metal industry, for example, the following service ranks or personal titles[121] were adopted pursuant to a decree of 20 March 1948 (VVS SSSR 1948, no. 12):

Highest Administrative and Technical Positions:

General-Director of Mines	Grade I
General-Director of Mines	Grade II
General-Director of Mines	Grade III

Senior Administrative and Technical Positions:

Director of Mines	(Special Grade)
Director of Mines or (Director of Mine Administration)	Grade I
(or Director of Mine Administration)	Grade II
(or Director of Mine Administration)	Grade III

Intermediate Technical Positions:

Mine Engineer	
(or Mine Technician)	Grade I
(or Mine Technician)	Grade II
(or Mine Technician)	Grade III

Lower Technical Positions:

Junior Mine Technician	
Senior Mine Master	
Mine Master	Grade I
Mine Master	Grade II
Brigadier	
(Underground brigades)	

If one disregards the brigadier there are fourteen ranks equivalent exactly to those which existed during the days of Peter the Great. They are patterned after the model of Soviet military organization. Pursuant to the decree of 24 July 1943 (VVS SSSR 1943, no. 28) a clear distinction was drawn between ordinary troops, noncommissioned officers, officers and generals of the Red Army, with staff officers (from major on up) enjoying a position of special prominence. Thus, in the mining industry, brigadier to junior mine technician would correspond to noncommissioned officers; mine engineer Class III to mine director would be equivalent to the officer corps; and general-director of mines Class I to Class III would equal the military rank of general. Mine directors would be the equivalent of staff officers.

The decree of 16 September 1943 (VVS SSSR 1943, no. 39) establishing ranks[122] in the state procuracy also has its military equivalent:[123]

Class	Rank	Corresponding Military Rank
	Higher Staff Positions	
1	Chief State Counselor of Justice	General of the Army
2	State Counselor of Justice, Class I	General
3	State Counselor of Justice, Class II	Lieutenant General
4	State Counselor of Justice, Class III	Major General
	Senior Staff Positions	
5	Senior Counselor	Colonel
6	Counselor	Lieutenant Colonel
7	Junior Counselor	Major
	Intermediate Staff Positions	
8	Attorney Class I	Captain
9	Attorney Class II	Lieutenant
10	Attorney Class III	1st Lieutenant
11	Junior Attorney	2nd Lieutenant

Ranks of inspector in the procuracy correspond to the service ranks of noncommissioned officers. The highest rank, reserved to the Procurator-General of the USSR signaled the return of the Secret Chief Counselor of tsarist Russia. The existing ranks in the Soviet diplomatic service shows that the Soviet system, even in those administrative areas where ranks have customarily existed, is significantly more complicated than in other countries:

USSR

Ambassador Extraordinary and Plenipotentiary
Envoy, Class I
Envoy, Class II

Counselor, Class I
Counselor, Class II
First Secretary, Class I
First Secretary, Class II
Second Secretary, Class I
Second Secretary, Class II
Third Secretary
Attache

The decree of 15 March 1946 (VVS SSSR 1946, no. 10) changing the name of the people's commissariates to ministries and the Council of People's Commissars to the Council of Ministers was also a reversion to traditional prerevolutionary terminology.[124] These service ranks were partially adopted in related areas of specialization, even though under the jurisdiction of another central authority.[125] This system of ranks was extended even further after Stalin's death. In the Ministry of Consumer Goods these unusual titles for milliners were introduced in November 1953: Colourist, Designer, and Master of Millinery, Classes I, II, and III.[126]

In the 1930s honorary titles of "Distinguished Teacher," "Distinguished Physician," and "Distinguished Scientist" were introduced. Later, titles such as "Hero of Socialist Labor" (1938), "People's Artist of the USSR" (1943), and "Heroine Mother" (1944) were also bestowed. After the war the following titles were created: "Laureate of the Stalin Prize" (1945), "Distinguished Zoo Technician" and "Distinguished Veterinarian" (1949), "Distinguished Agronomist" and "Master of Great Hunters" (1953), "Distinguished Test-Flyer and Helmsman" (1958), and "Distinguished Cosmonaut" (1961).

There is hardly a country in the world today which can even begin to compare itself to Bolshevik Russia in terms of the orders, titles, ranks it has conferred upon its citizens. Thus it can be observed that the bestowal of honorary titles and insignia is linked to corresponding privileges.

Even if one assumes that all this was calculated to spur men to higher achievement, as was certainly the case under Stalin, still the class system which finally emerged cultivated a bureaucratic mentality that rendered public life somewhat torpid.[127]

Next to the good will of the autocratic ruler, the service rank (the *chin*), modeled after that of tsarist Russia, was extolled as the measure of all things. These old-established symbols of privilege helped to consolidate the social position of the bureaucracy, especially its upper stratum, along with technocrats within the intelligentsia; the intelligentsia's intellectual components—writers, artists, and scientists—had cause for dissatisfaction in the postwar period, however.

All reforms in this system had been blocked by the top bureaucracy, the *nachalniki*, who feared that even limited liberalization of the regime might endanger the stability of the existing social order. For this reason, too, they opposed revolutionary experiments like those advocated by Khrushchev in the field of agriculture.[128]

During the war the rigidity of the kolkhoz system was somewhat relaxed. Kolkhoz peasants seized this opportunity, without authorization, to enlarge their private farm plots; pursuant to the 1935 model by-laws of the agricultural artel these were to be limited from 0.25 to 0.50 hectares, with one hectare permitted in exceptional cases.

After the war the reins were again tightened, although CC-Secretary A. A. Andreev was in favor of an agricultural policy that would measurably extend the system of individual work groups that more readily would take into account the familial ties of kolkhoz peasants. At the end of 1949 the direction of agrarian policy was taken over by Khrushchev, who wanted to combine around three to five kolkhozes into a large one, so as to produce working brigades of from 100 to 150 persons. After 1950, 252,000 small collective farm units were combined into 125,000 large kolkhozes[129] as Khrushchev pressed for the consolidation of smaller villages and individual farm plots into larger kolkhoz settlements called "agrocities." This plan for a "third agrarian revolution," which would have transformed the soil-bound kolkhoz peasant into a farm laborer, was regarded by Stalin and a majority of the Politburo as so risky that Khrushchev had to abandon the plan in March 1951.

The condition of both workers and minor white-collar employees, along with kolkhoz peasants, continued to worsen after the war. In 1948, despite the currency reform of 1947 and the subsequent drop in prices, real salaries dropped to the 1938 rate, which corresponded somewhat to the level of 1940. Nominally salaries were, on the average, twice as high as in 1938.[130] When prices fell still a third time after 1950, as the ruble was put on the gold standard, real wages neared the level of 1938 but did not reach it. After 1951 the situation deteriorated even more, especially in the country. Stalin wavered over what agricultural policy he should pursue.[131] According to Khrushchev, Stalin is said to have considered disbanding the state farms and annexing them to the kolkhozes.[132] After Khrushchev's temporary setback, which lasted from fall 1951 to spring 1952, Beria, who along with Malenkov appeared to be the most important advisor to Stalin, favored—subsequent to the dictator's death—the enlargement of the private farmland belonging to kolkhoz peasants.[133]

The special position of the Soviet state police, which was a "state within a state" in Stalin's time,[134] was related to the expansion of its economic rule and its role in numerous deportations. The result was a significant increase in the number of forced laborers pressed into service after the war. These workers were critically important to the development of the eastern part of the country which was rapidly getting underway in 1930, leading to the establishment, before the war, of the Ural-Kusnetsk-Kombinat. After hostilities broke out the War Economic Plan that was adopted by the Soviet government on 16 August 1941 provided for a massive shift of war-connected industries to the eastern zones. Because of the war this massive

eastward shift of the economy was greatly accelerated.[135] In 1941
alone 1,100 factories were evacuated; between 1942 and 1944
2,250 plants involving heavy industry moved their operations to
the new location. The labor supply was filled by moving 15
million persons to the eastern areas. A great many remained
there. Thus, accompanying the industrialization of the area was
a steady increase in the population of Siberia, Turkestan, and
the remote eastern regions. From 1939 to 1944 the urban population of these areas climbed from 15.6 to 20 million persons,[136]
producing a manifest change in the social and national structure
of the entire region.

Between 1939 and 1940 Stalin's policy of conquest expanded
the territory of the Soviet Union from 21.7 to 22.1 million
square kilometers. The population of the Soviet Union, 170.6
million on 17 January 1939, rose—on the basis of the 1939 calculation—to 190.7 million.[137]

The relation between urban and rural population changed
about one percent in favor of the rural population (68:32
instead of 67:33). In all of these areas, including the Baltic
states, which actually were more advanced than central Russia,
the social structure was adjusted to the Soviet model.

The continuation of the policy of conquest after World War
II led to the further enlargement of Soviet territory, which now
included northeast Prussia, from 22.1 to 22.4 million square
kilometers. Areas newly seized were subjected to the process of
Sovietization. Owing to the war and the misery caused by the
system of forced-labor camps, the Soviet population had suffered
immense losses. The entire population, estimated around 194.1
million on 1 January 1940, was cut down to 178.5 by 1 January
1950, notwithstanding the aggrandizement of territory. By 1
January 1953 it moved up again to an estimated 188.0 million,
remaining at a level which was under the 1940 figure. While the
urban population rose from 63.1 million (33 percent) to 80.2
million (43 percent) between 1940 and 1953, the rural popula-

tion dropped from 131 million (67 percent) to 107.8 million (57 percent).

Especially noteworthy was the preponderance of women in the country. In the cities this fact was related to the rising number of women represented in the working population. In 1936 women constituted 34 percent of workers and white-collar employees; between 1940 and 1942 this number increased from 37 to 45 percent. The figure was even higher among workers. It was 36 percent in 1936, 40 percent in 1940, and, as result of the war, 70 percent in 1942; after the war it was 45 to 47 percent. In Western Europe the corresponding figure was 20 to 30 percent and 15 percent in the USA.[138] Between 1939 and 1953, as the Soviet Union developed into the second most powerful military force in the world, she found herself simultaneously enveloped by a world more advanced in civility and culture. Stalin's fear of foreign influence prompted him to adopt in 1946 a policy of isolation toward the outside world while intensifying social controls from within.[139] This policy furthered the consolidation of the Soviet class society in the form of these established groups and also strengthened great Russian nationalism. At the same time, however, this policy hindered measures designed to expand the all too narrow socioeconomic base on which to maintain the Soviet Union as a world power.

5. The "New Course" and Khrushchevism (1953–1964)

In heavy industry, technical training, and natural science the Soviet Union had made great strides under Stalin; they were hailed by Soviet ideologues as shining examples of progress. The price paid for this progress was very high, however. It was obtained not only at the cost of millions of human lives and a low standard of living on the part of the broad masses, but also at the cost of individual liberty, owing to the omnipotence of the state together with stagnation in cultural and intellectual matters. In the last years of Stalin's life this paralysis extended to the economy, increasing social tensions as well as exacerbating the plight of the broad masses.

The tendency toward a state based on social ranks stifled, more and more, the creativity of the Soviet people. Moreover, the loss of social mobility and personal initiative that resulted from a regimentation of the body politic was not to be off-set by a system of social ranks and classes that the Vozhd ("leader") tried to install.

It appears that Stalin himself had become increasingly aware, in his last years, of these internal problems.[140] In any case, on the eve of his death, he favored a policy by which reforms were supposed to vary with individual revolutionary engagements. The first signs of "destalinization" were about to occur in several areas of Soviet life after the linguistic discussion of 1950.[141] After Stalin's death the retreat from the social system that bore his name occurred in three phases.

First were the "new course" measures taken by Malenkov to accommodate the popular demand for more consumer goods, more legal security, and more freedom in intellectual-cultural affairs.[142] The dissolution of most forced-labor camps was as significant in this regard, as were the more deeply felt "material interests" of working people in city and county, as well as the "thaw" in the literary-artistic sector.

The first great wave of the "destalinization" campaign was set off by Khrushchev's secret speech against Stalin at the Twentieth Party Congress of the CPSU (February 1956).[143] The second, and less successful, upsurge against Stalin was triggered by the Twenty-second Party Congress of the CPSU (October 1961), which adopted a new party program.[144]

Social development in Russia was very much influenced by these actions. Viewed in terms of power politics Khrushchev might well have pursued such risky policies with the following considerations in mind: (a) to bolster the Bolshevik one-party regime by loosening and modernizing the autocratic-totalitarian ruling system while giving greater consideration to the interests

of individual social strata; and (b) to increase the productivity
of the soviet economy by rationalizing and modernizing economic planning along with the simultaneous support of social
spontaneity.

Khrushchev's "destalinization" policy, which underwent frequent alterations, was incorporated in numerous reform measures—particularly policies affecting the administration of party,
state, and economy together with policies dealing with education, law, and military matters[145]—as well as in the Seven-Year
Plan (1959–1965) and the Twenty-Year Plan (1961–1980).[146]
This policy was associated with a revision in Marxist-Leninist
ideology, the role of which had undergone substantial change
under Stalin. The revision was expressed mainly in ideas such
as the "general peoples' republic" and the "general peoples'
party."[147] Important also was the further development of the
Marxist idea of contradiction, which will be discussed later. All
these measures, however, were only a partial accommodation to
reality, in no way comparable to Lenin's New Economic Policy.
Khrushchev's fall from power in October 1964 showed that
propaganda campaigns and organizational changes were not by
themselves sufficient to overcome certain social tensions and
economic difficulties of the Soviet Union.[148]

The sociological significance of Khrushchevism lies mainly in
the fact that the Soviet leader was under fire to move toward
a more open society by disavowing Stalin's isolationist policy
and by tolerating once again a measure of social pluralism.

The abolition of most distinctions of rank in nonmilitary
areas in July 1954 served this purpose, as was the case with the
establishment of boarding schools in February 1956, the restoration in July 1956 of the practice of admitting students to the
upper stage of general secondary schools without cost, along
with the education reform of December 1958 that was based
on the idea of polytechnical instruction.[149] These reforms were
expected not only to raise the number of qualified skilled
workers and foremen but also to terminate the practice of cater-

ing to the intelligentsia insofar as university education was concerned and to rid their children of a contemptuous attitude toward work.[150] At the same time the party expected to extend its influence over the newly emerging "creative intelligentsia," for whom special schools were being provided.

Also, the administrative reforms of 1957 (Economic Councils), 1958 (dissolution of the MTS), and the 1962 division of the party into two branches were calculated not only to increase industrial and agricultural production but also to enhance the social status of workers and kolkhoz peasants.[151] By accelerating the technical training of party functionaries in economics since 1956,[152] the party expected also to exert direct leadership over industry and agriculture and, thus, to render party functionaries less dependent upon members of the "technical intelligentsia."

Within the intelligentsia Stalin had largely elevated party functionaries to a position equal to that of the rest of the top bureaucracy. Khrushchev also favored the party *vis-à-vis* other ruling groups and assigned it a special place within the system.[153] However, he took measures to bolster the proletarian element within the main party apparatus in order to weaken the solidarity between party functionaries and other groups of functionaries that resulted from their common social membership in the intelligentsia. By introducing a rotating system he managed also to resist the practice of granting certain lifetime privileges to party functionaries.[154]

Khrushchev's policy of diminishing the terror of the regime by relaxing controls and providing more goods for people's needs not only endeared him to the broad masses, but also gained for him a measure of popularity among the upper and middle strata of the intelligentsia. On the other hand, by favoring the party apparatus, by disregarding the "well-earned rights" of other officeholders, and by seeking to reproletarianize the system, he multiplied his adversaries within the technocratic and intellectual segments of the intelligentsia. His attempt to reduce top wages to 1,200 rubles and to do away with individual bonuses threatened the incomes of all top functionaries.

Khrushchev's administrative reforms offended ministerial bureaucrats as well as plant and MTS directors. Economic managers, who had welcomed decentralized administration and greater plant autonomy, deeply resented Khrushchev's tightening of party controls over the economy and his granting more rights to unions. Planning experts were dismayed by Khrushchev's lack of realism. Workers and minor white-collar employees were generally regarded as the beneficiaries of "Khrushchevism." The pension increase of July 1956 was particularly to their advantage. The efforts of Khrushchev after the beginning of 1959 to increase monthly salaries by raising minimum salaries from 270 to 350 rubles and later from 500 to 600 rubles, and to cut high salaries so that they would approximate one another was likewise primarily in their interest.[155] He also sought to achieve this result through currency reform and his plan, announced in May 1960, gradually to abolish the income tax and substantially to shorten the working day.[156] But increasing economic difficulties, occasioned by rising defense costs, made it impossible for Khrushchev to realize these plans. In the summer of 1962 he was driven to raise the price of butter and meat about 25 to 30 percent, to impose a ceiling on wages, and to abandon plans for further tax decreases. A bad harvest in 1963 merely compounded the problem of providing the people with needed goods and services. The living standard of the broad masses, which inched upward because of prior salary increases, began once again to decline.[157]

The disappointed hopes of so many people could not adequately be compensated by improving the legal status of employees,[158] by expanding workers' rights in factory management,[159] by lowering certain retail prices, or by increasing social benefits.[160]

Kolkhoz peasants, whose taxes Malenkov reduced considerably, also owed much to Khrushchev.[161] Besides reorganizing the

MTS and incorporating the machine park within the collective farm, Khrushchev conceived of agricultural reforms which would introduce uniform prices for products delivered to the state,[162] increase substantially the income of the collective farm,[163] and introduce pensions for kolkhoz peasants.[164] On the other hand, Khrushchev's attempts to consolidate collective farms into gigantic collective enterprises or to convert them into state farms, to create collective farm associations, to raise the inapportionable fund, to abolish the field grass economy, and to limit private farmland generated increasing opposition.[165]

Decisive measures to cut back on the army of forced laborers were taken by Malenkov and Beria immediately after Stalin's death. According to Soviet reports 85 percent of all such prisoners had been released since March of 1953.[166] The conversion of most forced-labor camps into "labor colonies" was the result of a regulation passed by the USSR Council of Ministers on 25 October 1956. The system of forced-labor camps apparently had not been completely dissolved but was kept in existence for political prisoners.[167]

Between 1953 and 1959 the Soviet population increased from 188 to 208.8 million people and, according to Soviet estimates, would very probably reach 226.3 million by 1 January 1964.[168] The rise of the urban population between 1953 and 1959 went from 80.2 million (43 percent) to 100 million (48 percent), while the rural population increased from 107.8 million (57 percent) to 108.8 million (52 percent). At the turn of the decade (1960–61) the urban population exceeded for the first time, in absolute numbers, the rural population (percentage 50:50). On 1 January 1964 the urban population was estimated at around 118.6 million (52 percent), the rural population at 107.7 million (48 percent).

Women, who numbered 88.9 million in 1939 (as compared to 81.7 million men), totaled 114.8 million (against 94 million men) in 1959 and 123.1 million (against 103.2 million men) in 1964. The percentage of females, which in 1939 amounted to

52.1 percent of the population, went down between 1959 and 1964 from 55 to 54.5 percent.[169] Thus, women outnumbered men considerably, a fact that was particularly evident in rural areas. The natural population growth, which reached its zenith after the war with a rate of 18.1 births per thousand in 1958, declined to 14 per thousand in 1963.

Under Khrushchev the opening of the eastern territories had been brought about largely by the construction of the "Third Metallurgical Base"—provided by the Seven-Year Plan—in East Siberia and by new settlement in Kazakstan and West Siberia.[170] As a consequence, the population increase in these areas was somewhat higher than the average increase of the Soviet Union as a whole.

The social structure is in need of closer examination here. Between 1937 and 1959 white-collar employees had increased in number from 9.6 to 17.3 million (net total); during the same period the number of workers (including farm laborers) climbed from 17.3 to 39.6 million (net total).[171] The urban work force experienced a growth, though, that was considerably smaller than that of farm workers. In 1959, 44 to 55 percent of all production workers were employed only as assistant workers in Soviet industry. Forty-seven percent of all Soviet industrial workers were not running machines or other mechanical equipment actually, but were doing manual labor.[172] Kolkhoz farmers, whom Dallin estimated to number close to 40 million in 1940, dropped to 33 million in 1959. Together with 6 million farm laborers the population predominately employed in agriculture totaled about 39 million. By 1959 still 39.3 percent of all employed workers were involved in Soviet agriculture, as compared with 10 to 12 percent in the United States and 15 to 16 percent in West Germany.[173] Yet the productivity of Soviet agriculture lags considerably behind these two countries. It has been a matter of some concern in the Soviet Union that automation and especially the total mechanization of agriculture could lead to an excess labor supply.

Critically important for the intelligentsia, i.e., the mass of white-collar employees, was the fact that the number of specialists with a university education or advanced technical-school training had increased from 2.4 to 10.6 million between 1941 and 1964.[174]

The growing importance of university graduates served to reinforce those who had engineered a limited withdrawal from Stalinism. But they were still too weak politically to bring about greater change. Yet their strength in Soviet society was on the increase, while the tight grip of the party dictatorship began to loosen somewhat. Soviet citizens became more and more conscious of their inherent dignity as individuals, something that had been denied by the regime. Moreover, a kind of "public opinion" began to assert itself in the Soviet Union. Of course, this could hardly be compared to public opinion as we know it in the Western world. Yet it does appear in two distinct forms. First, there is the opinion of the top ten thousand, the *vyshie sloe* or the "higher circles," as the Russians say, whose opinions Stalin's successors could hardly ignore. This ten thousand includes mainly the top drawer of the main party apparatus—the party bosses—but it also includes people belonging to the higher strata of the Soviet intelligentsia. Second, there are the unarticulated opinions of the broad masses in Soviet society, opinions which are given expression mainly by the literati, only a portion of whom are members of the Soviet upper class.[175] Soviet writers constitute the large majority of those at the top of the progressive social forces in the Soviet Union. By "progressive" we mean all those people—really a heterogeneous group—who are seeking to relax the totalitarianism of the regime and to quicken the pace of social change. The social criticism which is exercised by the progressive Soviet literati and which is not put off by the party, is an expression of growing social conflict and a protest against social injustice and the lack of freedom which is all too manifest in the Soviet class society.

The progressives were joined in their struggle by representa-

tives of the older generation who during their youth, in the
1920s, were of cosmopolitan orientation (Paustovski, Ehrenburg, etc.) and by the established avant-garde of the younger
generation (Yevtushenko, Aksenov, etc.). Certain individuals
from the middle generation (Tvardovskii, Simonov, etc.) also
supported the progressives.

A counterattack was then launched, with the approval of the
party, by certain reactionary forces in the society. The latter
were largely older men of the middle generation who had risen
to power and influence during Stalin's time. Since this generational conflict embraces all segments of the cultural sphere, it
is a political event of the first magnitude.

The controversy even spilled over into the arts and letters;
the influence of the hard-liners here was strongest in the fields
of history and philosophy,[176] although their grip on law and economics was loosening somewhat.[177] "Marxist sociology" was
accompanied by a growing insistence upon an independent
"political science."[178]

Khrushchev tried desperately to curb these developments
shortly before his fall from power. In his speech of 8 March
1963 he made it quite clear that the party would not tolerate
dissent in these areas, and demanded of all writers and artists
that they rigidly adhere to the party line.[179] Ideological coexistence was no more admissible in the area of culture, according to
Khrushchev, than was the view that artistic endeavor could be
nonpolitical in character. Khrushchev sharply rebuked those
writers who insisted upon examining the nature of truth and
the problem of freedom as the essence of their creative work.

The problem of truth is concerned largely with the search
to overcome the past. The problem of freedom points to the
future. Both problems, connected as they are with the critique
of social abuses, have resulted in demands to change existing
conditions which do not correspond to the ethical standards
inherent in the concepts of truth and freedom. Thus the recent

debate about the idea of freedom in the Soviet Union combines the search for truth with immediate political reality.

Tarsis's "Legend of the Blue Fly"[180] taught that a revolution engineered by idealists would transform itself into a prisonlike socialism and thus into an established power which would be worse than an "oriental despotism." It only follows, therefore, that "where one party rules and all others are forbidden, tyranny is unavoidable." Tarsis believed that only the younger generation, untainted by the past, could be expected to overcome the totalitarian one-party state.

> Hence, one may contemplate a new beginning about fifteen years from now, around 1975, when the ghosts of the past have finally been exorcised; a new generation has grown up, and people really begin to think of the future instead of relying on scholastic dogmas and tottering authorities.

That freedom is to be understood primarily in terms of free elections Esenin-Volpin makes clear in these words:

> Freedom to us implies the possibility of holding elections, not simply because we want to hold an election (the necessity of holding an election is sometimes frightful and almost always unpleasant), but because we would like to be able to vote without coercion.[181]

Opinions of this sort, together with underground literary publications, such as the Moscow youth magazine *Feniks* [Phoenix] and the Leningrad student magazine *Kolokol* [The Bell], are symptoms of the ferment through which Soviet intellectuals and especially the younger generation are going today.[182] In this connection it is noteworthy that a similar phenomenon had occurred in Russia during the nineteenth century.

Besides the formal organization of the Bolshevik one-party system, an informal social order has developed in the Soviet Union. Like an iceberg, only its exposed part, namely the intellectual segment of the Soviet intelligentsia, has been visible. The mass of people is still largely apolitical, subservient to those in authority, the *nachal'stvo*, and somewhat alienated from the state. Gradually there evolved a group whose members, with a broad variety of backgrounds, were at home not only within the formal structure of the state, but also within this informal social structure that was now beginning to develop a sense of political identity. Because these people live and move in both interlacing spheres they have developed split personalities, as was clearly the case, for example, with Yevtushenko. Thus, what is taking place in the Soviet Union today is something that is not new for Russia. The intellectual segments of the Soviet intelligentsia are rebelling against the state. There are, however, notable differences between the old and new intelligentsia. First, the current generation of Soviet intellectuals is not yet as strongly pulled toward Europe as was the old Russian intelligentsia. Second, their critical capacities have yet to reach the sharp level of their predecessors. Finally, their social status is wholly different; in a society that has become more stratified, yet more sociologically compact, they are more inclined toward social conformity than was the case with intellectuals in tsarist Russia.[183]

II. THE SOCIAL STRUCTURE OF SOVIET SOCIETY

1. *The Formal Class Structure of Soviet Society*

According to Marx and Lenin a totally socialized system would have to lead to a classless society. In the Soviet Union, however, a new class society, exceeding that of capitalism and linked to the state even more firmly than was ever the case under the tsar, has evolved.[184] The Bolshevik regime has done everything possible to conceal in its statistical reports this contradiction between ideology and social reality. This was more easily achieved by taking several social groups and including them within a large social grouping through which the external image of Soviet society was more and more seen. One may observe from Tables 2 and 3 the progressive disappearance of several of these groupings from the official class structure (*klassovyi sostav*) of the Soviet population. The various groups which before the October Revolution constituted the upper and middle strata were simply designated as "capitalists" or members of the "bourgeoisie," or lumped together with rich and well-to-do farmers, namely, the kulaks. At the same time, workers and white-collar employees were collapsed into a larger group under the collective heading of the "proletariat." This classification had been adhered to even after the characterization "proletariat" was dropped and masses of white-collar employees had regarded themselves as part of the "intelligentsia." The size of both groups (along with family members) was revealed only for the years 1939 and 1959. In 1959, moreover, organized domestic workers (*kustari*), which included those left-over small industrial producers and petty artisans organized into cooperatives, were part of the total number of workers and employees. Until 1959 these domestic workers were included among kolkhoz farmers. The remaining peasants, working on their own, together with unorganized and privately employed homeworkers, were relatively unimportant. Thus, after the liquidation of the bourgeois-capitalist classes, only two main groups remained in Soviet society, namely (1) workers and white-collar employees, and (2) kolkhoz peasants.

To understand the ideological basis of this division one should mention the different forms of "socialist property" (state-owned property and cooperatively owned property) in the Soviet Union and the conflict between city and country. The distinction between workers and white-collar employees is based mainly on whether they perform physical or intellectual labor. When workers and peasants are grouped together as a "class" this usually means that they are both involved in the physical process of production; this is not the case with white-collar employees, among whom are the intelligentsia.

Considering Lenin's definition of classes the refusal to characterize white-collar employees as an independent class, like the other two groups: workers and peasants, seems hardly to be justified. (We shall discuss Lenin's concept of "class" a little later.) The distinction between the two forms of property just mentioned makes little sense when it is considered that the property of social organizations was recognized as a third form of "socialist property" in the newly revised civil code of 1961.[185]

That white-collar employees, or the intelligentsia in the broader sense, were regarded as equal in status to workers and farmers was to be seen from the intention of Khrushchev and his successors to give the former a special place next to the latter in the new USSR Constitution that has been under consideration since 1962.[186] The idea of a "general people's state" is designed mainly to bestow equal status upon the three social groups; in reality, however, it means putting the intelligentsia above the other two classes.

Soviet classifications permit us to describe the social structure of Soviet society only in rough outline. The foregoing observations about the three major social classes—workers, employees, and peasants—are nevertheless important since they not only reveal the general course of social change in Russia, but also contain vital information concerning the extent of social stratification in the Soviet Union.

The phases of social development in the Soviet Union, to which we have already alluded, are illustrated in Tables 2 and 3. Because of these revolutionary changes the percentage of workers and employees has risen astronomically (from 17.3 percent in 1928 to 34.7 percent in 1937 to 75.1 percent in 1964), while the percentage of peasants has declined appreciably (from 82.1 percent in 1926 to 55 percent in 1937 to 24.8 percent in 1964). The large number of workers and employees who, along with their families, make up two-thirds of the total population, shows the extent to which the Bolshevik regime carried forward the process of creating an industrial society that was actually

TABLE 2   The Social Composition of the Russian Population, 1917-1939
(Russian boundaries prior to 17 September 1939)

Classes	1913 Thousands	1913 %	1924 Thousands	1924 %	1928 Thousands	1928 %	1934 Thousands	1934 %	1937 Thousands	1937 %	1939 Thousands	1939 %
1. Workers and white-collar employees:	23,300	16.7	21,164	14.8	26,343	17.3	47,118	28.1	56,839	34.7	84,304	49.73
Workers:	--										54,566	32.19
Employees:	--										29,738	17.54
2. Kolkhoz peasants and cooperative homeworkers:	--	--	1,859	1.3	4,406	2.9	77,037	45.9	90,909	55.5	79,005	46.90
Kolkhoz peasants:											75,616	44.61
Homeworkers:											3,389	2.29
3. Individual peasants and private homeworkers:	90,700	65.1	107,822	75.4	111,131	72.9	37,902	22.5	9,172	5.6	4,414	2.60
Individual peasants:											1,396	0.82
Homeworkers:											3,018	1.78
4. Capitalists:	22,100	15.9	12,155	8.5	6,801	4.5	174	0.10			60	0.04
Kulaks:	17,100	12.3			5,618	3.7	149	0.09				
5. Others (Students, military, pensioners):	3,200	2.3			3,671	2.4	5,769	3.4	6,880	4.2	1,235	0.73
Balance											1,539	
Total Population	139,300	100	143,000	100	152,352	100	168,000	100	163,800	100	170,557	100

Source: *Sowjetunion 1935*, p. 77; *Pravda*, 29 January 1935; *Der sozialistische Aufbau der UdSSR 1933-1938* (Moscow, 1939) (Russ.), p. 138; for 1939 (not including the districts of the extreme Northern latitude), *USSR* (encyclopedia), p. 50. The figures for 1924 are based on percentages (*SSSR v tsifrakh v 1963 godu*, p. 21) of population totals for 1926. (A population increase of 4 million was estimated.)

begun during the tsarist regime. The outcome, quite apart from the special status and development of individual social groups, would hardly have been different had industrialization taken place by "capitalistic" methods. In such a case, even if development had proceeded at a slower pace, it is highly doubtful that it would have demanded such a high sacrifice.[187] We already saw how drastic was the impact of forced-labor camps on population growth in the Soviet Union. This is particularly clear from the figures contained in Table 2. From 1934 to 1937 the population of the Soviet Union, owing to the impact of Stalinist methods of industrialization, had increased by about two million only. At the same time there were sporadic increases of workers and white-collar employees without the number of peasants having receded very much. From 1937 to 1939 the total number of workers and white-collar employees (with family members) increased by a good 17.5 million (15 percent), although employed white-collar employees and workers had increased only by about 4.5 million from 1937 to 1940. The population growth between 1934 and 1937 (see Table 2) shows clearly the effects of Stalinist methods of industrialization.

To assume that in 1939, just as in 1940, there was on the average two dependents for every employed worker or white-collar employee means a discrepancy of 5.5 million in the above figures. This can only be explained by the fact that those forced laborers who, in terms of occupation and origin, belonged to other social categories were included among the number of workers and white-collar employees. Soviet statistics actually confirm the assumption that the number of forced laborers amounted to around 5 million on the eve of the Second World War. In the postwar period, too, Soviet statistics adhered to this manner of listing forced laborers.

Thus it should be noted that in the total figure for workers and white-collar employees (including family members) we are unable to determine exactly how many forced laborers are included.[188]

TABLE 3   The Social Composition of the Russian Population, 1939–1964
(Within the boundaries of 1941)

"Class"	1939		1955		1956		1959		1961		1962		1963		1964	
	Thousands	%	Thousands	%	Thousands	%	Thousands	%	Thousands	%	Thousands	%	Thousands	%	Thousands	%
Workers and white-collar employees:	95,732	50.2	113,335	58.3	117,750	59.5	142,700	68.3	155,160	71.8	161,699	73.6	165,763	74.3	169,951	75.1
Workers:							100,800	48.2								
Employees:							41,900	20.1								
Kolkhoz peasants:	90,010	47.2	80,093	41.2	79,160	40.0	65,000	31.4	60,508	28.0	57,781	26.3	57,114	25.6	56,138	24.8
Individual peasants and private homeworkers:	4,958	2.6	972	0.5	990	0.5	600	0.3	432	0.2	220	0.1	223	0.1	226	0.1
Total population:	190,700	100	194,400	100	197,900	100	208,800	100	216,100	100	219,700	100	223,100	100	226,315	100

Source: *Narodnoe khoziaistvo* for 1956 (Moscow, 1957), p. 19; for 1961 (Moscow, 1962), p. 27; for 1962 (Moscow, 1963), p. 14; for 1963 (Moscow, 1964), p. 28; *zapisnaia knizhka partiinogo aktivista 1966* [Registry of party activists for 1966] (Moscow, 1966), pp. 8–9; *Itogi vsesoiuznoi perepisi naseleniia 1959 goda. SSSR* (Moscow, 1962), pp. 90–92; *Istoricheskii s"ezd leninskoi partii* [The historic meeting of the Leninist party] (Moscow, 1961), p. 43. Absolute numbers are provided only for 1939 (within the boundaries prior to 17 September 1939) and 1959. The figures for 1939 (within the boundaries of 1941), 1955, 1956, 1961, 1962, 1963, and 1964 were calculated on the basis of population totals.

TABLE 4

Distribution of Population within the Class
Structure of 1959

Class	Millions	Percentages		
		Entire Population	Urban	Rural
Workers and employees:	142.7	68.3	46.2	22.1
Workers:	100.8	48.2	31.6	16.6
Employees:	41.9	20.1	14.6	5.5
Kolkhoz peasants:	65.5	31.4	1.6	29.8
Individual peasants and private homeworkers:	0.6	0.3	0.1	0.2
Total:	208.8	100	47.9	52.1

Source: S.A. Kugel, *Zakonomernost' izmeneniia sotsial'noi struktury obshchestva pri perekhode k kommunizmu* [The Lawfulness of socio-structural change in the transition to communism] (Moscow, 1963), p. 34.

We have already mentioned the increase in urban population brought about by forced industrialization and collectivization. The various "classes" within the urban and rural population are shown in Table 4. It shows that white-collar employees and "intellectuals" are more closely tied to the city than are the workers.

Additional information about the size and composition of these large social groupings can be obtained from statistics available on the occupational structure and educational attainment of the Soviet population.

The total labor force included in the national economy (109 million), as well as the number of people employed in the strict sense (99.1 million), is revealed in Table 5.[189] It is important to note that among those listed as employed in 1959 about 6.4 million were not of working age. As shown in Table 6 the women employed outnumbered men by 4.2 million.

TABLE 5

Employment of the Soviet Population in 1959

Employed Groups	Millions (1959)	Percentage (1959)	Percentage (1939)
1. Gainfully employed:	99.1	47.5	46.2
Of working age:	92.7	44.4	
Under military obligation:	3.6	1.7	
2. Relatives of kolkhoz peasants, workers, and peasants engaged in private economic activities:	9.9	4.7	4.9
Employed in the National Economy:	109.0	52.2	51.1
3. Family members engaged in household matters:	85.4	40.9	45.9
4. Pensioners:	12.4	6.0	1.3
5. Stipendiaries:	1.7	0.8	1.0
6. Other:	0.3	0.1	0.7
Total:	208.8	100	100

Source: Itogi vsesoiuznoi perepisi naseleniia 1959 goda,
pp. 96-99;   Narodnoe khoziaistvo SSSR v 1960 godu, p. 25;
Kugel, op. cit., p. 37;   P. G. Pod"iachikh,   Naselenie
SSSR (Moscow, 1961), p. 129.

With regard to the Soviet Union's potential labor force a
further breakdown of the above figures (Table 5) is presented
in Table 7, which is a more precise rendition of the occupational
structure of the Soviet population engaged in the national economy. Table 7 shows that in 1959 employees and workers constituted about half, while kolkhoz peasants made up a fourth of
the potential working force in the Soviet Union. It is important to note also that the high number of university and technical-school students is included in the gross and net totals of
workers, employees, and intellectuals.[190]

TABLE 6

Employment of Men and Women in 1959

Employed Groups	In Millions			%
	Men	Women	Total	
1. Those engaged in the national economy	52.4	56.6	109.0	52.2
2. Employed by individual persons	35.0	50.4	85.4	40.9
3. Employed by organizations (pensioners, stipendiaries)	6.5	7.6	14.1	6.8
4. Others	0.1	0.2	0.3	0.1

Source: Pod"iachikh, *op. cit.*, p. 128.

The 99.1 million people employed in the economy (including university students and persons not of working age, but excluding assisting family members) are further subdivided in Tables 8 and 9 by industry, social groups, and sex.

The outline of the social structure is even more manifest in Table 10, concerning which Soviet sources disclose only the percentages. It gives us an overview of those groups of working age who are employed in the national economy (including assisting family members but excluding university students and members of the armed services).

Table 10 records the percentages of the 94.6 million employed people by occupation and economic area.[191] Tables 8 and 10 disclose the total number of workers and employees on the job in 1959. The year-end figure of 56.9 million includes 39.6 million workers and 17.3 million white-collar employees. The gross number of workers (46.1 million) that appears in Table 8 seems about 0.6 million too high, but the gross number of employees (19.8 million) seems to be about 0.8 million too low when compared to the total number of "brainworkers" (20.5 million).[192]

TABLE 7

Laboring Groups within the Soviet Population in 1959

Professional Groups	Millions	%
Workers and white-collar employees and other gainfully employed:	66.6	52.1
Workers and employees:	63.0	49.3
Students and specialized pupils in the process of production:	4.4	
Kolkhoz peasants:	32.3	25.3
Individual peasants and private homeworkers:	0.3	0.2
Gainfully employed:	99.2	77.6
Relatives of kolkhoz peasants, workers, and peasants involved in private economic activities:	9.9	7.7
Employed in the National Economy:	109.1	85.3
Students and specialized pupils outside of production:	5.8	4.6
Family members engaged in the education of children and in housekeeping activities:	12.8	10.0
Others:	0.1	0.1
Total:	127.8	100

Source: *Itogi vsesoiuznoi perepisi naseleniia 1959 goda*, pp. 96-99; *Narodnoe khoziaistvo SSSR v 1960 godu*, p. 25; Pod"iachikh, *op. cit.*, p. 132.

Table 10 gives the number of cooperative homeworkers (1.2 million) and family members assisting workers and employees (3.4 million). Family members assisting kolkhoz peasants numbered around 6.5 million. Kolkhoz peasants (33 million) had only 0.8 million of their members in the military establishment;

TABLE 8   Employment in Various Branches of the Economy by Social Groups

Professional and Employed Groups	Thousands					Percentages			
	Total	Workers	White-collar employees	Kolkhoz peasants	Individual peasants and homeworkers	Workers	White-collar employees	Kolkhoz peasants	Individual peasants and homeworkers
Employed:	99,130	46,146	19,670	33,047	266	100	100	100	100
Engaged in material production:	80,172	38,912	9,514	32,181	255	84.3	48.4	97.4	95.8
Industry, construction, transportation, communications:	36,575	29,988	5,990	439	158	65.0	30.5	1.3	59.3
Agriculture:	38,426	5,918	693	31,723	92	12.8	3.5	96.0	34.4
Trade, supply:	5,171	2,534	2,625	11	--	5.5	13.3	0.1	0.1
Not engaged in material production (education, science, health, housing and welfare, state administration and administration of social organizations, credit and insurance):	14,453	5,328	9,018	97	10	11.5	45.9	0.3	3.6
Education, science, art, health:	9,793	3,289	6,418	85	--	7.1	32.6	0.3	0.1
Military:	3,623	1,823	1,033	767	--	4.0	5.2	2.3	0.1
Other:	191	83	105	2	1	0.2	0.5	0.0	0.5

Source: Itogi vsesoiuznoi perepisi naseleniia 1959 goda, p. 104 ff.

TABLE 9

Men and Women Employed in the Individual Branches
of the Economy
(as of 15 January 1959)

Occupational and Employed Groups	Thousands	%	% Men	% Women
Total Population:	208,827	--	45	55
Employed:	99,130	100	52	48
Material production:	80,863	81.6	53	47
Industry, construction, transportation, communications:	36,575	36.9	61	39
Agriculture:	38,426	38.8	46	54
Kolkhoz peasants:	31,723	32.0	43	37
Workers and employees on state farms:	6,611	6.7	59	41
Individual peasants:	92	0.1	35	65
Trade and supply:	5,171	5.2	39	61
Nonmaterial production (education, science, health, housing, welfare, state administration, credit, insurance, and the apparatus of social organizations):	14,453	14.6	36	64
Education, science, art, and health:	9,793	9.9	29	71
Military:	3,623	3.6	100	0.0
Other:	191	0.2	70	30

Source: *Narodnoe khoziaistvo SSSR v 1960 godu*, p. 26.

TABLE 10   Professional Structure of the Soviet Population

Professional and Employed Groups	Millions 1959	Percent 1959	Percentages								
			1940	1950	1955	1956	1957	1958	1961	1962	1963
Those engaged in material production (including goods, transportation, communications, and trade):	79.40	83.9	87.9	86.2	85.2	85.2	84.9	84.2	82.1	81.4	80.8
Workers:	31.78	33.6	19.4	25.6	31.6	32.2	33.3	33.6			
Engineering-technical personnel, white-collar employees, junior service personnel, trade personnel:	9.93	10.5	9.1	9.9	10.2	10.2	10.4	10.4			
Members of cooperative trades (associated homeworkers):	1.17	1.2	2.2	1.5	1.8	1.1	1.2	1.3			
Kolkhoz peasants engaged in the social economy and in private economic activities:	32.83	34.7	45.2	44.0	37.5	37.7	36.0	34.9			

Individual peasants and private homeworkers:	0.28	0.3	9.5	2.0	0.4	0.4	0.3	0.3	0.3	0.3
Family members of workers and employees engaged in private economic activities:	3.41	3.6	2.5	3.2	3.7	3.6	3.7	3.7	3.7	3.7
Those engaged in nonmaterial production:	15.23	16.1	12.1	13.8	14.8	14.8	15.1	15.8	17.9	18.6 / 19.2
Education, health:	9.84	10.4	6.0	7.7	9.1		9.5	10.1	11.9	12.6 / 13.1
Housing and welfare, public transportation, communications, administration of state and social organizations, credit and insurance:	5.39	5.7	6.1	6.1	5.7	5.6	5.7	6.0	6.0	6.1
Total:	94.63	100	100	100	100	100	100	100	100	100

Source: Percentages are from *Narodnoe khoziaistvo SSSR* for 1956, p. 202; for 1958, p. 655; for 1959, p. 584; for 1961, p. 565; for 1962, p. 451; for 1963, p. 473.

TABLE 11   Class Basis of the Employed Population in Urban and Rural Areas

"Classes"	Millions	Entire Population	Percentages	
			Urban	Rural
Workers:	46.1	46.6	31.4	15.2
Those engaged in industry, construction, transportation, communications:	30.0	30.3	23.8	6.5
Agriculture:	5.9	5.9	0.8	5.1
Employees:	19.7	19.8	14.5	5.3
Kolkhoz peasants:	33.0	33.3	1.2	32.1
Individual peasants:	0.3	0.3	0.1	0.2
Total:	99.1	100	47.2	52.8

Source: Kugel, *op. cit.*, p. 38.

86

TABLE 12

Education of the Soviet Population
(millions)

	Total	1959		1963
		Men	Women	
Complete university education	3.8	1.9	1.9	5.0
Incomplete university education	1.7	0.8	0.9	2.0
Advanced technical-school training	7.9	3.4	4.5	9.6
General secondary education	9.9	4.4	5.5	11.4
Complete education	23.3	10.5	12.8	28.0
Incomplete secondary education (at least 7 years of schooling)	35.4	17.1	18.3	40.6
Total	58.7	27.6	31.1	68.6

Source: *Narodnoe khoziaistvo SSSR* for 1959, p. 21; for 1962, p. 15; for 1963, p. 29.

TABLE 13   Education of the Soviet Population by "Class"
(as of 15 January 1959)

	Workers		Kolkhoz Peasants		White-Collar	
	Millions	Percent	Millions	Percent	Millions	Percent
Total Number within the "class" along with family members	100.8	48.2	65.6	31.4	41.9	20.1
University or advanced technical education (including incomplete university education)	1.4	1.4	0.5	0.7	11.6	27.6
General secondary education (10 years of schooling)	3.9	3.9	1.2	1.9	4.8	11.4
Complete education	5.3	5.3	1.7	2.6	16.4	39.0
Incomplete secondary education (at least 7 years of schooling)	19.1	19.0	8.2	12.7	7.8	18.6
Total:	24.4	24.3	9.9	15.3	24.2	57.6

Source: Computation by Wädekin (*op. cit.*, p. 323) is based on data from *Itogi vsesoiuznoi perepisi naseleniia 1959 goda*, p. 90.

TABLE 14

Classification of Employed by Type of Work

Employed Groups	1959		1963	
	Millions	%	Millions	%
Those engaged primarily in physical labor:	78.6	80.3	81.9	77.8
Workers:	45.6	47.1		
Kolkhoz peasants:	33.0	33.2		
Those engaged primarily in intellectual labor:	20.5	19.7	23.3	22.2
Total:	99.1	100	105.2	100

Source: *Itogi vsesoiuznoi perepisi naseleniia 1959 goda,*
pp. 161, 162; *SSSR v tsifrakh v 1963 godu,* p. 20.

this was relatively small when compared to workers and employees, whose members in the armed services constituted 1.8 and 1 million men respectively. This division of the employed urban and rural population among social groups is based on what could be determined earlier with reference to the division of the entire population. Two-thirds of white-collar employees and only half of the workers, as indicated by their occupation, labored in cities (See Table 11).

A more accurate picture of the social structure can be gleaned by looking at the educational attainments of the Soviet population.[193] Tables 12 and 13 delineate in significant detail the educational and occupational characteristics of white-collar employees and intellectuals. The 23.3 million people listed in 1959 as having a complete education tallies with the 20.5 million listed as "brainworkers"; among the former were 12.8 million women and 10.5 million men. Many more women than men had finished general secondary schools and technical training. An equal number of men and women, however, had completed their university education. Among those completing their uni-

TABLE 15

Employed Classified by Sex
(percentages)

	Men		Women		Total	
	1939	1959	1939	1959	1939	1959
Those primarily engaged in physical labor:	79.4	81.7	86.4	76.8	82.5	80.3
Those primarily engaged in intellectual labor:	20.6	18.3	13.6	23.2	17.5	19.7
Total:	100	100	100	100	100	100

Source: Pod"iachikh, *op. cit.*, p. 150. The erroneous percentages from Pod"iachikh for 1959 have been corrected.

versity and advanced technical training (including those with an incomplete university education) the ratio of white-collar employees to workers was 8 to 1 (11.6 million to 1.4 million); if those qualifying for the abitur examination are included the ratio would be 3 to 1 (16.4 to 5.3 million).

For more exact estimates of the number of white-collar employees and members of the intelligentsia, groups which overlap considerably, it is important to consider the educational level of the 99.1 million people employed in intellectual as well as manual labor. Table 15 reveals the number of men and women engaged in both intellectual and physical labor for the years 1939 and 1959. It is clear that the number of women engaged in intellectual work increased quite substantially. Indeed, women's participation in the general rise of the level of Soviet education —having resulted, even before the war, in the virtual elimination of illiteracy—was extraordinary. Since 1939 the number of fully educated citizens both among the gainfully employed and the entire population increased three and a half times. (See Table 16.)

The gap between the educational level of the gainfully em-

TABLE 16   Educational Level of the Employed Population According to Type of Work and Social Category

(per thousand group members)

	University and secondary education (including incomplete secondary education)		1959	
	1939	1959	University and advanced technical training (including incomplete university education)	General secondary education (including incomplete secondary education)
Entire population:	83	281	64	217
Employed population:	123	433	109	324
Those primarily engaged in physical labor:	43	316	14	302
Those primarily engaged in intellectual activity:	498	884	476	408
Workers:	82	386	20	366
Kolkhoz peasants:	18	226	9	217
White-collar employees:	519	893	490	403

Source: *Itogi vsesoiuznoi perepisi naseleniia 1959 goda*, pp. 111, 115, 116, 176; Pod"iachikh, *op. cit.*, p. 149.

TABLE 17

Total Number of Workers and White-Collar Employees
(in millions)

	Yearly average	End of year	Workers	Industrial workers	Rural workers	White-collar employees
1913 inside the boundaries at that time			8.6			
within the boundaries prior to 17 Sept. 1939	11.2	11.4	7.2	3.6	3	4.0
in the now-existing bondaries	12.9	12.9		4.3		
1917				3.0		
1918				2.5		
1919				2.5		
1920/21				1.5		
1921/22				1.2		
1922/23	6.6		4.2	2.0	1	2.4
1923/24	7.4			1.8		
1924/25	8.5			2.2		
1925/26	10.2			2.7		
1926/27	10.9			2.8		
1928	10.8	11.6	6.9	3.1	2.0	3.9
1929		12.2		3.4		
1930		14.5	9.5	4.3		5.0
1931				5.5		
1932	22.6	22.9		6.0		
1933	21.8	22.3	13.8	6.3		8.0
1934		23.6		6.5		
1935		24.6		7.1		
1936				7.7		
1937	26.7	27.0	17.3	7.9	2.4	9.6
1938						
1939						
1940	31.2	31.5	17.1	8.3	2.3	11.4
1941	31.0					
1942 (Plan)	32.7			9.2		
1943	19.3					
1945	27.3	28.3				
1946						
1947		31.4				

TABLE 17 continued

	Yearly average	End of year	Workers	Industrial workers	Rural workers	White-collar employees
1948		33.4				
1949		35.2				
1950	38.9	39.8	ca.26.3	11.3	ca.3.0	ca.13.5
1951	40.7	41.4			3.1	
1952	42.2	42.5				
1953	43.7	44.6		13.2	3.8	
1954	47.3	46.8		13.8		
1955	48.4	47.9		14.3	5.9	
1956	50.5	50.0		15.2	5.8	
1957	53.1	52.7			6.6	
1958	54.6	54.3		16.3	5.9	
1959	56.6	56.9	39.6	16.8	6.0	17.3
1960	62.0			18.6	6.7	
1961	65.9			19.5	7.4	
1962	68.3			20.2	7.7	
1963	70.5		ca.55.5	20.7	7.9	ca.25
1964	73.2					
1965 (Plan)	76.0					

Source: S. M. Schwarz, *Arbeiterklasse und Arbeitspolitik in der Sowjetunion* (Hamburg, 1953), pp. 42 ff.; Petroff, *op. cit.*, p. 69; Jugow, *op. cit.*, p. 286; Ch. Bettelheim, *L'économie soviétique* (Paris, 1950), p. 193; *Die Ergebnisse der Erfüllung des ersten Fünfjahresplanes* (Moscow, 1935) (Russ.); *Die Ergebnisse der Erfüllung des zweiten Fünfjahresplanes* (Moscow, 1939) (Russ.); *Narodnoe khoziaistvo* for 1956, pp. 50 and 203; 1958, pp. 654 ff.; 1959, pp. 585 ff.; 1960, pp. 633 ff.; 1961, pp. 181,461,566 ff.; 1962, pp. 368, 452 ff.; 1963, pp. 363 and 474 ff.; *Sel' skoe khoziaistvo* [Agriculture] (Moscow, 1960), pp. 450 ff.; *Ost-Probleme* 17 (1965), p. 515.

ployed and the population as a whole had, as a result, become a little larger. In this connection, the three large social groups (employees, workers, and peasants) in the Soviet Union did not develop in quite the same way. The general educational level of workers, for example, increased significantly when compared to that of white-collar employees, but the education of kolkhoz peasants increased even more so relative to workers.

In the area of higher "specialist" training, white-collar employees had considerably better opportunities than either workers or farmers. The advantages that employees and "brainworkers" had because of their education is clearly reflected in Table 16. Out of every thousand persons with a university education or advanced technical training (including those with some university training) who were gainfully employed, 490 were white-collar employees, while 476 were engaged primarily in intellectual work. The corresponding figures for workers and others involved mainly in physical work were 20 and 14 respectively.

The situation is much better for the fully trained worker; yet here too it is clear that the educational level of employed workers is substantially less than is the level of the worker class generally, including their families. On the other hand, the educational level of working white-collar employees is much higher than the level of the whole "class" (with their families).

These data on occupational and educational structure, which are helpful in determining the formal class structure of the Soviet Union, point clearly to the dominant position of white-collar employees in contrast to the other two large social groups which have been regarded as the basic classes in Soviet society. This observation, however, says nothing about the actual importance or influence of these groups inside the formal class structure. Hence, we proceed to a more detailed analysis of the makeup of these separate "classes" in the society.

2. The New Working Class

Statistical data on the social structure of the Soviet population that has accumulated so rapidly in recent years enables us to determine more precisely not only the size of separate classes but also their composition. Even so, we can give here only a limited discussion of each of these "classes." A more detailed analysis must await further research.

We begin with the working class which, until quite recently, had been touted as the exclusive ruling group in the Soviet Union ("dictatorship of the proletariat"). Today, however, the working class would seem to have only limited influence vis-à-vis other social groups in the "general peoples' state." Because the working class is closely related to those who are variously described as "white-collar employees" or "the intelligentsia," the former's general growth over time might best be appreciated by presenting the figures available for both groups. With regard to the number of workers and employees in Table 17 we have distinguished between the yearly average and the total at the year's end. It should be noted, however, that Soviet figures, particularly those having to do with the first two phases of development, are frequently in conflict.

Figures for several of the years represented in Table 17 are missing. The breakdown for industrial workers, however, is relatively complete; to a lesser extent in the case of farm workers. The latter will be dealt with more extensively in our treatment of the kolkhoz peasants.

The total number of workers in Russia has increased enormously since forced industrialization. In 1928 the total was 6.9 million men, the approximate size of the working force in 1913 (i.e., within Soviet boundaries as they existed prior to 17 September 1939). On the eve of World War II there were 17.1 million workers. Following the war the figure climbed from about 19.4 million in 1949 to 39.6 million in 1959, and then to around 55.5 million in 1963. It is to be observed from these figures that they include workers outside of production who perform distinct white-collar functions. On the other hand, foremen and highly trained technical workers are regarded as employees.[194] In addition to engineers and agronomists the total figure for 1963 also includes cooperative homeworkers; earlier they represented a self-sufficient group linked to kolkhoz peasants. In 1956 some industrial cooperatives were incorporated into state industry; the rest were incorporated in 1959–60. Since then cooperative homeworkers have constituted an essential part of the "working class."

From a quantitative and even from a qualitative perspective the Soviet working class can be compared to that of the older industrialized nations. This is particularly the case for industrial workers, who numbered 3.1 million in 1928, a figure below that of the 3.6 million mark achieved prior to the war (within the boundaries before 17 September 1939). By 1939 this number totaled 8.3 million; in the postwar period it shot up to 11.3 million in 1950, 16.8 million in 1959, and 20.7 million in 1963.

Soviet workers, when compared to prerevolutionary workers, constituted a new and distinctive class.[195] Only a relatively small segment of this "new working class," which emerged out of the process of forced industrialization, was actually employed prior to the revolution, or traced its origin to the workers of that time. Only among metal workers, the nucleus, really, of industrial laborers, is the percentage of prerevolutionary workers and their children greater. Metal workers, who currently number 9.3 million men, have both the strongest feeling of class consciousness among Soviet workers and the firmest link to the revolutionary and trade union tradition. The overwhelming majority of new workers, however, trace their origin to the peasantry.

Stalin, with raw cruelty, transplanted the Russian peasant from his village into the factory. The remaking of these farmhands—they were often unable to read or write, knew nothing at all about modern machinery, and were highly undisciplined in their work habits—into urban workers was an extremely difficult task.[196] The tight hold of the land on the Russian peasant was mainly dislodged by forced collectivization. Yet the style or outlook of these new workers had been deeply molded by their natural love of the soil. Of some importance too was the fact that these new workers did not enjoy the assistance and encouragement of idealistic intellectuals who had earlier contributed so much to the Russian labor movement.

Also, the new working class, because its largest segment was made up of women and younger men, was too weak effectively to resist the state bureaucracy. In 1940 around 40 percent of all industrial workers were women, 30 percent were younger men (under 23 years of age), while only 30 percent were men in higher age brackets (as compared with the 1914 worker force, of which 62, 27, and 11 percent were, respectively, older men, women, and younger men). Perhaps this, together with a weakly developed class consciousness and the brutality of a totalitarian ruling apparatus, are the reasons why no strong revolutionary sentiment developed in the working class, notwithstanding the abject misery of the 1930s. Also of importance in this regard was the stratification within the working class itself; this was mentioned earlier in our discussion of the training of a "worker aristocracy," consisting of foremen and highly qualified technical workers. High specialization, which was accompanied in 1937 by the introduction of more than 2,000 occupational titles and technical specialities in the metal industry alone,[197] had also contributed to a highly differentiated work structure, blunting even more the development of class consciousness. In the course of time the worker and his family developed a firm link to the factory; it became an integral part of his tiny universe, along with the social groups to which he belonged.[198] Some industries were promoted and favored by the regime; when this happened the workers in these industries tended to benefit, actually increasing their influence in the most important administrative and industrial centers. This was particularly true of large enterprises in the vicinity of Moscow and Leningrad. Conformity to the system was strongest among middle-aged workers, but less so among the young working generation which had not experienced the terrors of the past.

Hindus very graphically describes the average worker in his middle years:

> The working man of rural origin, coming from the village, knew nothing about the Western concept of the rights of labor. Still today he knows little about it. He has undergone both a physical

and psychological discipline that no trade union in the West
would tolerate. He is a closely watched ward of the state and of
the party; he lives in a community that, though not as closed a
society as a Moscow auto plant, is largely a world of its own,
along with the party, Komsomol, or Trade union, always ready,
when necessary, to conform and change its opinion in accordance
with the outlook and views of the Kremlin.[199]

Hindus's analysis leads him to conclude that the regime does
not have to fear the political opposition of workers. But he is
also of the view that the young working generation is too well
educated to allow itself to be victimized by the Soviet bureaucracy. In this respect the men of this generation are freer than
their parents, for they are not disposed patiently to withstand
abuses of authority. This generation seems prepared to set forth
its wishes and demands in clear and bold language.

The success of poetry readings in manufacturing plants sug-
gests that many of the young workers have rather thoroughly
absorbed the ideas of progressive writers. Moreover, it can be
seen from reports of strike actions[200] that the worker's relationship to the regime is more problematical than Hindus supposes.
Recent research by Soviet sociologists has disclosed that young
workers are highly dissatisfied with their work and frequently
with their occupation.[201] This explains the increasing mobility
among workers in industrial areas. On the other hand, it shows
that workers today possess more freedom of movement than
under Stalin, when they were actually shackled to a given
industry by the Draconian legal measures that regulated their
lives. Investigations by the Laboratory for Sociological Research
at Leningrad University, the results of which appeared in 1963,
found that a high percentage of Leningrad workers (59 percent)
were indifferent to or dissatisfied with their own work. An
almost equally high percentage (57 percent) were indifferent
to or dissatisfied with their occupation.[202] Another study in
the same year revealed that 36.4 percent of the respondents
switched jobs because of bad working conditions, while 30 per-

cent did so because of unsatisfactory housing and living conditions. Twenty-three percent of these respondents expected higher earnings in their new places of work.[203]

As far as the social stratification of workers is concerned, skilled workers, along with the relatively small group of foremen and highly qualified workers, are of particular importance. The working masses, however, are, in the main, still partially trained or even unskilled. Then there is a group of trainees, whose exact number is fixed by the "workers' aristocracy" that enjoys white-collar employee status. In 1959 the number of foremen (masters) totaled 753,521, while highly qualified personnel numbered 881,786.

Earlier we saw that around 1958–59 some 50 percent of all production workers in Soviet industry (15.9 out of 31.8 million) were semiskilled. Among the remaining 50 percent the number of skilled workers was somewhat less than that of partially skilled workers. In highly developed industries especially, such as the metal and machine construction industry, as well as the areas of trade, registration, and supply, the number of skilled workers is probably substantially higher. Already in 1930 a check of more than 100,000 workers in the machine industry showed that 19.7 percent of them were skilled workers.

Khrushchev's education reform of 1958 was instituted for the primary purpose of overcoming the shortage of foremen and skilled workers;[204] this he sought to accomplish by overhauling the system of occupational training. How far he succeeded in accomplishing his objective is still very difficult to say.

The nature of the Soviet working class has been determined, first, by its historical evolution and, second, by the special character of the Soviet economy. The Soviet worker lives and works in an economic system that is exclusively based on state ownership of industry. On the other hand, he is totally dependent upon the state, his only employer, whose ruling structure determines his own social position. Soviet "state workers" are therefore caught in the clutches of their rulers and are subject to exploitation that is far more severe than that of unionized workers in the developed areas of the "capitalistic world."

3. The Kolkhoz Peasants

We have already discussed in some detail the social revolution which was engineered on the land as a result of the forced collectivization of agriculture. The free peasantry, "the last capitalist class" in Lenin's view, was liquidated almost entirely. In its place there arose a "class" of so-called kolkhoz peasants. In addition, there are paid workers on state farms (the sovkhozes) who are regarded as members of the working class along with those workers formerly employed by machine-tractor stations (MTS) and now employed by repair-technical stations (RTS). An overview of the development of these groups (less family members engaged in supplementary enterprises) is contained in Table 18. The data here, relative to employees in the kolkhozes, diverge somewhat from the yearly number of kolkhoz peasants (including family members) engaged in social production; the size of the latter group was calculated on the basis of monthly averages.[205] For example, in 1959 the number was 24.1, not 24.5 million. Using this more exact annual figure as our base the total number of kolkhoz peasants (including 9.9 million family members engaged in private economic enterprises on the side) was 33 million. In 1959 a like number of people were engaged as full-time workers in the agricultural sector.[206] A typical Soviet "peasant" (kolkhoz peasant and farm worker) on 1 January 1960 was able to provide, in a country with a population of 213 million, for the needs of 6.43 persons including himself, while an American farmer (farmers and farm workers) in July 1959 produced enough to feed himself and 23.69 persons.[207]

The kolkhozniki, as members of a compulsory association, are certainly no less dependent upon the state than are paid workers who labor upon the land. The kolkhoz system that Stalin introduced has been aptly described as a "feudal-militaristic

TABLE 18

Total Number (Yearly Average) of Agricultural Workers
(in millions)

Year	Total number engaged in agrarian sector	Kolkhoz	State farms and other agriculture organizations	State farms alone	MTS RTS	Total number gainfully employed in agriculture	Kolkhoz	State farms and other agriculture organizations	State farms alone	MTS RTS
1913 (within boundaries prior to 17 Sept. 1939)										
1922/23			3							
1928			1							
1934			2.0							
1937			2.4 (+MTS)						1.5	
1940	31.3	29.0	1.8	1.3	0.5	27.8	25.8	1.6	1.2	0.4
1945										
1950	30.7	27.6	2.4	1.7	0.7	27.9*	25.1*	2.2	1.0	0.6
1952										
1953	29.4	25.6	2.6	1.8	1.2	26.2	22.9	2.3	1.5	1.0
1954	30.7	24.8	2.8	1.8	3.1	27.5	22.1	2.6	1.6	2.8
1955	31.5	25.7	2.9	1.9	2.9	28.5	22.9	2.7	1.7	2.6
1956	30.9	24.3	4.0	2.1	2.6	27.5	21.5	3.7	1.8	2.3
1957	30.8	24.9	4.6	2.2	1.3	27.3	22.0	4.3	2.0	1.0
1958	30.0*	24.5	5.0*	3.2	0.5	26.9*	22.1*	4.6*	2.0	0.2
1959	29.0	22.3	6.3	3.8	0.4	26.1	20.1	5.8	3.0	0.2
1960	28.1	20.7	7.4			25.5	18.7	6.8	3.6	
1961	27.7	20.0	7.7			25.2	18.1	7.1		
1962										
1963	27.3	19.4	7.9			24.9	17.6	7.3		

Source: Sel'skoe khoziaistvo SSSR [Agriculture in the USSR] (Moscow, 1960), pp. 450, 451; Narodnoe khoziaistvo SSSR for 1961, p. 461; for 1963, p. 363.
*The original figures have been corrected in view of the latest available figures.

structure." Kolkhoz land is assigned to a specific agricultural artel only for the revenue that it brings, since the sole owner of the land is the state. Yet it would be wrong to compare the kolkhoz peasant to a farm laborer.

Thanks to the private farm plots of the kolkhoz peasants and their close link to nature, rural skills, rural virtues, and a rural life-style have been preserved to a very large extent, even by the young generation.[208] These qualities one finds present also in the farm laborer directly involved in agriculture on state farms; he is likewise occupied in large measure with his private economic activity. Because of his work he too is much closer to the kolkhoz peasant than to the city worker.

One could safely maintain, therefore, that in 1959 there were some 41 million people represented in the farm community, and not just the 33 million kolkhoz peasants.[209] Less those in the military service, students working in industry, and organized home workers, this would mean that the size of the peasantry, numerically, is equal to the sum of both workers and white-collar employees. The private farm plots can especially be regarded as the economic basis of the peasant community. The number of private farm plots—around 20 million—has remained surprisingly stable since the end of forced collectivization, although in recent years this number has declined from 20.5 (1959) to 16.1 million (1963).[210] This change, engineered by Khrushchev, is linked with the conversion of the kolkhozes into state farms. But this need not have led to an actual reduction in private plots, since the small private enterprises of farm workers are not separately treated in Soviet statistics.

In this connection it should be pointed out that agricultural production in the Soviet Union owes much to these private farm plots. Although they consist only of some 3 percent of the entire acreage, in 1962 these small economic units produced 44 percent of all meat products, 45 percent of all milk, 76 percent of all eggs, 70 percent of all potatoes, 42 percent of all vegetables, and 28 percent of all wool produced in the Soviet Union.[211]

The largest part of this produce was consumed by the peasants themselves. Yet they sold 23 percent of the meat, 10 percent of the milk, 48 percent of the eggs, 56 percent of the potatoes, 14 percent of the vegetables, and 16 percent of the wool they produced.[212] The urban food supply was largely dependent upon the surplus production of these private farm plots. Notwithstanding the downfall of Khrushchev, who had never completely given up his "agrocities" project, one must still bear in mind that private farm plots will continue to remain an important element in Soviet agriculture, and, in the process of reducing the size of state farm operations, a return to the individual group system and the transformation of some state farms into collective farms could take on greater significance.[213] This development is already underway, and it is wholly conceivable that these private farm plots will be enlarged, along with guarantees of greater autonomy for collective farms. This increasing emphasis upon autonomous administration by cooperatives, as well as upon the broadening of the private sector of the economy, would, in any case, magnify the relative importance of the farm component within the social structure of the Soviet Union. Actually, the middle generation of kolkhoz peasants seems to be making a much greater effort to preserve and extend private farmlands than the young generation.[214] But this is more a matter of avoiding the disadvantages of the village vis-à-vis the city and a matter of living one's own life, an objective that could only be reached by breaking down the coercive character of the kolkhoz. Yet the importance of the young generation of kolkhoz peasants as a factor in social change should not be underestimated. The same goes for peasant women whose emancipation, due largely to the kolkhoz system, has been largely overlooked. Since young men are resigned to leaving the village, young women have a special interest in seeing to it that rural conditions change.[215]

Kolkhoz peasants and farm workers can also be differentiated by class.[216] The first category comprises the rural intelligentsia, which consists of the chairmen of collective and state farms, agro-technical directors, highly qualified agro-technical assistants, and special categories of white-collar employees. In 1959 there were 102,768 chairmen (and officers) of collective farms, 278,544 agronomists and engineers in addition to some 30,000 veterinarians and 70,000 verterinary technicians and assistant medical officers in the agrarian sector. The second category is made up of directors of cattle and poultry farms (143,097), brigadiers of tractor brigades (120,804), agricultural farm brigades (74,487), and other agrarian brigades (142,084). The third category consists of section leaders (156,505), tractor operators (2,035,965), and combine drivers (353,327). In the fourth group are the LKW-drivers, persons servicing farm machinery, etc. (212,716), and several other occupational groups among whom dairymen were singled out for special recognition by Khrushchev.[217] The bottom category consisted of kolkhoz peasants and farm workers who had no special occupational training. These numbered around 19.3 million.

Kolkhoz peasants exhibited the characteristics of a professional estate to a far greater extent than workers or employees. The peasant's official relation to the kolkhoz is, however, considerably different from his earlier attachment to the mir. If a member of a kolkhoz takes it upon himself to secure a job in an urban-industrial area he violates the rules of the agricultural artel and may, as a consequence, be expelled by vote of the general membership. The kolkhoz is not, however, in a position to prevent a kolkhoz peasant from becoming a member of another professional group.[218]

4. White-Collar Employees and the Intelligentsia

According to the formal class structure of the Soviet Union, which is only of limited value when viewed sociologically, the only established classes are workers and kolkhoz peasants. The third large social group—from which, for ideological reasons, the designation "class" has been withheld—breaks down into two categories: white-collar employees and the intelligentsia. The decisive criterion for distinguishing the latter groups from workers and peasants is not the functions they perform, but whether they are engaged primarily in physical or intellectual labor. This was noted in comments accompanying the results of the Soviet census of 1959:

> By the activities of workers we mean work that predominately involves an expenditure of manual labor; by the activities of employees we mean work that is mainly intellectual in nature.[219]

Official Soviet statistics treat white-collar employees as a special social group corresponding to the whole number of "brainworkers" (20.5 million). The 1959 census numbered these employees at 19.7 million. The remainder were presumably "workers." The question of how to classify white-collar employees generally has troubled Marxist-Leninist sociologists both in Russia and in other parts of the world, as was clearly manifested by the 1961 and 1962 discussions contained in the journal Probleme des Friedens und des Sozialismu.[220] At international conferences most Soviet sociologists have turned out to be adherents of a "Marxist middle-class theory."[221] They were unable to agree with the contention of some discussants that white-collar employees are to be regarded as members of the working class. The top Soviet authority on white-collar employees, V. S. Semenov, was not even willing to classify engineering and technical personnel as workers, although he was obliged to add that they were involved directly in the process of production and, hence, from a Marxist point of view, had participated in the creation of "surplus value." He based this conclusion on the fact that engineers, technicians, and other skilled personnel are in a position to assist owners of capital to exploit the working class as much as possible for the purpose of obtaining the highest profits. Semenov declared:

> Engineering-technical personnel, together with office clerks, mercantile employees, state employees, and members of the indepen-

dent professions collectively constitute the intelligentsia and white-collar employees. On the basis of their concrete role in the productive process the intelligentsia and white-collar employees stand somewhere between the antagonistic classes of the bourgeoise and the proletariat, and belong to the middle and intermediate ranks of capitalist society.[222]

Conferences with foreign colleagues have recently driven Soviet sociologists into intensive studies of the sociological nature of white-collar employees and the intelligentsia in the Soviet Union.[223] In these writings white-collar employees have been newly designated as a "stratum" (sloi), although formerly such concepts of social stratification had not been applied in their analysis of Soviet society.[224] Soviet sociologists, however, do not yet venture to speak of a stratification of white-collar employees, who with members of their families constitute a fifth of the entire population. The term "intermediate stratum" (prosloika), a concept that dates back to Stalin, continues to be applied to the intelligentsia.[225] This "intermediate stratum" still included around 15.7 million people in 1959, according to official statistics; if students outside the productive process are included the total was probably around 21.5 million.

Efforts to distinguish white-collar employees as a whole from the intelligentsia have given Soviet sociologists particular difficulty. With regard to the distinction between employees and the intelligentsia, Rutkevich remarks:

> By the intelligentsia one ordinarily understands a rather broad social stratum consisting of those professionally engaged in intellectual activity. Today the line which divides intellectual and physical labor is so interwined that it is difficult to produce clearcut statistics on any one group. Even the members of intellectual occupations customarily refer to themselves as "employees." By "employees" one ordinarily means all those who are employed in state industries and offices, together with those working within the apparatus of social organizations—that is, the party, cooperatives, the Komsomol, sporting associations, etc.—and not workers, i.e., persons who are mainly engaged in physical labor. . . .

Thus, in the broadest sense, the intelligentsia is characterized by its social position, causing its members to be bracketed with white-collar employees as a stratum. In a narrower sense, the intelligentsia is made up of specialists devoted to intellectual work.[226]

Before the war, the intelligentsia was broadly conceived—as indicated by statements of Molotov at the eighteenth Party Congress of the CPSU in March 1939—and grouped together with white-collar employees. Since Stalin's death, however, official statistics, as shown in Table 19, have treated the two groups separately. In 1959 only 15.7 million (77 percent) of the "brain-workers"—white-collar employees as a whole—were included in the intelligentsia. The remaining 4.8 million (23 percent) were distributed among occupations in third-ranking public service areas. Semenov, like Rutkevich, has taken another route in distinguishing the intelligentsia as a separate class. He writes:

> From an intermediate stratum which had no actual share in the means of production under capitalism, the intellectuals developed into a social stratum with rights and prerogatives equal to those enjoyed by workers and peasants. From an intermediate stratum which under capitalism was not characterized by a unified social interest, intellectuals and white-collar employees evolved into a stratum with social interests common to those of workers and peasants.[227]

If this assertion is accepted it is hard to understand why those intellectuals and white-collar employees involved directly in production—especially engineering-technical personnel—are not to be counted as members of the working class. Or should not there be any change under "socialism" in their function as "assistants of exploitation"? Semenov himself is thoroughly aware of the weakness of his own argument, but for political reasons does not venture to depart from the distinguishing criterion used up to now. Thus, he attempts to qualify his original theory by distinguishing between "predominately intellectual labor" and "nonphysical labor." Under this distinction only the

TABLE 19   Composition of the Soviet Intelligentsia and Workers Engaged in
Intellectual Activity (White-Collar Employees)
(in thousands)

	1926 (Molotov)	1926 (CSO)	1937	1939	1956	1959
1. Political and economic leaders:	384.6	365	1751.0	(1813.4)	2240	(2142.0)
A. Leaders of state administration, social organizations and their administrative units:				445.2		392.1
B. Managers of production plants and their work departments:				757.0		955.2
C. Directors of trade organizations:				244.9		334.8
D. Directors of supply organizations:				366.3		459.9
2. Engineering and technical personnel:	(206.8)	225	(1060.0)	1656.5	2570	4205.9
A. Engineers, architects, etc. (those not plant directors):	31.5		250.0	247.3		834.3
B. Middle-level technical personnel:	175.3		810.0	1409.2		3371.6
3. Agricultural-technical personnel:	(31.3)	45	(176.0)	294.9	376	477.2
A. Agronomists, veterinarians, etc.:	18.0		80.0	196.8		323.4
B. Middle-level agricultural personnel:	13.3		96.0	98.1		153.8
4. Medical personnel:				679.6	(1376)	1702.5
A. Physicians (including directors of medical institutions):	70.0	57	132.0	152.8	329	413.6
B. Middle-level medical personnel:	129.8	128	382.0	(527.6)	1047	1288.9
5. Teachers and scientists:				1553.1		2835.6
A. Scientists (including directors of scientific institutes):	13.5	14	80.0	111.6	231	316.4
B. Teachers (including directors of schools), sport functionaries:	347.6	381	969.0	1441.5	2080	2519.2

	1	2	3	4	5	6
6. Men of letters and cultural leaders:	(112.3)	90	(456,0)	(486,3)	572	(757,0)
A. Writers and journalists:	}58.5		}297.0	58		104.0
B. Political and adult-education instructors:				285		462.3
C. Artists:	53.8		159.0	143.3		190.6
7. Planners and bookkeepers:	(607.4)	650	(2439,0)	3102.0	2161	3501.9
A. Economists, comptrollers, etc.:	250.0		822,0	1037.3		1271.5
B. Accountants, etc.:	375.4		1617,0	2064.7		2230.4
8. Juridical personnel:	27.1	27	46.0	62.4	67	78.7
9. University students:	168.0	168.0	550.0	550.0	1178	
10. Other groups among the intelligentsia (including the military):		575	1550.0		2609	
Total "intelligentsia"	2116.4	2725	9591.0	9648.2	15466	15700.8
Communications (postal service, etc.):				265.4		476.4
Trade and supply (less directors):				1014.9		1473.5
Municipal industries and services:				202.5		277.1
Office personnel (including bureau heads):				489.4		535.9
Agents and dispatchers:				176.4		146.0
Other:				2024.6		1885.3
Total white-collar employees:				13821.4		20495.0

Source: Compiled from Molotov's statements regarding the Soviet "Intelligentsia" in 1926 and 1937 at the 18th Party Congress of the USSR (V. M. Molotov, *Der dritte Fünfjahresplan* [Moscow, 1939], pp. 44–45 (Russ.); *The Land of Socialism Today and Tomorrow* [Moscow, 1939], p. 149); *Narodnoe khoziaistvo SSSR v 1958 godu* [The USSR economy in 1958] (Moscow, 1959), p. 672; *Itogi vsesoiuznoi perepisi naseleniia 1959 goda*, pp. 164–166; *Narodnoe khoziaistvo SSSR v 1960 godu* [The USSR economy in 1960] (Moscow, 1961), pp. 33–35. The figures of the Central Statistical Office (CSO) for 1926 are not congruent with Molotov's data.

intelligentsia is engaged professionally in purely intellectual work. Semenov says:

> The intelligentsia and white-collar employees are not identical categories. The concepts of "intelligentsia" and "employee" are quite distinct. They are not identical groups because of their differing perspectives toward their employment. "Members of the intelligentsia" are men who actually think about the content of their labor and thus are engaged basically in an intellectual endeavor. Employees are men who perform certain kinds of service work for the state or state-supported social organizations; they are fulfilling prescribed tasks, functions, or duties for a given salary. . . . under socialism the overwhelming majority of the intelligentsia are really employees in this sense. Yet not all white-collar employees are to be grouped together with those performing intellectual tasks; a large number of employees fall outside of this group.[228]

Semenov includes among those employees who do not belong to the intelligentsia men who mainly pursue "service work" (trud obsluzhivaniia).[229] Yet he does not go so far as to designate intellectuals and these employees as distinct groups. He emphasizes rather their common characteristics, stemming from the nonphysical aspect of their work, uniting them in one social class. He writes:

> This division of service functions and intellectual labor presupposes a rather close nexus between both types of work. The intelligentsia and service workers have one key characteristic in common which makes them members of a unified social stratum of intellectuals and white-collar employees; they do not engage in physical labor [rabotniki nefizicheskogo]. In this respect they are basically distinct from workers and farmers, for the latter are engaged chiefly in physical labor.[230]

Semenov, on the basis of 1959 census data, divides the intelligentsia into the following groups: (1) leading cadres in public administration and social organizations (2.4 million); (2) the technical and economic intelligentsia (5.0 million); and (3) the scientific and cultural intelligentsia (5.3 million).[231]

Altogether these figures add up to 12.7 million persons, or

TABLE 20

Number of Soviet Specialists in the National Economy
with University and Advanced Technical-School
Training (Outside the Military)
(in thousands)

Year	Total	University Education	Advanced Technical-School Training
1913	190	136	54
1928	521	233	288
1941 (1/1)	2401	909	1492
1953 (1/7)	4279	1848	2431
1954			
1955 (1/7)	5133	2184	2940
1956 (1/12)	6257	2633	3624
1957 (1/12)	6821	2805	4016
1958 (end)	7476	3027	4449
1959 (1/12)	8017	3236	4781
1960 (1/12)	8784	3545	5239
1961 (1/12)	9433	3824	5609
1962 (1/12)	9956	4050	5906
1963 (end)	10598	4312	6286

Source: *Narodnoe khoziaistvo SSSR* for 1958, p. 673; for
1963, p. 486; *SSSR v tsifrakh*, p. 149.

60 percent of all white-collar employees. To arrive at this figure
Semenov subtracts from the total official figure of 15.6 million,
2.9 million office employees who were included (by official
statistics) among the technical-economic intelligentsia. This
roughly corresponds to the number of leading political and
economic personnel represented in Table 19, which clearly
underscores the rapid increase of white-collar employees and
intellectuals between 1926 to 1959.

These figures are further subdivided below. There is nothing
new about this classification. Up to now the "technical intelligentsia" (*tekhnicheskaia intelligentsiia*) has been distinguished
from the "creative intelligentsia" (*tvorcheskaia intelligentsiia*).[232]
White-collar employees, who perform "service functions," totaled 8.5 million; according to Semenov, they can be divided
into the following categories:[233]

a) Office employees   2.9 million
b) Employees in transportation   0.3 million
c) Employees in communications   0.5 million

TABLE 21   Classification of Specialists with University and Advanced Technical-School Training, According to Profession (Outside of Military) (in thousands)

	1928	1941 (1/1)	1955 (1/7)	1956 (1/12)	1957 (1/12)	1959 (1/12)	1960 (1/12)	1961 (1/12)	1962 (1/12)	1963 (1/12)
All specialists with university training:	233.0	909.0	2184.0	2633.1	2805.5	3235.7	3545.2	3824.0	4049.7	4282.6
Engineers:	47.0	289.9	585.9	721.0	816.1	986.6	1135.0	1236.0	1325.1	1420.5
Agronomists, zoologists, veterinarians, and foresters:	28.0	69.6	158.7	179.5	193.1	222.4	222.3	243.8	255.2	267.1
Economists, statisticians:	13.0 }	57.0 }	113.8 }	130.2	145.2	177.6	197.7	218.3	235.8	252.7
Trade personnel:	}	}	}	11.0	12.3	16.3	19.3	21.6	24.1	26.1
Jurists:	13.0	20.9	47.1	56.5	57.8	65.5	69.8	74.0	76.6	77.8
Physicians:	63.2	141.8	299.0	329.4	346.0	378.6	400.6	424.2	441.9	460.1
Teachers, librarians, and men of letters:	59.0	300.4	906.4	1116.7	1144.9	1278.9	1378.1	1473.8	1548.0	1629.1

All specialists with advanced technical-school training:	288.0	1492.2	2949.1	3624.4	4016.1	4781.1	5238.5	5609.1	5906.1	6200.9
Technicians:	51.0	320.1	804.9	1049.8	1257.3	1679.5	1955.8	2156.9	2292.7	2446.4
Agronomists, zoologists, veterinarians, and foresters:	31.0	92.8	254.4	295.4	310.0	360.7	356.3	389.4	409.6	410.6
Planning experts, statisticians:	⎱6.0	30.9	⎱186.1	205.0	237.4	299.6	337.5	379.1	414.9	451.6
Trade personnel:	⎰	5.3	⎰	46.9	57.2	88.0	106.7	127.0	145.6	165.2
Jurists:	2.0	6.2	23.2	23.0	20.4	18.1	17.2	16.5	16.2	15.2
Medical personnel:	48.0	393.2	731.1	900.2	980.3	1119.7	1187.3	1222.5	1251.9	1294.4
Teachers, librarians, and men of letters:	137.0	536.4	818.6	934.3	971.5	1018.4	1061.9	1096.6	1143.3	1178.8

Source: *Narodnoe khoziaistvo SSSR* for 1956, p. 209; for 1959, p. 604; for 1960, p. 650; for 1961, p. 576; for 1962, p. 465; for 1963, p. 487.

113

TABLE 22   Classification of Employed Specialists with University and Advanced Technical Education, According to Branch of Industry or Administration (in thousands)

	/January 1941			/December 1957			/December 1959			/December 1963		
	All Specialists	With University Education	With Advanced Tech. Education	All Specialists	University Education	Advanced Tech. Education	All Specialists	University Education	Advanced Tech. Education	All Specialists	University Education	Advanced Tech. Education
Total specialists:	2400	908	1492	6821	2805	4016	8017	3236	4781	10483.5	4282.6	6200.9
Industrial plants:	311	153	158	1102	354	748	1468	443	1025	2118.6	612.2	1506.4
Construction organizations:	41	17	24	174	62	112	248	82	166	404.2	133.9	270.3
Kolkhozes, MTS:	29	5	24	278	71	207	240	48	192	} 415.7	} 105.5	} 310.2
State farms and agricultural organizations:	21	7	14	93	32	61	126	43	83			
Transport and communication enterprises:	62	17	45	215	56	159	280	68	212	404.5	90.1	314.4

114

Trade and supply organizations:	13	2	11	151	32	119	281	57	224	420.4	73.7	346.7
Health institutions:	465	114	351	1262	307	955	1431	341	1090	1657.4	418.7	1238.7
Schools for cadre training, general schools, and cultural institutions:	944	344	600	2132	1138	994	2284	1240	1044	2830.3	1594.1	1236.2
Scientific, teaching, and research institutes:	123	91	32	552	356	196	691	449	242	1122.8	731.3	391.5
State and economic administration, administrative organs of social organizations, credit and insurance institutions:	281	135	146	539	255	284	599	295	304	750.4	381.5	368.9

Source: *Narodnoe khoziaistvo SSSR* for 1958, p. 675; for 1959, p. 605; for 1963, p. 488. Those on military duty are not included in these figures.

115

d) Employees in trade and supply   2.5 million
e) Municipal and service trade employees   2.3 million

Rutkevich understands by the intelligentsia only those specialists who have a university education or advanced technical-
school training. Thus, he limits the intelligentsia to a much
narrower group than does Semenov.

Between 1928 and 1963 the total number of such highly
trained specialists (less members of the armed services) increased from 0.5 million to 10.6 million (Table 20). In 1959 the
number was 8 million and, thus, 4.7 million less than the number of intellectuals included in Semenov's figures.

Tables 21 and 22 classify these specialists by occupation and
by the branch of industry or public administration in which
they are employed. The tabular data demonstrate clearly the
Soviet strength in the engineering, technical, medical, and
teaching fields. But the considerably lower number of economists, by comparison, and the all too few lawyers are likely to
have a detrimental effect upon an industrial society that is striving for a higher rate of development. In 1963 economists constituted only one-eighth of the specialists employed in the entire
economy; lawyers comprised only one-seventh of the specialists
in administration. Meanwhile, contemporary Soviet leaders
appear to have grown aware of the dearth of economists, but
less so of lawyers. Among specialists academicians are of special
significance. Between 1928 and 1963 their number increased
from 200,000 to 4.3 million. Many of the 1.4 million graduate
engineers, who are the real prototypes of the Soviet system,
belong to the political and economic elite. Together with certified agronomists they play a larger role in the administration of
public affairs than economists or lawyers.

In 1959, besides the above-mentioned specialists, there were
still 2.8 million persons who had university (including those
who did not graduate) or advanced technical-school training.
Of these, 1.7 million were white-collar employees and 1.1 million were workers.[234] Among the 1.7 employees were an esti-

mated 400,000 university graduates working in civilian areas or for the military. In 1959 gainfully employed university graduates totaled approximately 3.6 million (3.2 + 0.4 million).[235] They constituted 20 percent of the political and economic leadership personnel (2.2 or 2.4 million) and around 20 percent of the technical-economic intelligentsia (5.3 or 5 million), less office clerks, and 40 percent of the scientific-cultural intelligentsia (5.2 or 5.3 million).[236]

The high percentage of university graduates among the scientific and cultural intelligentsia gives this group more influence than is generally assumed. Progressive writers, artists, and scientists who comprise the nucleus of the "creative intelligentsia" are a prestige elite. The leadership cadres of the bureaucracy are recruited mainly from the technical and economic intelligentsia; their intellectual orientation, however, is much like that of certified engineers. As a consequence, the conflict of interest between the power elite and economic managers, whose outlook is governed much more by economic rationality, has not entirely been eliminated. If the academic nucleus of the technical-economic intelligentsia were built around a greater number of qualified political scientists and economists, the influence of the technical-economic intelligentsia engaged directly in the economic sphere would increase significantly.

The special status that university graduates hold today in Soviet Russia has been described by Hindus in these words:

> As an elite of an elite, university graduates are in a group all by themselves, the most exclusive social stratum in the whole of Russia. They frequently hold lectures in factory club houses, yet they do not really mingle with the masses. When the trade unions took over health and vacation resorts, except those that belong to the army, they built their own private summer bungalows in quiet and distant places in the South, far away from where the masses of men tended to congregate. In the winter some of them fly to their southern cottages on weekends. They represent the celebrated braintrust of the Kremlin; they are the key figures in a conscious effort to surpass America in industrial

production and scientific leadership. Due to their single-minded purpose and coordinated endeavors they produced sensational results, in a very short period of time, in supersonic flight and in the production of missles, atomic and hydrogen bombs, interplanetary rockets, and space ships. If during this time they have fallen behind in the liberal arts and the social sciences, still it has to be said that in natural science and technology they are among the leading men of the time.[237]

If this description applies only to top-drawer university graduates it is nevertheless true that Soviet academicians generally perceive themselves as an elite group among specialists who, in turn, clearly place themselves, as a group, several notches above other white-collar employees.

The same elite consciousness exists also among political and economic leaders—the nachalniki—among whom academically trained persons are currently only a minority. It is customary in the Soviet Union to characterize these top groups of white-collar employees as "leading cadres." When used by Soviet Communists the military term cadre refers to those trained men who carry out those functions more relevant in a politico-technical sense.[238] All specialists, along with a large number of other white-collar employees, are included within this concept. But the cadres include also skilled laborers and qualified personnel who work on collective farms. The heart of the bureaucracy is made up of the cadres from the intelligentsia and white-collar employees.[239] Besides the top political and administrative leaders the bureaucracy includes those who hold administrative positions in departments concerned with cultural matters as well as lower-level office employees. The total number of people in the bureaucracy—the apparatchiki—increased from 5.5 to 6.2 million during the late Stalin period. By 1959 it dropped back to 5.5 million, only to rise again since then. This might be the reason why no Soviet statistics on these employees have been published since 1960.

In 1959 the total number of bureaucrats may have been as

TABLE 23

The Soviet Bureaucracy
(thousands)

Year	Total Number	
1941 (June)	5515	
1952 (1 April)	6232	
1954 (1 April)	6104	(6213)
1955 (1 January)	5697	(5807)
1958 (1 September)	5579	(5696)
1959 (1 September)	5554	(5645)
1960 (15 September)	5753	

Source: *Narodnoe khoziaistvo SSSR* for 1959, p. 595; for 1960, p. 644. Competing figures taken from the 1959 year-book are in parentheses.

much as 6 million, or 30 percent of all white-collar employees, for Table 23 does not include all relevant administrative areas. Of these 6 million, 2.4 million were trained persons in the political and economic areas, while 2.9 million were "office employees." The remaining employees were hired by bureaus administering cultural and other specialized affairs.

Under Stalin's ranking system the "leading cadres" thus included the top bureaucracy as well as those holding office in higher and intermediate levels of service who were either representatives of the state or had special career qualifications.[240] The rest of the bureaucracy included similarly qualified personnel in lower-level state positions together with bureaucratic assistants.

To the "leading cadres" belong all those officeholders who are included in the "nomenclatura" of the party's cadre departments and of the personnel departments of state and social organizations dependent on them.[241]

The cadre division of the Central Committee of the CPSU is responsible for preparing the "nomenclatura" of the top bureaucracy.[242] In the Soviet Union there are conflicting models of bureaucratic organization. One is based on patronage, the other on merit.[243] Moreover, the tendencies of a bureaucratic caste, stemming from the late Stalin period, can still be observed. The Soviet officeholder is caught in a conflict of social roles.[244] First, there is a latent conflict between the expectations linked to his official position and his social role. Second, there is the conflict between his loyalty to his patron—the party—and his duty vis-à-vis society, which expects from him a high measure of competence. The individual officeholder will often resolve the conflict, to a lesser or greater extent, by making decisions now in favor of the "total state," and thus the ruling party, and now in favor of the larger society.

Sociological studies by Western scholars have employed "functional theory" to distinguish between white-collar employees and workers. For example, Fritz Croner has identified the following four functions as having the character of white-collar work: managerial, constructive or analytical, administrative, and commercial.[245]

It is hardly likely, as Croner supposes, that all these task areas have developed out of a comprehensive managerial function, owing to the "theory of delegation."[246] It is also questionable whether in a developed industrial society it is possible, with the aid of a "theory of function," to draw such a clear distinction between employees and workers, since in many areas their responsibilities overlap.[247] Yet we can say that despite their overlapping functions in given areas white-collar employees and workers constitute distinct social groups by virtue of their differing social statuses.[248] Hence, in an industrial society not as highly developed as that of the Soviet Union, Croner's functional theory would doubtless seem to be a better criterion for differentiating between white-collar employees and workers than the mere distinction between manual and nonmanual labor. With the aid of this theory one could probably show that the number of white-collar employees in the Soviet Union is markedly greater than Soviet statistics would have us believe. Functional theory enables us, in any case, to identify those activities which a great part of the "leading cadres" characteristically perform, namely the functions of policy-making, social planning, and social control.

The carrying out of these functions, which are not the "functions of work,"[249] refers always to the organization of society as a whole and not to the organization of work alone or to any segment of it. Consequently, these functions, which are performed by the party bureaucracy as well as those state and social agencies politically and ideologically linked to it, possess a character wholly different from the functions carried out by directors and branch managers in plants, who—apart from differences in the economic system, do not essentially differ from Western economic managers.[250]

That segment of the "leading cadres" which carries out these political functions indeed belongs to the bureaucracy but not to the category of white-collar employees. It personifies, moreover, the total state, upon whom, as exclusive property owner and employer, all workers depend. In 1959 the entire top bureaucracy included nearly 400,000 persons, as indicated in Table 19. About half of them belonged to the party bureaucracy.[251] At that time there were also around 1.7 million leading economic managers. Other state officeholders (jurists, economists) numbered some 300,000.[252] Out of this ruling elite of some 2.4 million persons, it was estimated in 1959 that 500,000 had a university education, of whom some 100,000 were top-level bureaucrats. The other 3.1 million university graduates were, in the main, employed in the higher civil service in different areas of the Soviet state. The entire upper stratum, made up principally of top bureaucrats and university graduates, may have included, in 1959, as many as 3.8 million persons.[253]

The remaining leadership personnel and other functionaries with only secondary technical-school training constituted about 6.5 million persons,[254] while the working staff and officials in middle levels of civil service totaled 2.4 million persons. Of the 8.4 million persons who, according to Semenov, render "service functions," about a third (2.8 million) comprise officials and functionaries in lower levels of service. Two-thirds (5.6 million) are bureaucratic assistants and low-level employees.[255]

The majority of these 8.4 million white-collar employees, among whom number 60 percent of the bureaucracy, are hardly better educated than trained workers.

In this connection an experienced student of Soviet affairs has remarked:

> While the working conditions of Soviet workers are almost comparable to those in the West, white-collar employees work in poorly ventilated, sparsely furnished, and uncongenial crowded offices. The white-collar employee is clearly at a disadvantage. Many of them are heard to say that they have not even yet played second fiddle. Naturally this is not the case with higher-ranking employees among the elite who differ considerably from the average employee in both appearance and standard of living. The difference does not, however, show up in their intellectual capacity. Their degree of education does allow them to discuss matters of intellectual interest on equal terms with Western visitors.[256]

As we already saw, 39 percent of all white-collar employees (including their families) in 1959 had the benefit of a full education (in contrast to 5.3 percent of the workers and 2.6 percent of the kolkhoz peasants). It was this awareness of being fully educated that bridged the large gaps between various groups of white-collar employees, generating among them a feeling of having a special social place vis-à-vis the other two classes (workers and peasants) in Soviet society.

5. Social Stratification in the Soviet Union

The Soviets do not dispute the existence of classes in their country, even though the private ownership of the means of production has long been abolished and despite the transition from socialism to communism. What they do assert is that, because of the socialization of the country, vertical stratification has taken the place of the old horizontal class structure.[257] This change was brought about by the harmonious cooperation that workers and kolkhoz peasants received from white-collar employees and the intelligentsia with whom they were closely bound.

The workers were supposed to have a definite ideological preference within the framework of the "general people's state" that was eventually to take the place of the "dictatorship of the proletariat;"[258] moreover, this state was not to experience either social stratification or class antagonism. With the gradual narrowing of the difference between city and country, just as between intellectual and physical labor, social differentiation was also to disappear in the course of the "construction of communism" and was to be replaced by a "classless society" built on the principle of "commonly owned property."

Indeed, social contradictions would continue to exist in a socialist society.[259] But these would not be of an antagonistic nature. It would, therefore, be possible to resolve them without social conflict in an evolutionary way.[260]

At the same time it was declared that the Communist Party of the Soviet Union, which meanwhile has transformed itself into the "avant garde of the proletariat," will continue to exist as the bearer of "social power" and will exercise its distinct political as well as economic functions.[261] The question of the extent to which under these circumstances the desired ideal society can generally be realized is one that will be answered in the future. As a substitute for an answer it is only asserted that there would not be any "social stratification" in the Soviet Union.

Our treatment of the formal class structure has already clearly shown that there are far-reaching differences between the large single social groups which are conditioned by their occupational and educational status. These differences are related to distinctions of authority, prestige, income, life-style, and social consciousness, as well as to those of social behavior conditioned by these factors.[262] This difference in the values and life condition of individual groups of persons has produced in the Soviet Union, just as in every other society, a manifest stratification. Chief among the factors that, on the basis of occupational function and level of education, have conditioned this stratification are authority and prestige; these are of greater significance than is income. Authority is identified more with the social roles that accompany general positions of leadership than with occupying a given public office within the domain of the state.[263]

Leadership and rulership can only be distinguished from one another by marking clearly the difference between state and society.[264] Only when the interrelationship as well as the independence of these two realms is clearly recognized is it possible to find an answer to the difficult problem of the nature of social change under totalitarian rule.

The leadership relation, as Herbert Krüger has pointed out,[265] is essentially of a different kind than the "power relation" that is characteristic of the state. The latter pertains to order and obedience while the former is associated with authority and the willingness to follow. Leadership normally implies an institutionally secured position of authority, while rulership is always concerned with institutionalized power.[266] Not only does a certain degree of influence flow from the authority associated with the social function of leadership, but it is also linked to reputation, that is, to the recognition of the superiority and originality of a person or groups of persons independent of whether they occupy a power position.

The basis of both authority and reputation in a modern industrial society is knowledge.[267] This applies to the Soviet Union, where the industrial society has not yet entirely stripped off the eggshells of a developing society and hence still exhibits many primitive features, as much as it does to the rest of the world. The decisive difference consists in the fact that the Soviet

Union is a totalitarian society, while the advanced industrial nations in the Northern Hemisphere today are, without exception, democracies.

At this point let us first limit ourselves to the industrial society based on achievement; later we shall take up the totalitarian model that is associated with the power structure of Soviet society. Hans Dreitzel has correctly underscored the elitist social structure of modern industrial societies.[268] In this society nearly all production areas are professionalized and the methods of selecting the elite for occupational careers are predetermined and regulated by educational or bureaucratic-organizational screening. They represent the institutionalized selection mechanism for recruiting the elite members of industrial society. Qualification in terms of knowledge, which Dreitzel characterizes as the most important means of production in modern society,[269] is not only the normative criterion but also the real functioning basis for selecting elites. Ability to produce, which is based on knowledge, is not the only way of getting top positions in society, however. It is also a matter of personal success, where in addition to the individual's power to convince, adjustment to ruling social norms as well as personal relations within society loom as important means of selection over and above all performance standards.[270] This way of getting ahead prevails to a far greater extent in the highly bureaucratized society of the Soviet Union, with its totalitarian one-party system, than in democratic industrial societies. Here a knowledge of ideological doctrines and power techniques and organizational skill is critically important, along with the patronage exercised by the party leaders (nomenclatura system).

This larger role of success vis-à-vis ability, especially as it relates to filling the top positions in society, conditions the marked class character of Soviet society and the partially elite character of the Soviet upper stratum.[271] To this extent the progressive Western industrial societies, despite all their structural weaknesses, represent a society based much more markedly on ability than the Soviet Union, where the principle of ability manifests itself particularly as a basic principle in the organization of work.

In the Soviet Union there are, above all, specialists with university and advanced technical-school training who have the ability that an industrial society needs in an atomic age. They hold all the important positions of leadership and, in addition, occupy some of the ruling positions. Because of the important social functions they exercise they are also capable, even were they not part of the ruling elite, of influencing the norms and sanctions that condition the rank ordering of society.[272]

Along with leading party cadres who are chosen by a special recruitment procedure, these members of the Soviet elite come mainly from the upper and upper-middle classes. Writers, artists, and scientists occupy a position of prestige within this elite that permits them significantly to influence the attitudes of the whole society, beyond the members of their own class, and partly in opposition to the ruling group.[273] The values of Soviet society are in some cases shaped more by the intellectual influences of this prestige elite than by the accomplishments of economic managers or by the norms of the ruling elite and the bureaucracies that are dependent upon them.[274] This was clearly shown in a sociological study conducted by the Philosophical Institute of the Soviet Academy of Sciences, an organization dedicated to the study of the values, ideals, and aspirations of an elite group of Soviet youth.

This study was carried out during the winter of 1961–62 in Moscow and Leningrad, immediately after the Twenty-second Party Congress of the CPSU.[275] The average 27-year-old respondent defined the ideal citizen as one who is "an always cooperative person," a "conscientious worker," and a "genuine specialist." Neither the "ambitious and successful economic functionary"—held up as a model for the best workers—nor the "all too submissive worker" were very positively evaluated by the respondents. Both the egotist and the person who shrinks responsibility were emphatically rejected. Topping the list of positive values favored by respondents were "interesting work" (22 percent) and "private and familial happiness" (18 percent). Next in line of preference for male respondents was "freedom of thought and action;" female respondents ranked a "clear conscience" third in their scale of preferred values. On the other hand, no one regarded fame and "power over other men" as positive social values.

To test the validity of these results a follow-up survey showed that 23 percent of the respondents emphatically rejected "power over other men" as a social goal; 18 percent rejected the "acquisition of wealth" and 13 percent rejected fame as larger aims of life. Only 0.7 percent of the respondents rejected "freedom of thought and action" as a desirable human goal.

When questioned about their children, respondents regarded "moral qualities" (27 percent), attributes of "a true man" (17 percent), and musical and athletic ability (9 percent) more important than any technical qualification; only 4 percent of the respondents preferred a "qualified skilled worker" and 3 percent a "conqueror of the cosmos." These values, which differ markedly from the ideological standards set by the party, rather clearly express the humanitarian influence of the classical Russian literature that is still read by all strata of the Soviet people. The individual's incorporation into the informal social order is the by-product of a deepening of traditional behavior patterns that bear witness to the unbroken continuity of Russia's intellectual life.[276]

With certain qualifications this is also true in the religious sphere. In the survey mentioned above only 3 percent of the respondents characterized themselves as occasional church-goers. But over half of the married respondents permitted their children to be baptized.[277] The question regarding the relationship of a representative cross section of the Soviet people to property was not, understandably, clearly raised in the above-mentioned sociological inquiry.[278] However, Soviet press reports make very clear that Russians of every social class want higher incomes[279] and more private property.[280] The party leadership has to take these desires into account and cater to these "material interests." On the other hand, the party is doing everything possible to parry this thrust toward more private enterprise, if necessary by the employment of Draconian criminal sanctions.[281]

How low the income of salary and wage earners is can be seen from Soviet statistics of 1959; they show that 40 million, i.e., more than two-thirds of all workers and white-collar employees, had a monthly average wage of 60 rubles or less (1 new ruble is equal to $1.10).[282] Until 1965 a rise in the average salary to 99 rubles per month was considered.[283]

According to Soviet sources all wages and salaries in 1959 amounted to 26.1 percent of industry's contribution to the entire social product (in 1960 equal to 76.4 billion rubles out of a total of 146.7 billion).[284] Thus industry had the lion's share when compared to agriculture.

In the Federal Republic of Germany (excluding the Saarland and Berlin) the wage quota, i.e., gross income of employed labor, amounted to 60.8 percent of the popular income in the same year and 61 percent in 1960.[285] Were the income of the self-employed to be included, the working population's share of the total social product would be even higher. These figures show that Soviet society has been subjected to a high degree of exploitation. This can be seen from the fact that a very large portion of the entire social product that can be diverted to satisfy consumer needs has been held in reserve.

Because of this the income gap between the upper and other social strata is all the more pronounced; men in the top brackets of the bureaucracy and some select intellectuals receive a particularly high portion of the rewards conferred by society, which do not entirely relate to cash income;[286] the income level of regular members of the upper stratum was also considerable when compared to the income of the stratum immediately following.[287] It is considerably more difficult to differentiate the two middle strata from each other since a skilled worker or technical laborer, who belongs to the lower middle class, often earns more than a doctor or high-school teacher who on the basis of other characteristics clearly belongs to the upper-middle stratum.[288] Income is more of a factor in distinguishing the lower-middle from the lower stratum. On the other hand, it is not easy to use income as a measure for differentiating groups within the lower stratum, since it is hard to determine the exact earnings of kolkhoz peasants,[289] whose cash income is considerably less than unskilled laborers[290] and petty clerks.

Though income is a meaningful basis of social stratification in the Soviet Union, social prestige is generally more important in view of the relatively low standard of living. Class consciousness in Soviet society is determined as much by education as by occupational status. Thus, the office employee often perceives himself the equal of an ordinary skilled worker, even though he earns much less and is officially classified as lower in social status.

The life style of the upper stratum in the Stalin era—apart from the exceptions—seemed no less bourgeois than the two categories of the middle stratum. Gradually more modern tendencies, patterned after Western habits and attitudes, began to appear.[291]

The social stratification of Soviet society today is quite different from the Russian social structure that existed prior to the 1917 Revolution. These differences are substantial.

First, the social pyramid in the Soviet Union is much lower and, at the same time, considerably more balanced than in tsarist Russia. The standard of living and life style of those groups at the top of the Soviet pyramid do not approach that of the old upper stratum. Second, the Soviet pyramid begins at a much lower level. Forced laborers, while fortunately having dwindled in number since the death of Stalin, still constitute a distinct social group which has suffered a greater injustice than the most destitute elements of the old order. If we ignore this group, unskilled workers, petty clerks, and the large mass of kolkhoz

peasants (including individual peasants) occupy the lowest
levels of the pyramid. Then come trained workers, office employees, and qualified kolkhoz peasants. The lower-middle stratum is composed of skilled workers as well as the "worker aristocracy" (foremen and highly qualified skilled workers), together
with white-collar employees of equal rank. The upper-middle
stratum includes "specialists" with advanced technical-school
training who are not members of the top bureaucracy. The
upper stratum is made up of persons in the top bureaucracy,
independent of their level of education, and university graduates. In this respect it is essentially more extensive than the
prerevolutionary upper stratum.[292]

The social stratification of the whole population might possibly correspond in essential detail to the stratification of the
employed population, which cuts right across the large social
groups.

It is relatively easy to identify those who belong to the upper
stratum and both segments of the middle stratum. The composition of these three strata is largely confined to intellectuals
and white-collar employees. Less precise measurements are available for differentiating between the two lower strata, except
that kolkhoz peasants are relatively easy to identify and classify. Only field research in the Soviet Union, however, would
help us more precisely to identify the individual strata. Since
such research is not currently possible Table 24 seeks merely
to identify the Soviet social stratification in terms of gross
characteristics.

6. The Real Class Structure of the Soviet Union

Modern industrial society is highly mobile. If the Soviet
Union exhibits a lesser degree of social mobility than highly
developed Western nations this is due principally to the over-
centralization and overbureaucratization that has grown out of
an autocratic-totalitarian system. In order not to be forced to

TABLE 24

Stratification of the Soviet Population 1959

Stratum	Employed Population (millions	Percentage	Total Population (millions)
Upper stratum	3.8	3.8	7.9
Upper-middle stratum	6.5	6.6	13.8
Lower-middle stratum	15.5	15.7	32.8
Upper-lower stratum	27.3	27.5	57.4
Lower-lower stratum	46.0	46.4	96.9
Total:	99.1	100	208.8

The estimates for the upper stratum (3.8 million) and the upper-middle stratum (6.5 million) are based on the section on "white-collar employees" and the "intelligentsia." The lower-middle stratum (15.5 million) embraces 2.4 million white-collar employees (1.6 million are highly qualified workers, among whom some 0.6 million have not completed their university or advanced technical-school training) and 13.1 million skilled workers (among whom there are some 7.7 million production workers), i.e., 28.4 percent of the gross number of workers (46.1 million), among whom the larger part of some 1.1 million workers has advanced technical-school training. The upper-lower stratum (27.3 million) includes 2.8 million "office employees" and white-collar employees of equal rank, 15 million trained workers (among whom are some 8.2 million production workers) (32.5 percent of the gross number of workers) and 9.5 million qualified kolkhoz peasants (brigadiers, tractor operators, etc.), among whom a small number has advanced technical-school training. The lower-lower stratum embraces 4.2 million "petty office employees," 18 million unskilled workers (39.1 percent of the gross number of workers) and 23.5 million ordinary kolkhoz peasants. The difference of 0.3 million consists of individual peasants and artisans who are members of the three lower strata. Statistics pertaining to the social stratification of the entire Soviet population are estimates based on percentages of the employed population in each social stratum. Compare these figures to those of Wädekin (*op. cit.*, p. 329), which are much larger in the case of the two highest strata: upper stratum, 5.8 million (here 7.9 million); upper-middle stratum, 19–24 million (here 13.8 million); lower-middle stratum, 33–36 million (here 32.8 million); the entire lower stratum, 144–148 million (here 154.3 million).

give further details about the interrelationship between the
governing structure and the system of social inequality, Soviet
sociologists have up to now avoided every discussion concerning
the question of the linkage between social mobility and social
stratification.[293] Currently only some of the literati have had
the courage to identify power as the main source of class difference introduced more in the postwar period.[294] Contemporary
Soviet literature reveals, as sharply as social reality itself, that
Soviet society has gone beyond an industrial elitism based on
ability alone; it is unmistakably a class society. The unique features of this society can be understood by the use of a totalitarian model that does justice both to the unchanging as well
as the dynamic qualities of the Soviet system.[295]

Up to now the discussion of totalitarianism has suffered from
the fact that the importance of mass terror, owing to the experience with the Hitler regime and Stalinism, has been overem-
phasized.[296] At the same time the decisive characteristics of an
autocratic-totalitarian ruling system have not adquately been
perceived.[297] The first principal characteristic of such a regime is
the unlimited party autocracy that stems from a permanent one-
party dictatorship. The unlimited character of the party autocracy, together with the other two main features, is the principal
thing that distinguishes it from an authoritarian regime, which
nowadays also rests mostly on a one party dictatorship.[298]

The second characteristic feature is total control "from
above." It extends, with the aid of a well-known transmission
system, not only to all mass media and related informational
activities. Within the framework of this total control "from
above" terror simply serves to demonstrate the effectiveness of
the control apparatus. A totalitarian system will not renounce
fear and terror as methods of achieving social integration. This
does not mean the employment of mass terror. Not an extensive
form of terror but comprehensive control over thought and
action in all spheres of life is to be regarded as the unique feature of totalitarianism. The development of recent years has

been, owing to the efforts of Khrushchev, one of adjusting totalitarian one-party rule, along with the maintenance of comprehensive social controls "from above," to a changed internal situation, thus permitting a certain degree of social spontaneity and personal initiative.

The third characteristic feature is total planning, involving not only the economic sphere but also the domains of politics and culture. Such planning is dictated by the need for the deep-seated social changes required by Marxist-Leninist ideology. In this sense a "socialist society" is merely a transitional state along the way to a perfect "communist society." The question is only how the "classless society"—apart from its utopian character—is to be realized, since the basic ideological assumption—the absence of controls—was rejected as a dogma with the adoption of the thesis of the "immortality of the party" contained in the CPSU's new party program.[299] In theory socio-structural change was to have been brought about by revolutionary means in the Soviet Union. Actually, evolutionary, not revolutionary, means have been the preferred way of bringing about social change. It would not be wholly accurate to describe Soviet totalitarianism as a "permanent revolution from above," particularly since evolutionary methods of social change have been advocated by Khrushchev and his successors.

Ludz is certainly correct in regarding the social dynamics of a totalitarian society not simply as a process engineered and directed by the party.[300] He goes too far, however, in his criticism of the theory of "permanent revolution"—developed mainly by Richard Löwenthal—since it has not excluded this.[301] About all that can be said for it is that it overestimates the revolutionary and hence the violent character of a process oriented toward ideology. As long as the party has the will and the power to keep under control autonomous social processes as well as the social spontaneity generated by these processes, society will remain—despite certain relaxations—under totalitarian rule. This statement in no way means that the basic conflict of Soviet

society, which exists between the ideological totalitarian claims
of the party and the developmental necessities of an industrial
society, can be settled in this way. In this respect "oscillations
in the execution of sanctions," to which Ludz refers,[302] are important signposts for any assessment of the current condition
of this conflict. It would be hardly correct to assume, however,
that the totalitarian party will develop into an "authoritarian"
party merely through the inconsistent application of executive
sanctions.[303] This would be the case only in the event that the
party autocracy were limited.

The function of commanding and deciding the social policy
that is carried out by top state and party officials is based on an
unlimited party autocracy along with an absolute monopoly of
economic power that is derived from the state's ownership of
all land and means of production.[304] The functions of social
planning and social control that are carried out by the top
bureaucracy are linked to the process of total control emanating
"from above" and to an ideologically conditioned process of
social planning. In fact, the main party apparatus represents the
core of this top bureaucracy; it is to be regarded as the real
source of totalitarian rule. The "power elite" represents—as we
have already seen in our treatment of white-collar employees
and the intelligentsia—around 400,000 persons. If we include
the remaining bureaucratic and military segments of the intelligentsia we have a power elite of some 700,000 persons. The
greater measure of power possessed by the Soviet elite is not the
only factor that distinguishes it from power elites in the West.
It is actually somewhat alien to the elite structure of an industrial society, since it is not at all governed by the economic
rationality that is so characteristic of an industrial society based
on merit. The goal of "providing for existence and growth"
(Forsthoff), or for the necessities of society, is for them only of
secondary importance. The primary objective is the consolidation and expansion of their base of power.

Because of its absolute monopoly of power and its unrestricted control of all the means of production it is in a position to divert a disproportionately large share of the national product for the purpose of achieving this objective and of obtaining at the same time a higher personal income for its members.[305] Thus the ruling group derives considerable personal advantage from its control over the *state* and, hence, over state property. It would lose many of these advantages if a larger portion of the national product were to be diverted for investment in the economy and for mass consumption.[306] This general situation has led to sharp conflicts of interest, within the "leading cadres," between the power elite and economic managers who would give greater recognition to economic considerations and who want to consolidate and expand industrial autonomy and "personal property." More serious is the conflict of interest between the ruling group and the prestige elite which endeavors to enlarge the sphere of personal freedom by limiting the omnipotent state.

Economic managers and most of those who belong to the prestige elite hold state offices that simultaneously place them in ruling positions. Yet they are much closer to the other strata of Soviet society than is the power elite, whose core is markedly parasitic in character.[307]

Hence we are justified in speaking of an antogonistic conflict of interest between the greater part of the power elite and the other strata of Soviet society. The conflict is even sharper in the case of the "creative intelligentsia," since the technical intelligentsia, as it were, constitutes the base group of the top-level bureaucracy. Thus, Russia today is not only stratified socially, but is also split along class lines.

Can the ruling power elite and the top-level bureaucracy with which it is closely associated be regarded, sociologically, as a "class"? Are we justified in speaking of Soviet society as a "class society"? These questions can only be answered on the basis of a class theory that takes into account the peculiarities of totalitarian rule and the changed conditions of a developed industrial society.

Neither of these factors is considered in the class theory of Marx,[308] to which Soviet sociologists constantly revert. Moreover, the theory is fragmentary since the last chapter (52) of Volume III of *Das Kapital*, entitled "The Classes," was never completed, because of Marx's death. Its importance lies primarily in the fact that it draws attention to the interrelations existing not only between the pattern of ownership and social system, but also between the power system and the social structure. Marx defined as classes those politically organized social groups that are determined by the consciousness of a common class situation and by the class interests commonly associated with this consciousness. The last criterion for distinguishing between classes is association with, or exclusion from, functioning private property and the resulting power relations that make possible the misappropriation of labor's product and hence the exploitation of working men. The inexorable result of this unjust situation is, in Marx's theory of class warfare, conscious struggle among conflicting interest groups, bringing about a revolutionary change in the existing social structure.

The weakness of the Marxian theory of class lies primarily in the fact that political rule is by no means simply the product of property relations and that socio-structural changes are not solely attributable to class conflict. To define political power in terms of property, as Dahrendorf has rightly pointed out, is to define the whole in terms of one of its parts.[309]

The right to control and, therefore, to dispose of the means of production, a process that need not be linked to the legal right to own property, is only one aspect of power.

Lenin's definition of classes contained in his 1919 essay, "The Great Initiative," is much more realistic. He writes:

Classes are those large human groups which can be differentiated by their place in a historically determined system of social production, by their relationship to the means of production (to a large extent fixed and formulated by law), by their role in the social organization of work, and thereby the manner and extent to which they share in the wealth they produce. Classes are groups of men concerning whom one group can misappropriate the labor of another as a consequence of its role in a given economic system.[310]

Lenin, far more than Marx, was concerned with defining classes in terms of the place and rank of individual social groups within a given social system. It is clear from his definition of class that also in the Soviet Union, so long as the conditions of political rule continued to exist, there would be a rank ordering of social groups which would manifest itself in social stratification. The question is simply whether the Soviet Union has a dual or a triple class structure. A critical analysis of Marx's conception of class makes relatively clear that the authoritative way for determining the real class structure of society is by looking at the nature of power. Dahrendorf has followed this route in shaping his own theory of conflict and power.[311] He maintains that in every industrial society there are a great number of political interests which more or less interact with one another. Within each of these ruling organizations there are two groups: (1) a group in possession of power that wants to preserve the existing power structure and therefore the status quo and (2) a group that is excluded from power and seeks to alter the existing power structure.

For Dahrendorf, then, it is not the possession or nonpossession of private property in the means of production, as Marx assumed, but participation or exclusion from ruling political positions that is the decisive criterion for measuring the significance of classes.

Because of the unequal allocation of institutionalized power, Dahrendorf assumes that every society divides itself into these two groups.

As a result of this dichotomy and the social roles which result therefrom, the two classes, as representatives of fundamental manifest interests—i.e., of conscious purposes—always stand opposed to one another.[312]

Applying this theory to the Soviet Union, all those holding official ruling positions—not only the power elite but also the entire intelligentsia—form a closed "ruling class" that the governed popular masses confront as an opponent. This conclusion simply fails to accord with the complexity of social reality in Russia. This reality can only be grasped when the theory of (political) rulership and the theory of function are considered together, and only when the difference between political rule and leadership is considered. There are two ways of getting to the bottom of the Soviet class structure. If we start out not only by bearing in mind the distinction between positions of institutional power and social leadership but also by granting the possibility of people being excluded from leadership and ruling positions, we can arrive at a threefold division of society and, thus, can speak of a threefold class structure.[313] In this instance the "ruling class" is made up of those who occupy positions of political power, that is, those who do not simultaneously hold positions of social leadership in the sense of constituting an elite structure of modern industrial society. This means that only the larger part of the power elite is to be regarded as the "ruling class."[314] All occupants of genuine leadership positions, independent of whether they simultaneously hold positions of political power, constitute, on the other hand, a second class, which occupies an intermediate position between the governors and the governed.[315]

The largest part of the intelligentsia, particularly economic managers and the prestige elite, may be incorporated into this second class, which is closer to the remaining strata of the population than the power elite.[316] Whether the remaining social strata in this instance are to be regarded as elements of a third class, or whether it is more correct to differentiate between an urban and a rural proletariat remains an open question.[317]

That there are social tensions between the rulers and their main subjects as well as between the intelligentsia and the popular masses certainly cannot be denied.[318] But these tensions are, for the most part, nonantagonistic in character. Thus also, a modified dualistic class structure, whereby all those who are ruled constitute a unity from the point of view of class, is a plausible thesis. The prevailing academic leadership stratum within the "intelligentsia" would assume the role of a counter-elite, in opposition to the ruling power elite.[319]

In evaluating the possibilities of social change under the conditions of totalitarian rule it is irrelevant, in the final analysis, whether the intelligentsia constitutes a distinct class or whether its top group is perceived as a counterelite. In either case the intelligentsia must be regarded as the force pushing the reform efforts associated with "destalinization," which are in part openly directed against the party bureaucracy as the nucleus of the "ruling class." The conflict of roles with which the "intelligentsia" must live has, to be sure, so far prevented it from becoming the dynamic force that would have enabled Soviet society to embark upon a post-totalitarian phase of development.

Because of the special position of all those in an industrial society who primarily exercise leadership and not power, we cannot really accept Dahrendorf's thesis that social conflict arising out of the power structure itself is the most important source of social change.

Schelsky is entirely right in pointing out that it is not possible to reduce a theory of social conflict merely to the power conflict based on the relationship of political rule and thus to analyze social conflict as though it were only a theory of power.[320]

According to Dahrendorf a power conflict in a totalitarian society is resolved only by revolution, which makes genuine social change possible. Of decisive importance here is the fact that potential conflict groups have the possibility of independent organization.[321] When this happens the entire structure of the totalitarian state breaks down. In this connection he quite rightly underscores the fact that the rulers continually fear that the party, as the only legitimate political organization, will itself generate opposition and revolutionary conflict.

Dahrendorf's theory of conflict gives insufficient attention to the power and influence of those who exercise primarily the function of social leadership, not the function of institutionalized power. His theory ignores the role of ideals and spiritual forces in bringing about social change.[322] These factors do bring about, in an evolutionary way, a gradual undermining of the autocratic-totalitarian ruling system, which makes possible the acceleration of social change.

Important also in this connection are conflicts that take place within the ruling class, since the latter contains elements which view power in terms of social leadership. This is particularly true of the military and many government officials. The power elite in Bolshevik Russia is not at all as unified as often assumed. Frictions exist between the party and the government apparatus as well as between the state police and the armed forces.[323]

In each case we are dealing with organizations of a distinct kind which, vis-à-vis the party, have greater influence than the Soviets, trade unions, the Komsomol, and other mass organizations.[324]

A searching analysis of the Soviet power elite, which up to now has not been carried out, would yield valuable information about the sources and nature of these conflicts.[325] The conflicts which contribute to social change cut both vertically and horizontally across Soviet society.[326] A democratic society is characterized by open competition among elite groups. In a totalitarian society this is not permitted. Yet there is evidence of a limited pluralism of elites within an autocratic-totalitarian system. Up to now the Bolshevik state party, buttressed by ideology and totalitarian methods of control, has succeeded in keeping the classes from splitting apart and from integrating into a unity divergent social groups and forces. This will become much more difficult, however, in view of the fact that Soviet society is becoming, from a sociological point of view, ever more complex and compact. The number of those who regard the party in its totalitarian form as a hindrance to the further development of Russia and who are striving to overcome the exploitative features of the Soviet class society is steadily increasing.

III. SUMMARY AND OUTLOOK

Soviet society, which is the product of two deep-seated social revolutions, exhibits a double face. On the one hand it is a relatively primitive industrial society that must grapple with difficult problems of development. On the other hand, it is a class society, organized along totalitarian lines, with a high degree of social tensions. The social situation in contemporary Russia is distinguished by the efforts of progressive social forces to liberate Soviet society from the tutelage of the party and the totalitarian state and, thus, to build a more open society from within and without.

The struggle between progressive and reactionary forces is taking place primarily between the bureaucratic and intellectual sectors of the intelligentsia.

Also the power elite, which together with the bureaucrats directly dependent upon it, constitutes the "ruling class," also exhibits inner conflicts.

The main conflicts in the Soviet upper stratum are occurring between the top bureaucracy, economic managers, and the prestige elite. The upper-middle stratum has been less preoccupied by these conflicts. In its bureaucratic sector Stalinist resistances of inertia predominate. If the "progressive forces" in the economic leadership and prestige elite should prevail, the top bureaucracy will hardly be able to evade the consequences of such a development without a return to Stalinism. The "progressive" forces among the "technical intelligentsia" are those striving for greater economic rationality, stronger attention to "material interests," higher standards of living and social welfare. The progressives among the "creative intelligentsia" are those revolting against social injustice, demanding a renunciation of the Stalinist past, and standing up for human dignity, more freedom of opinion, scientific objectivity, and political freedom.

As a result of this struggle a latent conflict has come into being, between the main party apparatus, as the real representative of totalitarian rule, and those parts of the Soviet upper stratum which are seeking greater autonomy and a larger share in political power in order to realize their special interests.

Of decisive importance here for progressive change in the society is the relationship between the inertia of the governed and the pressure that is generated by all those forces striving for change. The difficulty lies in accurately assessing the impact of these variables within the framework of a "closed society" in the absence of intensive field research.

The statement that social change is taking place in the Soviet Union, something we can document with much evidence, says nothing about the direction of such change.

This change does not have to involve in any way a genuine liberalization or even democratization in the sense of a regime based more on the principle of the rule of law.

The transformation of a totalitarian into a more humane authoritarian rule, such as that contemplated by theories of state and society which were advocated by reform Communists, would already be an immense advance from the standpoint of Soviet society.

Whether such a development, in view of the strength of Russian nationalism, will lead to a narrowing of the rift between East and West is still very uncertain.

A Russian national communism could easily adapt to fascist characteristics.

Soviet society has reached a crossroad in its development. Even if the direction which it will take is momentarily in doubt, still one thing seems certain. The fate of Russia will be shaped decisively by those groups who today, within the framework of an industrial society based on achievement, are fulfilling the role of a genuine leadership stratum.

NOTES

1. See C. E. Black, *The Transformation of Russian Society* (Cambridge, Mass., 1960) and K. Thalheim, *Grundzüge des sowjetischen Wirtschaftssystems*, 1st ed. (Cologne, 1962), p. 22 ff.; see also K. H. Ruffmann's article in this volume.

2. See G. von Rauch, *Die Geschichte des bolschewistischen Russland* (Wiesbaden, 1955), p. 91 ff.

3. See B. Meissner, "Sowjetdemokratie und bolschewistische Parteidiktatur" in R. Löwenthal, *Die Demokratie im Wandel der Gesellschaft* (Berlin, 1963), p. 153 ff.

4. For the sociological effects of Soviet economic policy see K. Thalheim's article in this volume.

5. See B. Meissner, "Fortschrittsgedanke und gesellschaftliche Transformation" in E. Burck, ed., *Die Idee des Fortschritts* (Munich, 1963), p. 107 ff.

6. See G. Wagenlehner, "Karl Marx und der Aufbau des Kommunismus," *Osteuropa* 11 (1961), p. 249 ff.

7. See Thalheim, *op. cit.*, p. 25 ff. and H. Raupach, *Geschichte der Sowjetwirtschaft* (Reinbek, 1964), p. 34 ff.

8. See H. Lambert, *Die Entwicklung der Nationalisierung von Industrieunternehmen in Sowjetrussland* (Berlin-Breslau, 1928), p. 109.

9. See J. and P. Petroff, *Die Wirtschaftliche Entwicklung der Sowjet-Union* (Berlin, 1926), p. 69, and F. Pollock, *Die planwirtschaftlichen Versuche in der Sowjet-Union, 1917 to 1927* (Leipzig, 1929), p. 105.

10. N. I. Luchenko, *Sovetskaia Intelligentsiia* [The Soviet intelligentsia] (Moscow, 1962), p. 5, and W. Hofmann, *Die Arbeitsverfassung der Sowjetunion* (Berlin, 1956), p. 492.

11. L. Trotsky, *Terrorismus und Kommunismus* (Hamburg, 1923), p. 133, and Hofmann, *op. cit.*, p. 492.

12. Luchenko, *op. cit.*, p. 6.

13. I. P. Kim, *Razvitie soiuza rabochego klassa i krest'ianstva v SSSR* [The Development of the alliance between the working class and Peasants in the USSR] (Moscow, 1958).

14. See P. I. Liashchenko, *Istoriia narodnogo khoziaistva SSSR* [History of the national economy in the USSR], vol. III (Moscow, 1956), p. 46; Tsentral'noe Statisticheskoe Upravlenie [Central Statistical Office] *Narodnoe khoziaistvo SSSR: statisticheskii sbornik* [The national economy of the USSR: statistical compilation] (Moscow, 1956), p. 97; A. Jugow, *Die Volkswirtschaft der Sowjetunion und ihre Probleme* (Dresden, 1929), p. 102: O. Auhagen, "Die Landwirtschaft" in G. Dobbert, *Die Rote Wirtschaft* (Königsberg, 1932), p. 98.

15. *Die UdSSR* [special volume of the Great Soviet Encyclopedia] (Leipzig, 1959), p. 774. According to *Narodnoe khoziaistvo SSSR*, p. 97, the figure is 367 million hectares. See also E. Kochetovskaia, *Natsionalizatsiia zemli v SSSR* [The nationalization of the soil in the USSR] (Moscow, 1962), p. 146.

16. *Die UdSSR*, p. 774. According to *Narodnoe khoziaistvo SSSR*, the figure is 215 million hectares and therefore 58.2 percent. One may assume that over and above the land of peasant communities (*mir*) and privately owned peasant property, which in 1907 totaled 28.7 million hectares in the 45 regions of European Russia, this figure also includes land leased by landowners and the state (totaling in 1917 some 38.8 million hectares) but not Cossack property.

17. *Narodnoe khoziaistvo SSSR*, p. 97.

18. *Die UdSSR*, p. 774. According to *Narodnoe khoziaistvo SSSR*, p. 97, the figure was 152 million hectares, and hence 41.8 percent.

19. N. Oganoskii, *Skizzen der Wirtschaftsgeographie Russlands*, pp. 105–109; Jugow, *op. cit.*, p. 102. The landowner's property included, moreover, leased land. Within the 45 regions of European Russia the property of the nobility amounted, in 1907, to 52.2 million hectares; in the 50 regions of European Russia in 1905 the property of merchants, entrepreneurs, and the petty bourgeois amounted to 22.3 million hectares.

20. This figure includes the property of the army and self-governing corporations (cities, etc.), which in 1903 amounted to 6.6 million hectares in the 50 regions of European Russia; presumably it includes also Cossack property (15.8 million hectares in 1905). The property of churches, cloisters, and spiritual leaders totaled 3.2 million hectares in 1905 within the 50 regions of European Russia. The property of the state and the crown consisted largely of forest land and included only a limited amount of agriculturally usable land.

21. Cossack land is not included in this figure.

22. This figure is from Sokolow, *Die Agrarpolitik der Sowjetregierung* (Moscow-Leningrad, 1927), p. 59.

23. See O. Schiller, *Das Agrarsystem der Sowjetunion* (Tübingen, 1960), p. 14. He also accepts this figure, although he does not begin with these statistical data. His estimates rely on Soviet statements that the increase in the 36 regions of European Russia on 1 November 1920 amounted to 23 million hectares (22.6 percent). In this regard see also Raupach, *op. cit.*, p. 38. Jugow, *op. cit.*, p. 103, refers to a Soviet upheaval in 29 regions of European Russia resulting in a 24 percent increase.

24. See S. N. Prokopovich, *Russlands Volkswirtschaft unter den Sowjets* (Zürich-New York, 1944), p. 63.

25. See Jugow, *op. cit.*, p. 103; B. Brutzkus, *Agrarentwicklung und Agrarrevolution in Russland* (Berlin, 1925), p. 151. In the 29 regions of European Russia the usable land per capita before the revolution amounted to 1.87

desyatin; after the Revolution it was 2.26 desyatins. The difference of 0.39 desyatin would correspond to an average increase of 21 percent. In the Ukraine it was around 40 percent.

26. See Liashchenko, *op. cit.*, vol. III, p. 47.

27. See *The Economic Stratification of the Peasantry in 1917 and 1919*, published by the Central Statistical Administration in 1922 (Russ.); see also Jugow, *op. cit.*, p. 103 ff.

28. See Brutzkus, *op. cit.*, p. 160 ff.; Prokopovich, *op. cit.*, p. 68 ff.; Thalheim, *op. cit.*, p. 26 ff.; Raupach, *op. cit.*, p. 40 ff.

29. According to official Soviet statistics 5 million men died of starvation. The well-known agrarian statistician, Prof. A. N. Celincev, put the figure at 9 million. See Brutzkus, *op. cit.*, p. 166 ff.

30. See Tsentral'noe Statisticheskoe Upravlenie [Central Statistical Administration], *Narodnoe khoziaistvo SSSR v 1963 godu. Statisticheskii ezhegodnik* [The national economy of the USSR in 1963: Statistical yearbook] (Moscow, 1965), p. 7.

31. See W. Markert, "Marxismus und russisches Erbe im Sowjetsystem" in *Der Mensch im kommunistischen System* (Tübingen, 1957), p. 63.

32. Arthur Rosenberg, *Geschichte des Bolschewismus* (Berlin, 1932), p. 116 ff.

33. See Rauch, *op. cit.*, p. 173 ff.; I. Ia. Trifonov, *Klassy i klassovaia bor'ba v SSSR v nachale NEPa* (Leningrad, 1964).

34. See Lenin's address to the all Russian Association of Transport Workers on 27 March 1921 in V. I. Lenin, *Ausgewahlte Werke*, vol. II (East Berlin, 1953), p. 809 ff.

35. See Thalheim, *op. cit.*, p. 29 ff.; Raupach, *op. cit.*, p. 47 ff.

36. See B. Meissner, "Die sowjetischen Gewerkschaften als Instrument des sozialistischen Staates" in *Auslandsforschung*, no. 2 (Darmstadt, 1953), p. 22.

37. See Arthur Rosenberg, *op. cit.*, p. 157.

38. The sources for the following figures are to be found in the second part of this article.

39. See R. Feldmesser, "The Persistence of Status Advantages in Soviet Russia," *The American Journal of Sociology* 59 (July 1953), p. 21 ff.

40. See O. Anweiler's article in this volume.

41. In this connection see the presentation in the second section of this article.

42. See B. Meissner, *Das Parteiprogramme der KPdSU, 1903 to 1961* (Cologne, 1962), p. 98 ff.

43. These figures are from Jugow, *op. cit.*, p. 143.

44. Figures are from Jugow, *op. cit.*, p. 150. See also A. Gajster, *Die Schichtung des Sowjetdorfes* (1928).

45. See Schiller, *op. cit.*, p. 18.

46. *Narodnoe khoziaistvo SSSR v 1963 godu*, p. 7.

47. See A. V. Golikov, *Vazhneishii etap razvitiia sel'skokhoziaistvennoi kooperatsii v SSSR* [The principal stage in the development of the agricultural association in the USSR] 1921–1929 (Moscow, 1963).

48. See Jugow, *op. cit.*, p. 130.

49. See Liashchenko, *op. cit.*, vol. III, p. 257 ff.; Raupach, *op. cit.*, p. 48.

50. See Rauch, *op. cit.*, p. 235 ff.; Liashchenko, *op. cit.*, vol. III, p. 209.

51. From Prokopovich, *op. cit.*, p. 191.

52. See Liashchenko, *op. cit.*, vol. III, p. 263.

53. See B. Meissner, *Russland im Umbruch: Der Wandel in der Herrschaftsordnung und sozialen Struktur der Sowjetunion* (Frankfurt a. M., 1951), p. 16 ff.

54. See I. Stalin, *Fragen des Leninismus* (Moscow, 1947), p. 140; *Werke* vol. 8, January to November 1926 (East Berlin, 1952), p. 19.

55. See R. Löwenthal, "Totalitäre und demokratische Revolution," *Der Monat*, November 1960, p. 35 ff.

56. See B. Meissner, "Shdanow," *Osteuropa* 2 (1952), p. 15.

57. "Über die Aufgaben der Wirtschaftler" in Stalin, *Fragen des Leninismus*, p. 399.

58. See G. Malenkov, "Informationsbericht über die Tätigkeit des Zentralkomitees der Kommunistischen Partei der Sowjetunion" (Bolscheviki), *Neue Welt* 2, no. 23 (1947), p. 10.

59. See K. Mehnert, "Die Wandlungen in der soziologischen Struktur des russischen Volkes," *Osteuropa* 8 (1932–33), p. 451 ff.

60. See Thalheim, *op. cit.*, p. 32 ff.; Raupach, *op. cit.*, p. 75 ff.; Schiller, *op. cit.*, p. 18; Liashchenko, *op. cit.*, vol. III, p. 262 ff.

61. See B. Brutzkus, *Der Fünfjahresplan und seine Erfüllung* (Leipzig, 1932), p. 46 ff.

62. O. Auhagen, *Die Bilanz des ersten Fünfjahresplanes der Sowjetwirtschaft* (Breslau, 1933), p. 43 ff.

63. According to Prokopovich, *op. cit.*, p. 34, 9 million human lives were lost in the famine of 1933 and 1934.

64. At the first meeting of Churchill and Stalin in August 1942 in Moscow. See W. S. Churchill, *The Second World War: The Hinge of Fate* (Boston, 1950), p. 498. Stalin spoke of a relentless battle involving 10 million people.

65. The percentages which follow are from Prokopovich, *op. cit.*, p. 121; *Narodnoe khoziaistvo SSSR*, p. 99.

66. The figures are from Prokopovich, *op. cit.*, p. 313.

67. These figures are from Pollock, *op. cit.*, p. 174, and E. Lokschin, "Die Industrie" in *Union der Sozialistischen Sowjetrepubliken* (Encyclopedia), vol. I (East Berlin, 1950), p. 834 ff.

68. Figures are from *Die Ergebnisse der Erfüllung des ersten Fünfjahresplanes* (Moscow, 1935), p. 25.

69. Figures are from Mehnert, *op. cit.*, p. 455.

70. *Narodnoe khoziaistvo SSSR v 1963 godu*, p. 7 ff. The figures quoted by the Central Statistical Office refer to the Soviet Union up to 17 September 1939. In the special volume *UdSSSR Grosse Sowjetenzyklopädie*, 1st ed., vol. I, p. 46, the urban population for 1927 and 1939 is listed at 26.3 million (17.9 percent) and 55.9 million (32.8 percent) respectively. This is a total increase of 29.6 million, which amounts to a rise of 112.5 percent.

71. Figures are from E. Dawydow, "Bevölkerung" in *UdSSR* (encyclopedia), vol. I, p. 46 ff.

72. *Ibid.*

73. See H. Schmidt, "Das Bau- und Wohnungswesen" in Dobbert, *op. cit.*, p. 191.

74. Figures are from Prokopovich, *op. cit.*, p. 309, and *Private Houses in the Soviet Union, Newsletters from behind the Iron Curtain*, vol. II, no. 93 (1948).

75. Schmidt, *op. cit.*, p. 190.

76. These figures are from Prokopovich, *op. cit.*, p. 306 ff.

77. Prokopovich, *op. cit.*, p. 304 ff.

78. The gap between fixed prices and sales at cost is the Bolshevik regime's most important source of finance. Under Stalin the turnover tax accounted for almost 75 percent of the revenue in the unified budget of the USSR. See R. Kerschagl, "Das Steuersystem der USA und UdSSR," *Schmollers Jahrbuch für Gesetzgebung, Verwaltung und Volkswirtschaft* 69, no. 3 (1949), p. 97 ff.; K. Thalheim, *Betrachtungen zur wirtschaftspolitischen Lage der Sowjetunion* (Hannover, 1961), p. 30.

79. Figures taken from Prokopovich, *op. cit.*, p. 310.

80. Figures taken from Prokopovich, *op. cit.*, p. 148; see also his *Der Vierte Fünfjahrplan der Sowjetunion 1946–1950* (Zürich-Vienna, 1948), p. 70.

81. Prokopovich, *Der Vierte Fünfjahrplan*, p. 70.

82. See N. DeWitt, *Soviet Professional Manpower* (Washington, D.C., 1955); O. Anweiler and K. Meyer, *Die sowjetische Bildungspolitik seit 1917* (Heidelberg, 1961), and the article by O. Anweiler in this volume.

83. See D. Dallin, *Das wirkliche Sowjet-Russland* (Hamburg, 1948), p. 139, n. 1; H. Jaeger, *Staatsmacht und Bürokratismus in der Sowjetunion* (Darmstadt, 1952), p. 42.

84. Sources can be found in the second section of the present article.

85. See Stalin, *Fragen des Leninismus*, pp. 637 and 730.

86. "Neue Verhältnisse—Neue Aufgaben des wirtschaftlichen Aufbaus" in Stalin, *Fragen des Leninismus*, p. 402 ff.

87. See B. Meissner, "Die Entwicklung der Ministerien in Russland," *Europa-Archiv* 3 (1948), p. 1204.

88. See Anweiler-Meyer, *op. cit.*, pp. 165 and 171.

89. Figures are from DeWitt, *op. cit.*, p. 577. See also in this connection Anweiler, *op. cit.*

90. See B. Meissner, "Der Wandel im sozialen Gefüge der Sowjetunion," *Europa-Archiv* 5 (1950), p. 12 ff.

91. See Stalin, *Fragen des Leninismus*, p. 594.

92. *Ibid.*, p. 613.

93. *Ibid.*, p. 636. By 1894 Kautsky, in his article, "Die Intelligenz und die Sozialdemokratie" had also refused to regard the intelligentsia as a class. See A. N. Weiss, *Die Diskussion über den historischen Materialismus in der deutschen Sozialdemokratie 1871 bis 1918* (Wiesbaden, 1965), p. 107.

94. See N. Berdyaev, *Sinn und Schicksal des russischen Kommunismus* (Lucerne, 1937), p. 23 ff.; the articles by M. Malia, L. Schapiro, and B. Elkin in R. Pipes, ed., *The Russian Intelligentsia* (New York, 1961); G. Fischer, "The Intelligentsia and Russia" in Black, op. cit., p. 253 ff., and *Russian Liberalism: From Gentry to Intelligentsia* (Cambridge, Mass., 1958); S. R. Tompkins, *The Russian Intelligentsia* (Norman, 1957); K. v. Beyme, *Politische Soziologie im zaristischen Russland* (Wiesbaden, 1965).

95. See Rauch, op. cit., p. 320 ff.

96. This figure is from Meissner, *Russland im Umbruch*, p. 10 ff.

97. See G. Brunner, *Das Parteistatut der KPdSU 1903–1961* (Cologne, 1965), p. 35 ff.

98. See B. Iakovlev, *Konsentratsionnye lageri SSSR* [Concentration camps in the USSR] (Munich, 1955); D. Dallin and B. Nicolaevsky, *Arbeiter oder Ausgebeutete: Das System der Arbeitslager in Sowjet-Russland* (Munich, 1948); *Amerikanischer Gewerkschaftsbund (AFL): Sklavenarbeit in Russland*, n.d.; H. S.: "Bericht über sowjetische Lager, bearbeitet aufgrund der offiziellen Protokolle der Internationalen Kommission zum Kampf gegen das Regime der Konzentrationslager," *Ost-Probleme* 3 (1951), p. 1102 ff.; M. Mihajlov, *Moskauer Sommer 1964* (Bern, 1965), p. 40, points out that the first concentration camps had been constructed by the Bolshevik regime in 1921.

99. According to statements by GPU-officer Kiselev-Gromov this figure came to 662,257 on 1 May 1930. See Dallin-Nicolaevsky, op. cit., p. 11.

100. Salomon Schwarz, "Stastistik und Sklaverei," *Ost-Probleme* 3 (1950), p. 1562 ff.; a recognized authority on the history of the Russian working class calculated that there were 100 million in 1939; Naum Jasny, "Authentisches Material über die Zwangsarbeit," *Ost-Probleme* 3 (1951), p. 132, on the basis of the plan for 1941 estimated at least 3.5 million; Dallin-Nicolaevsky, op. cit., p. 17, accepted the figure of 15 million. Mihajlov, op. cit., pp. 37 and 49, estimates the total number by 1956–57 to be around 8 to 12 million. According to the calculations of the author the number of forced laborers in 1939 might have totaled about 5 million. As a result of deportations that Stalin ordered after the outbreak of the war this figure might even be higher. See R. Conquest, *The Soviet Deportations of Nationalities* (London, 1960). Since all authorities agree that 85 to 90 percent of concentration camp inmates in the Stalin era were men, the sharp

drop in the birthrate at this time may not be attributable exclusively to the war.

101. See Jasny, *op. cit.*, p. 1559. The secret plan for 1941 was captured by the Germans and later utilized by the Americans.

102. See Rauch, *op. cit.*, p. 439 ff.; K. Mehnert, *Weltrevolution durch Weltgeschichte* (Kitzingen-Main, 1950).

103. See Meissner, *Russland im Umbruch*, p. 42.

104. See K. Mehnert, *Der Sowjetmensch* (Stuttgart, 1958), p. 184 and G. P.: "Ein Nachtgespräch in Moskau," *Christ und Welt*, 4 April 1957.

105. The thesis that Bolshevism was a substitute for an incipient capitalism has been developed by G. F. Achminow in his book, *Die Macht im Hintergrund* (Ulm, 1950), (2nd ed., *Die Totengräber des Kommunismus* [Stuttgart, 1964]). Except for the fact that Russia was much further along in its economic development before the Bolshevik seizure of power than Achminov seems to accept, his thesis is much too narrow because it fails to consider the full impact of Stalin's "ersatz Bonapartism." Moreover, it overestimates the role of the "technical intelligentsia" and, therefore, of the economic manager as an element of social change. The idea of "ersatz Bonapartism" brings to mind Isaiah Berlin's essay, "The Silence in Russian Culture," *Foreign Affairs* 36 (1957), p. 1 ff.

106. See Hofmann, *op. cit.*, p. 382 ff.; A. Inkeles, "Social Stratification and Mobility in the Soviet Union 1940–1950," *American Sociological Review* 15 (1950), p. 470 ff.; H. Laeuen, "Die soziale Differenzierung in der Sowjetunion" (Beilage zur Wochenzeitung), *Das Parlament*, 17 August 1955, p. 494 ff.; K. Mehnert, *Der Sowjetmensch*, p. 51 ff. and 114 ff. The tax reform of 1943 was an effective device for the progressive taxation of higher monthly incomes. The direct income tax on a monthly income of 500 rubles for a married couple with two children was 5.7 percent; an income of 1,000 rubles was taxed at 7.7 percent, 2000 rubles at 11.1 percent, and higher incomes around 13 percent.

107. Ever since the finance reform of 1934 Soviet banks and savings accounts paid interest, just as the state had granted a tax preference for gains made on investments. See Laeuen, *op. cit.*, p. 495.

108. Figures from Laeuen, *op. cit.*, p. 496.

109. Quoted from the report published by the ECA-Mission in West Germany, p. 15. Examples: in 1937 an engineer received bonuses of 8,320 and 8,000 rubles for quickly assembling two drilling machines (*Industriia*, 31 December 1937). In 1939 a director received a bonus of 12,000 rubles for fulfilling his plan at an early date and for reducing production costs (*Predpriiatie*, 29 August 1939). In 1942 managers of leading industrial firms received Stalin bonuses, which went as high as 50,000 to 150,000 rubles (*Pravda*, 11 April 1942). See G. Bienstock, S. M. Schwarz, and A. Jugow, *Management in Russian Industry and Agriculture* (London, 1944), p. 95. For additional examples see Mehnert, *Der Sowjetmensch*, p. 114 ff.

110. See Dallin, op. cit., p. 98 ff. Dallin overestimates the percentage of forced laborers in the professional population. The workers share of the national income vis-à-vis the intelligentisia might therefore have been higher.

111. See Mehnert, Der Sowjetmensch, p. 52. Regarding these privileges it is interesting to note that under Stalin special pensions were granted to widows and children of well-deserving members of the top bureaucracy. See examples in Inkeles, op. cit., p. 470. See also M. Djilas, Die Neue Klasse (Munich, 1958), p. 86.

112. According to Soviet sources (Pravda, 27 June 1937) artists living in the RSFSR in 1937 earned the following: 14 persons received more than 10,000 rubles, 11 persons between 6,000 and 10,000 rubles, 39 persons between 2,000 and 3,000 rubles, 114 persons between 1,000 and 2,000 rubles, and 400 persons lower than 500 rubles. See also in this connection A. Bergson, "On the Inequality of Incomes in the USSR," American Slavic and East European Review (April 1951), p. 95 ff.

113. Decree of the Presidium of the Supreme Soviet of the RSFSR of 12 June 1945 concerning changes in the Civil Code of the RSFSR (VVS RSFSR 1945, no. 38).

114. Decree of the Presidium of the Supreme Soviet of the RSFSR of 26 August 1948, concerning the right of the citizen to buy and erect private houses (Izvestiia, 31 August 1948).

115. On the basis of the tax reform of 1943. See Inkeles, op. cit., p. 471. In place of the inheritance tax a relatively low registration fee was required.

116. See the chapter by O. Anweiler.

117. See B. Dennewitz and B. Meissner, Die Verfassungen der modernen Staaten, vol. I, (Hamburg, 1947), p. 144 ff.

118. See the chapter by K. H. Ruffmann.

119. The author has already drawn attention to this noteworthy development in 1950–1951. See Russland im Umbruch, p. 4.

120. The decrees marked with * have been repealed by the ukase of the Presidium of the Supreme Soviet of the USSR of 12 July 1954, while the decree marked with ** was abolished by the ukase of 11 October 1956. See Sbornik zakonov SSSR i ukazov Prezidiuma Verkhovnogo Soveta SSR 1938–1961 (Moscow, 1961), p. 556 ff. For personnel involved in railway traffic, inland navigation, and civil air transport only the shoulder insignia were done away with.

121. Russian: personal'nye zvaniia.

122. Russian: klassnye chiny.

123. This rank was abolished by the ukase of 12 July 1954.

124. A revival of traditional forms in the area of education meant the reintroduction of citations for the best secondary-school graduates with the conferral of a gold and silver medal in 1943 and a memorial medal for graduates of state universities in 1945.

125. See, e.g., the assignment of service ranks and insignia of the managerial and engineering-technical personnel in the Ministry of Geology to members of the Geological Service of the MVD pursuant to the decree of 4 August 1950 (VVS SSSR 1950, no. 22).

126. See *Pravda*, 11 November 1953.

127. See Laeuen, *op. cit.*, p. 496.

128. See Rauch, *op. cit.*, p. 530 ff.; Raupach, *op. cit.*, p. 103 ff.; Schiller, *op. cit.*, p. 51 ff.

129. By 1952 there were already 97,000 of these, each averaging about 1700 hectures (including fallow land). See Raupach, *op. cit.*, p. 104.

130. See the round-table discussion by American scholars, "How Strong is Soviet Russia?" *New Republic*, May 1949. "Rubel und Preissenkung," *Ost-Probleme* 2 (1950), p. 310 ff.; "Kaufkraft des Rubels," *Ost-Probleme* 2 (1950), p. 414 ff.

131. See R. Löwenthal, "Stalins Vermachtnis," *Der Monat* 5, no. 55 (1953), p. 20 ff.

132. See B. Meissner, "Chruschtschowismus ohne Chruschtschow," *Osteuropa* 15 (1965), p. 8.

133. After his downfall Beria had been rebuked for shaking the kolkhoz system. See B. Meissner, "Nach Stalins Tod," *Osteuropa* 3 (1953), p. 284. His intention to enlarge private farmland had been mentioned in the Soviet press.

134. See Meissner, *Russland im Umbruch*, p. 28 ff.

135. See A. Sieger, "Die drei Zonen der sowjetischen Wehrwirtschaft," *Europa-Archiv* 4 (1949), p. 2399 ff.

136. These figures are from Sieger, *op. cit.*, p. 2402.

137. Figures from *Narodnoe khoziaistvo SSSR v 1963 godu*, p. 8.

138. See J. Towster, *Political Power in the USSR, 1917–1947* (New York, 1948), p. 330 ff.

139. Regarding "zhdanovshchina" see Rauch, *op. cit.*, p. 532; Meissner, Shdanow," p. 20 ff.

140. See E. Boettcher, *Die sowjetische Wirtschaftspolitik am Scheidewege* (Tübingen, 1959), p. 245 ff.

141. See Boettcher-Lieber-Meissner, *Bilanz der Ära Chruschtschow* (Stuttgart, 1966).

142. See W. Leonhard, *Kreml ohne Stalin* (Cologne, 1959), p. 122 ff.; Thalheim, *Grundzüge des sowjetischen Wirtschaftssystems*, p. 41 ff.

143. Text in Meissner, *Das Ende des Stalin-Mythos* (Frankfurt a. M., 1956), p. 175 ff.

144. See B. Meissner, "Die Ergebnisse des 22. Parteikongresses der KPdSU," *Europa-Archiv* 19 (1962), p. 73 ff.; and by the same author *Das Parteiprogramm der KPdSU 1903 bis 1961* (Cologne, 1962).

145. See B. Meissner, *Russland unter Chruschtschow* (Munich, 1960); see also his "Die Innenpolitik Chruschtschows," *Osteuropa* 11 (1961), p.

81 ff.; "Die Grosse Verwaltungsreform Chruschtschows," *Osteuropa* 13 (1963), p. 81 ff.; "Zweifrontenkampf der KPdSU," *Osteuropa* 13 (1963), p. 577 ff.; and "Chruschtschowismus ohne Chruschtschow," *Osteuropa* 15 (1965), p. 1 ff.

146. Analysis and text of the Seven-Year Plan appears in B. Meissner, *Russland unter Chruschtschow*, pp. 203 ff. and 472 ff.; for the Twenty-Year Plan see Meissner, *Das Parteiprogramm der KPdSU*, pp. 72 ff. and 189 ff.

147. See F. C. Schroeder, "Inhalt und Entwicklung von Staat und Recht nach dem neuen Parteiprogramm der KPdSU," *Jahrbuch für Ostrecht*, III/1, (1962), p. 45 ff. and III/2, (1962), p. 49 ff. See also Meissner, *Das Parteiprogramm der KPdSU*, p. 98 ff.

148. See B. Meissner, "Chruschtschowismus ohne Chruschtschow," *Osteuropa* 15 (1965), pp. 1 ff., 138 ff., and 217 ff.

149. See Anweiler-Meyer, *op. cit.*, p. 44 ff.; Meissner, *Russland unter Chruschtschow*, pp. 115 ff. and 226 ff.

150. See R. A. Feldmesser, "Equality and Inequality under Khrushchev," *Problems of Communism* 9, no. 2 (1960), p. 35 ff., and the article by O. Anweiler in this volume.

151. With regard to administrative reforms see B. Meissner, *Russland unter Chruschtschow*, pp. 20–85, and "Die Grosse Verwaltungsreform," p. 89 ff. See also "Wandlungen im Herrschaftssystem und Verfassungsrecht der Sowjetunion" in Boettcher-Lieber-Meissner, *op. cit.*, p. 148 ff. As a result of the partial reform of 13 March 1963 the great administrative reform of Khrushchev was changed in the direction of greater centralization, and in a way that he had not desired; the division of the party administration into an urban-industrial and a rural-agrarian branch was abolished after Khrushchev's downfall. See Meissner, "Zweifrontenkampf der KPdSU," p. 578 ff. and also his "Chruschtschowismus ohne Chruschtschow," p. 148 ff.

152. See W. Leonhard, "Party Training after Stalin," *Survey* no. 20 (October 1957), p. 10 ff., and "Internal Developments: A Balance Sheet," *Problems of Communism* 12, no. 2 (1963), p. 4.

153. See S. Bialer, "But Some Are More Equal than Others," *Problems of Communism* 9, no. 2 (1960), p. 48.

154. See Bialer, *op. cit.*, p. 45 ff. Regarding the rotation system see Meissner, *Das Parteiprogramm der KPdSU*, p. 107.

155. See Feldmesser, *op. cit.*, p. 34, and Bialer, *op. cit.*, p. 43.

156. See K. Thalheim, *Betrachtungen zur wirtschaftspolitischen Lage in der Sowjetunion*, p. 30 ff.

157. See the program draft by Professor Aganbegian, the director of the economic department of the Siberian branch of the USSR Academy of Science, in *Socialist Commentary* (October 1965). Estimates by E. Nash ("Purchasing Power of Workers in the USSR," *Monthly Labor Review*, 1960, no. 4) indicates that the typical Soviet worker had to work 8 percent longer in 1959 than in 1928 in order to provide his family with basic needs.

158. See W. Meder, "Liberalisierungstendenzen im sowjetischen Arbeitsrecht," *Jahrbuch für Ostrecht*, I/2 (1960), p. 85 ff.

159. See Meissner, *Russland unter Chruschtschow*, pp. 83 ff. and 107 ff.; K. Thalheim, "Die Veränderungen im sowjetischen Wirtschaftssystem in der nachstalinistischen Ära" in Boettcher-Lieber-Meissner, *op. cit.*, p. 123 ff.

160. See A. Nove, "Social Welfare in the USSR," *Problems of Communism* 9, no. 1 (1960), p. 1 ff.

161. See Schiller, *op. cit.*, p. 55 ff.

162. See Schiller, *op. cit.*, p. 70 ff., and Thalheim, *Betrachtungen zur wirtschaftspolitischen Lage*, p. 25 ff.

163. See Feldmesser, *op. cit.*, p. 34, and Bialer, *op. cit.*, p. 41 ff. The average monthly income of the kolkhoz peasant (in money and production) was in 1958, despite this increase, lower than the minimum wage of 270 rubles for agrarian workers and employees.

164. See Meissner, "Chruschtschowismus ohne Chruschtschow," p. 10.

165. See O. Schiller, "Die sowjetische Landwirtschaft im Zeichen des Uberganges zum Kommunismus," *Osteuropa- Wirtschaft* 7 (1962), p. 162 ff. The number of kolkhozy decreased between 1954 and 1959 from 89,000 to 54,600.

166. See Meissner, *Russland unter Chruschtschow*, p. 225 ff.

167. See Meissner, "Verwaltungsumbau," *Osteuropa* 4 (1954), p. 285.

168. These figures are from *Narodnoe khoziaistvo SSSR v 1963 godu*, p. 8.

169. Figures are from *Narodnoe khoziaistvo SSSR v 1963 godu*, p. 9.

170. See Meissner, *Russland unter Chruschtschow*, p. 219.

171. Sources are indicated in the second section of this article.

172. See *Planovoe khoziaistvo* [Planned economy], 1960, no. 3, p. 45 ff.; *Voprosy ekonomiki* [Economic questions], 1960, no. 1, p. 36 ff. The number of machine workers and those maintaining and repairing equipment had increased between 1948 and 1958 from 44.3 to 50 percent, while the number of manual workers declined from 55.7 to 50 percent during the same period. See *Trudovye ressursy SSSR* [Manpower in the USSR] (Moscow, 1961), p. 58.

173. Sources for these figures are found in the second section of this article.

174. Figures from *SSSR v tsifrakh v 1963 godu* [1963 statistics for the USSR] (Moscow, 1964). There were 10.6 million specialists at the end of 1963.

175. See H. von Ssachno, *Der Aufstand der Person* (Berlin, 1965); L. Froese, *Der Mensch in der neueren russischen Literatur* (Ratingen, 1962); K. Mehnert, *Humanismus in der jungsten Sowjetliteratur* (Wiesbaden, 1963); Mihajlov, *op. cit.*, p. 6 ff.; essays by Haimson and Hayward in Pipes, *op. cit.*, pp. 101 ff. and 111 ff.; M. Hayward, "Soviet Literature in the Doldrums," *Problems of Communism* 8, no. 4 (1959), p. 11 ff.; A. Zr., "The

Conscience of a Generation," *Problems of Communism* 10, no. 3 (1961), p. 7 ff.; D. Burg, "The 'Cold War' on the Literary Front," *Problems of Communism* 11, no. 4 (1962), p. 1 ff.; no. 5, p. 33 ff.; vol. 12, no. 1 (1963), p. 44 ff.; R. Hingley, "The Cultural Scene," *Problems of Communism* 12, no. 2 (1963), p. 41.; V. Frank, "The Literary Climate," *Survey*, July 1965, p. 46 ff. See also the reports of Barbara Bode in *Osteuropa*.

176. See H. Dahm, *Die Dialektik im Wandel der Sowjetphilosophie* (Cologne, 1963) and K. Marko, *Sowjethistoriker zwischen Ideologie und Wissenschaft* (Cologne, 1964).

177. See K. Westen, "Rechtsreform nach dem Tode Stalins," in Boettcher-Lieber-Meissner, *op. cit.*, p. 189 ff. and H. Raupach, "Die Wiederbelebung der ökonomische Theorie seit 1953," p. 132 ff.

178. See A. Brodersen, "New Trends in Soviet Social Theory," *The American Slavic and East European Review* 17 (1958), p. 282 ff.; G. Fischer, *Science and Politics: The New Sociology in the Soviet Union* (Ithaca, 1964); R. Ahlberg, *Die Entwicklung der empirischen Sozialforschung in der Sowjetunion* (Berlin, 1964) and "Die Entwicklung der Beziehungen zwischen der sowjetischen Gesellschaftswissenschaft und der westlichen Soziologie" in Boettcher-Lieber-Meissner, *op. cit.*, p. 278 ff. The most important findings of this recent sociological research in the Soviet Union is to be found in a two-volume collective work, *Sotsiologiia v SSSR* [Sociology in the USSR] (Moscow, 1965). Regarding the Soviet argument with Western sociology see G. V. Osipov, *Sovremennaia burzhuaznaia empiricheskaia sotsiologiia* [Modern bourgeois empirical sociology] (Moscow, 1965).

179. See P. Johnson, "The Regime and the Intellectuals," *Problems of Communism* 12 (1963), Special Supplement.

180. See V. Tarsis, *Skazanie o sinei mukhe* [Legend of the blue flies] (Frankfurt a. M., 1963), pp. 35 and 37 ff.

181. Quotation is from K. Alexandrow, *Ausbruch in die Freiheit* (Freie Rundschau, 1961), p. 18. Soviet writers who have made themselves vulnerable because of their demand for greater freedom, such as Esenin-Volpin, Tarsis, and Nariza were confined to mental hospitals by Khrushchev as being "mentally deranged." After Khrushchev's downfall all three were released. Tarsis spoke of his experiences with foreign journalists in Moscow (*Kölner Stadt-Anzeiger*, 28 October 1965) shortly after the arrest of the Soviet writers Andrei Siniavskii and Iulii Daniel, who, as Abram Tertz and Nikolai Arzhak, had published stories in the Polish monthly magazine "Kultura," which appears in Paris. Esenin-Volpin took part, at the beginning of September 1965, in student demonstrations against the arrest of Siniavskii and Daniel in Moscow. He carried a placard with the inscription, "Respect the Constitution!" See *New York Times*, 18 December 1965. Siniavskii and Daniel were meanwhile sentenced to seven and five years imprisonment respectively. See *Neue Zürcher Zeitung* 16 and 26 February 1966. After

Tarsis went to England his Soviet citizenship was withdrawn. See *Kölner Stadt-Anzeiger*, 22 February 1966.

182. On the generational problem and the situation of youth and students in the Soviet Union see L. Haimson, "Three Generations of the Soviet Intelligentsia," *Foreign Affairs* 37 (1959) p. 235 ff.: "Das Generationsproblem in Osteuropa," *Osteuropäische Rundschau* 11, no. 9 (1965) pp. 2 and 3; *Molodezh Sovetskogo Soiuza* [Youth in the Soviet Union] (Munich, 1959); *Youth in Ferment* (Munich, 1962); Sojetische Jugendprobleme" (Special Number) *Sowjet-Studien*, 1963, no. 14; A. Kossof, "Youth vs. the Regime: Conflict in Values," *Problems of Communism* 6, no. 3 (1957), p. 15; S. V. Potechin, "Patterns of Nonconformity," *ibid.*, p. 23 ff.; A. Z.: "The Conscience of a Generation," *Problems of Communism* 10, no. 3 (1961), pp. 7 ff.; *Russland unter Chruschtschow*, p. 7 ff. and 116 ff.; D. Burg, "Observations on Soviet University Students" in Pipes, *op. cit.*, p. 80 ff. The students of Stalin's time are described in the novel by Jury Bondarev Tishina, *Vergiss wer Du bist* (Munich, 1962). On the Russian student movement prior to 1917 see G. Kiss, *Die gesellschaftspolitische Rolle der Studentenbewegung im vorrevolutionären Russland* (Munich, 1963).

183. On the lack of critical thought and the existence of a conforming petty-bourgeois "semi-intelligence" see Mihajlov, *op. cit.*, pp. 94 and 98. For a discussion of the problem of conformity in the established Soviet order see also H. J. Lieber, "Ideologie und Gesellschaft in der Sowjetunion" in Boettcher-Lieber-Meissner, *op. cit.*, p. 241 ff.

184. See D. Sering (R. Löwenthal), *Jenseits des Kapitalismus* (Nürnberg, 1947), p. 147 ff.

185. See D. Pfaff, *Das sozialistische Eigentum in der Sowjetunion* (Cologne, 1965), p. 140.

186. See Meissner, "Wandlungen im Herrschaftssystem und Verfassungsrecht der Sowjetunion" in Boettcher-Lieber-Meissner, *op. cit.*, p. 161.

187. See W. W. Rostow, *Stadien wirtschaftlichen Wachstums* (Göttingen, 1960), p. 117 ff.

188. Polish exile sources recently presented evidence that there were 56 forced-labor camps in the Soviet Union. See *Neue Zürcher Zeitung*, 23 April 1965; *Der aktuelle Osten*, 15 May 1965, no. 20, p. 7 ff. On the question of forced-labor camps see also P. Barton, "Les transformations du systeme concentrationnaire sovietique," *Saturne*, January-February 1956. A realistic description of life in a concentration camp in the Stalin era appears in the novel of the Soviet writer A. Solzhenitzyn, *One Day in the Life of Ivan Denisovich* (New York, 1963). See also the memoirs of General A. V. Gorbatov in *Novyi Mir*, 1964, no. 3–5; Mihajlov, *op. cit.*, p. 37 ff.

189. Already in 1959 the Soviet Union could point to the fact that 47.5 percent of the entire population, a very high percentage, was employed. In the Federal Republic of Germany this percentage reached 46.6 percent in 1964. In the other European Common Market countries the figure was con-

siderably lower: France 42.6 percent; Italy and Luxembourg 40.3 percent; Belgium 39.6 percent; the Netherlands, 36.4 percent. See *Die Welt*, 19 November 1965.

190. Of the 5.8 million students and advanced specialized students who are not involved in production, 2.2 million are university students, 2.7 million are studying in specialized technical schools, 0.7 million are engaged in independent study by permission, and 0.2 are engaged in other activities. Of the 4.4 million students and advanced specialized pupils who are engaged in production 1 million are university students, 1.4 million attend specialized technical schools, 0.4 million are engaged in independent study by permission, 1.6 million are common professional pupils and engaged in other activities. For figures regarding these students see *SSSR v tsifrakh v 1963 godu*, pp. 158 and 160. The figure of 4.4 million was calculated by the author. Pupils involved in production who attend general secondary schools are not included here.

191. This number comprises those able-bodied employees (92.7 million) and family members engaged in private side pursuits (9.9 million), less the military (3.6 million) and students or specialized pupils associated with the process of production (4.4 million).

192. The gross number of workers (46.1 million) embraced 31.8 million workers in the more immediate areas of production (including agricultural workers), 2.5 million workers in the area of trade and supply, 5.3 million workers outside of production, 1.2 million cooperative homeworkers, 1.8 million military personnel, 219 students and specialized pupils involved in the process of production, as well as the 0.6 million difference mentioned in the text. As for the 19.8 million white-collar employees, 7.4 million are engineering and commercial personnel, 9.9 million are outside the process of production, 1 million are in the military, and 1.5 million are students and specialized pupils linked to the production process. The membership of the 4.4 million students and specialized pupils associated with production in both social groups is based on the author's estimates.

193. See the chapter by O. Anweiler in this volume.

194. See the illustrations in *Itogi vsesoiuznoi perepisi naseleniia 1959 goda*, p. 10. Members of the armed forces together with students and specialized pupils are not included in the figures given above (see Table 10).

195. See S. Schwarz, *Arbeiterklasse und Arbeitspolitik in der Sowjetunion* (Hamburg, 1953), along with his "Entwicklung der Arbeiterschaft," *Ost-Probleme* 15 (1963), p. 776; M. Ia. Sonin, *Vosproizvodstvo rabochei sily v SSSR i balans truda* [The Reproduction of the work force in the USSR and the labor balance-sheet] (Moscow, 1959); S. Strumilin, ed., *Izmeneniia v chislennosti i sostave Sovetskogo rabochego klassa* [Alterations in the number and composition of the Soviet working class] (Moscow, 1961); R. P. Dadykin, ed., *Formirovanie i razvitie Sovetskogo rabochego klassa 1917–1961* [The formation and development of the Soviet working class, 1917–

1961] (Moscow, 1964). Regarding developments in various regions of the Soviet republics see Z. A. Astanovich and K. V. Gusev, *Razvitie rabochego klassa v national'nykh respublikakh SSSR* [The evolution of the working class in the national republics of the USSR] (Moscow, 1962).

196. See M. Hindus, *Haus ohne Dach: Russland nach viereinhalb Jahrzehnten Revolution* (Wiesbaden, 1962), p. 200 ff.

197. See S. Jenkner, *Arbeitsteilung, allseitige Entwicklung des Menschen und polytechnische Bildung* (Dissertation, Göttingen, 1965), p. 134.

198. See H. C. Berlinius, *Die Sowjets—wie sie denken, fühlen, handeln* (Stuttgart, 1963), p. 41.

199. Hindus, *op. cit.*, p. 203; on the current situation of the Soviet working class see P. Barton, "The Current Status of the Soviet Worker," *Problems of Communism* 9, no. 4 (1960), p. 18, and the accompanying discussion in which E. C. Brown, M. Dewar, and S. M. Schwarz took part, *Problems of Communism* 9, no. 6 (1960), p. 38 ff.; see also J. B. Sorenson, "Soviet Workers: The Current Scene—Problems and Prospects," *Problems of Communism* 13 (1964), p. 25.

200. See A. Boiter, "When the Kettle Boils Over," *Problems of Communism* 13 (1964), p. 33 ff.

201. For a detailed presentation of this research and a critical evaluation of the methods used, see G. Wagenlehner, "Die empirische Sozialforschung in der Sowjetunion," *Moderne Welt* 6 (1965). Especially interesting is the research carried out in the Leningrad and Sverdlovsk plants. See V. A. Zdravomyslov, "Otnoshenie k trudu i tsennostnye orientatsii lichnosti" [Attitude toward work and value orientation of personality], *Sotsiologiia v SSSR*, vol. II, pp. 189–208; G. I. Popov, "Konkretnye sotsial'nye issledovaniia v praktike ideologicheskoi raboty" [Concrete social inquiries in the exercise of ideological labor], *Sotsiologiia v SSSR*, vol. I, pp. 74–84; *Erfahrungen und Methoden der konkret-soziologischen Forschung* (Moscow, 1965), pp. 144–196; N. V. Golubeeva and E. S. Kuz'min, "Opyt izucheniia proizvodstvennykh kollektivov" [An exploratory study of production collectives], *Sotsiologiia v SSSR*, vol. II, pp. 388–408; and L. I. Kogan, "Problema likvidatsii professional'noi ogranichennosti rabochego" [Overcoming the occupational narrowness of workers], *Sotsiologiia v SSSR*, vol. II, pp. 57–75. On the relationship between formal organization and informal order in plants see N. G. Valentinova, "Vliianie vzaimootnoshenii v proizvodstvennom kollektive na povyshenie indeksa k trudu" [The influence of interpersonal relations on interest in work], *Sotsiologiia v SSSR*, vol II, pp. 442–457. On the matter of the workers' cultural-technical competence and their use of leisure time see S. T. Gurianov, "Dukhovnye interesy sovetskogo rabochego" [The intellectual interests of the soviet worker], *Sotsiologiia v SSSR*, vol. II, pp. 153–188; M. T. Iovchuk, "Sotsial'noe znachenie pod'ema kulturno-tekhnicheskogo urovnia rabochikh" [The social significance of the rise of the cultural and technical standards of workers], *Sotsiologiia v SSSR*,

vol. II, pp. 28–56; B. T. Kolpakov and G. A. Prudenskii, "Opyt izucheniia v nerabochego vremeni trudiashchikhsia" [An exploratory study of the workers' use of leisure], *Sotsiologiia v SSSR*, vol. II., pp. 209–224; and G. V. Osipov and S. F. Frolov, "Vnerabochee vremia i ego ispol'zovanie" [Leisure and its uses], *Sotsiologiia v SSSR*, vol. II, pp. 225–242.

202. See Zdravomyslov and Iadov in *Sotsiologiia v SSSR*, vol. II, *op. cit.*, p. 196 ff.; *Erfahrungen und Methoden der konkret-soziologischen Forschung*, p. 144 ff.; Wagenlehner, *op. cit.*, p. 416. The analysis is based on a representative cross section with respect to the age, sex, education, income, and party membership of 2,665 workers up to the age of 30 from 25 plants in Leningrad. Less reliable are two surveys by Golubeeva and Kuz'min (*Sotsiologiia v SSSR*, vol. II, p. 392) which in 1965 were also carried out in several Leningrad plants of various sizes; here the work brigades researched were divided into three categories. But the replies of 13 percent in the highest category were irrelevant or indifferent; the same was true of 50 percent in the intermediate category and 86 percent in the lowest category. The corresponding percentages of the second survey were 26, 30, and 38 percent respectively.

203. See M. Popov, *Sotsiologiia v SSSR*, vol. I, p. 75; *Erfahrungen und Methoden der konkret-soziologischen Forschung*, p. 177 and 202 ff. In January of 1963 a total of 10,792 workers from 25 large industries were asked why they would like to change jobs. Golubeeva and Kuz'min reported, on the basis of the surveys mentioned in the previous note, that 8 percent in the higher category, 48 percent in the middle group, and 81 percent in the lower group expressed a desire to change their place of work. In the area of Sverdlovsk (with some 4 million inhabitants) some 350,000 workers changed their jobs yearly. See Kogan in *Sotsiologiia v SSSR*, vol. II, p. 66 ff.; Wagenlehner, *op. cit.*, p. 416.

204. See B. Meissner, *Russland unter Chruschtschow*, p. 226 ff.; Jenkner, *op. cit.*, p. 172 ff. The sociological aspect of Khrushchev's educational policy is not given its full significance by Jenkner. From the new Soviet writing dealing with the sociological significance of the better technical training and qualification of workers see M. Ia. Sonin, *Vosproizvodstvo rabochei sily v SSSR i balans truda* [The reproduction of the work force in the USSR and the labor balance-sheet] (Moscow, 1959), p. 265 ff.; S. L. Seniavskii, "Podgotovka i povyshenie kvalifikatsii industrial'nykh rabochikh kadrov SSSR v 1953–1961" [The education and raising of qualifications of USSR industrial workers in 1953–1961] in R. P. Dadykin, *Formirovanie i razvitie Sovetskogo rabochego klassa 1917–1961*, p. 187 ff.; G. L. Smirnov, "Dinamika rosta rabochego klassa i izmenenie ego professional'no-kvalifikatsionnogo sostava" [The dynamic of growth of the working class and structural changes in its professional qualifications] in *Sotsiologiia v SSSR*, vol. I, p. 344 ff.; A. P. Osipov, "Tekhnicheskii progress i izmeneniia professional'noi struktury rabochego klassa" [Technical advances and changes in the professional structure of the working class] in *Sotsiologiia v SSSR*, vol. II, p. 10 ff.

205. See *Sel'skoe khoziaistvo SSSR: statisticheskii sbornik* (Moscow, 1960), p. 459.

206. *Ibid.*, p. 450. The number is derived from the amount of work performed by the 13 million family members of kolkhoz peasants, workers, and white-collar employees who are engaged in private enterprise activities. Of these family members 9.9 million are kolkhoz peasants while 3.7 million are workers and white-collar employees.

207. Figures are from Hindus, *op. cit.*, p. 214.

208. See O. Schiller, "Die sowjetische Landwirtschaft nach Chruschtschow," *Osteuropa* 15 (1965), p. 379; Berlinius, *op. cit.*, p. 49.

209. To the 33 million kolkhoz peasants (including 9.9 million family members engaged in their own agricultural pursuits) we would add 4.7 million agrarian workers from the sovkhozes and RTS as well as some 3.3 million (from a total of 3.7 million) family members of workers and employees engaged in private agricultural activity.

210. *Narodnoe khoziaistvo SSSR v 1963 godu*, p. 226.

211. Figures are from *Narodnoe khoziaistvo SSSR v 1962 godu*, p. 238. The 1963 figure is not contained in the statistical compilation for 1963.

212. Figures from *Narodnoe khoziaistvo SSSR v 1963 godu*, p. 230.

213. See Schiller, "Die sowjetische Landwirtschaft nach Chruschtschow," p. 383.

214. See Hindus, *op. cit.*, p. 244; Schiller, "Die sowjetische Landwirtschaft nach Chruschtschow," p. 381, and R. A. Bauer, A. Inkeles, and C. Kluckhohn, *How the Soviet System Works* (Cambridge, Mass., 1957).

215. See Berlinius, *op. cit.*, p. 51. For an account of the activities of those who wanted to transform the kolkhozes into genuine cooperatives and of those who were against party regimentation see B. Lewytzkij, "Warten auf einen neuen Lenin," supplement to the weekly newspaper *Das Parlament*, 3 November 1965. The faults of the current kolkhoz system are uncovered in the novel by F. Abramov, *Ein Tag im "Neuen Leben"* (Munich-Zürich, 1963).

216. Figures are from *Itogi vsesoiuznoi perepisi naseleniia 1959 goda*, p. 164 ff.

217. See Hindus, *op. cit.*, pp. 211 and 228.

218. See F. I. Kurilov, *Zakonodatel'stvo o pravakh i obiazannostiakh kolkhoznikov* [Legislation on the rights and duties of kolkhoz peasants] (Moscow, 1956), p. 61ff. The view of K. E. Wädekin ("Zur Sozialschichtung der Sowjetgesellschaft," *Osteuropa* 15 [1965], p. 322), and Mihajlov (*op. cit.*, p. 96) that kolkhoz farmers could change either their place of work or place of residence is not true. That depended wholly on whether the individual, through sheer skillfulness, succeeded in finding a place of work. It was difficult for the kolkhoz peasant to move to a new job because he usually lacked a passport. The contrary assumption of Mihajlov is an error. Recently there has been an increase in the number of people who have supported the right of the kolkhoz peasant to have an individual passport to leave the collective

farm. See Arkhipov in *Pravda*, 21 July 1965, and Chubukov in *Ekonomicheskaia Gazeta*, 4 August 1965, p. 30.

219. See *Itogi vsesoiuznoi perepisi naseleniia 1959 goda*, p. 10 and Wädekin, *op. cit.*, p. 321.

220. See the articles concerning the theme "Welche Veränderungen gehen in der Arbeiterklasse von sich?" in *Probleme des Friedens und des Sozialismus* 1960, no. 5, p. 43 ff.; no. 9, p. 70 ff.; no. 12, p. 65 ff.; 1961, no. 4, p. 439 ff.; no. 5, p. 451 ff.; no. 6, p. 543 ff.; no. 9, p. 818 ff. For a report on this exchange of opinion see the detailed report that R. Ahlberg gave at the second German Conference on Eastern Sociology in Berlin (30 September to 2 October 1965). See "Die Sowjetische Angestelltendiskussion," *Osteuropa* 15 (1965), p. 771 ff.

221. See also A. A. Arzumanian, ed., *Gorodskie srednie sloi sovremennogo kapitalisticheskogo obshchestva* [The urban middle strata in modern capitalistic society] (Moscow, 1963). On the evolution of the middle class in the Western sense see R. König, *Soziologie Heute* (Zürich, 1949), p. 53 ff.

222. *Probleme des Friedens und des Sozialismus*, 1961, no. 5, p. 456.

223. See A. L. Lutchenko, *Sovetskaia intelligentsiia* (Moscow, 1962); G. E. Glezerman, ed., *Izmenenie klassovoi struktury obshchestva v protsesse stroitel' stva sotsializma i kommunizma* [The change in the class structure of society during the construction of socialism and communism] (Moscow, 1961), p. 299 ff.; M. I. Rutkevich "Stiranie klassovykh razlichii i mesto intelligentsii v sotsial'noi strukture sovetskogo obshchestva" [The elimination of class distinctions and the status of the intelligentsia in the social structure of the soviet society] *Filosofskie nauki* [Philosophical sciences], 1963, no. 5, p. 22 ff., and "Izmenenie sotsial'noi struktury sovetskogo obshchestva i intelligentsiia" [The transformation of the social structure of Soviet society and the intelligentsia], *Sotsiologiia v SSSR*, vol. I, p. 393 ff.; V. S. Semenov, "Ob izmenenii intelligentsii i sluzhashchikh v protsesse razvernutogo stroitel'stva kommunizma" [Transformation of the intelligentsia and white-collar employees during the expansion of communism] *Sotsiologiia v SSSR*, vol. I, p. 416 ff.

224. See G. M. Andreeva, *Kritika sovremennykh burzhuaznykh revizionistskikh teorii klassov* [Critique of modern bourgeois revisionist class theories] (Moscow, 1959), p. 5.

225. See Glezerman, *op. cit.*, p. 299; Rutkevich, *Sotsiologiia v SSSR*, vol. I, p. 314. This characterization was adopted also by Hofmann, *op. cit.*, p. 495.

226. *Sotsiologiia v SSSR*, vol. I, p. 394; *Filosofskie nauki*, 1963, no. 5, p. 23.

227. *Sotsiologiia v SSSR*, vol. I, p. 416.

228. *Sotsiologiia v SSSR*, vol. I, p. 419.

229. Semenov emphatically asserts that this designation is not limited to the service area.

230. *Sotsiologiia v SSSR*, vol. I, p. 420.

231. *Sotsiologiia v SSSR*, vol. I, p. 418.

232. See L. Labedz, "The Structure of the Soviet Intelligentsia" in R. Pipes, *op. cit.*, p. 63 ff. Regarding the Soviet intelligentsia see also Bauer-Inkeles-Kluckhohn, *op. cit.*, p. 174 ff.

233. *Sotsiologiia v SSSR*, vol. I, p. 418. According to official statistics working white-collar employees not considered to be part of the intelligentsia amounted to only 4.8 million in 1959.

234. The division of the above-mentioned figure of 2.8 million into white-collar employees and workers is based on the data concerning the share of brain and manual workers with higher training contained in the tables. Of 1.7 million white-collar employees, 1 million were estimated to be in military service (0.4 million in military intelligence, 0.6 million in obligatory service) and 0.7 million active as nonspecialists. Of 1.1 million workers, 0.4 million were in the military service (including those doing obligatory service) while 0.7 worked in civilian areas.

235. Out of a total of 3.8 million university graduates in 1959, some 0.2 million might possibly have been nonemployed family members of white-collar employees.

236. The figures which appear in parentheses are based on the table and calculation of Semenov. Those with some university training are estimated to comprise about 15 percent of political and economic leaders; this is derived from Soviet statements that 11.1 percent of the delegates to the Twenty-second Party Congress of the CPSU had university degrees. Among factory directors and chief engineers (1 million) this percentage could at least be doubled. For 1959 the average percentage was 20 percent (1956: 15 percent). For the educational status of party members see Meissner, *Russland unter Chruschtschow*, p. 193. On 1 January 1965, 1.8 million party members (15 percent) had a completed university education, while 5.6 million (47.7 percent) had a completed school education. In 1964, 5.1 million party members (46.2 percent) were white-collar employees, 4.1 million (37.3 percent) were workers, and 1.8 million (16.5 percent) were kolkhoz peasants. These data are from *Zapisnaia knizhka 1966*, pp. 40–44.

237. Hindus, *op. cit.*, p. 367. See also D. Joravsky, "Soviet Scientists and the Great Break" in Pipes, *op. cit.*, p. 12 ff.; J. A. Armstrong, "Der Sowjetgelehrte," *Sowjet-Studien*, 1958, no. 6, p. 56 ff.

238. On the idea of the cadre see J. Schultz, *Der Funktionär in der Einheitspartei* (Stuttgart-Düsseldorf, 1956), p. 4 ff.

239. On bureaucracy see F. Morstein-Marx, *Einführung in die Bürokratie* (Neuwied, 1959), p. 33. It may not be justified, despite the intelligentsia's total dependence on the state, to describe, as W. W. Kulski does in "Class-Stratification in the Soviet Union," *Foreign Affairs*, 1953, no. 1, p. 145, every educated person in Russia as a "bureaucrat." Also, G. Barrington Moore's view that white-collar employees and the intelligentsia are to be identified with the bureaucracy is wide of the mark. See *Soviet Politics—The Dilemma of Power* (Cambridge, Mass.), p. 280 ff.

240. Regarding the notion of an officeholder or an official person (*dolzh-nostnoe litso*) see S. S. Studenikin, V. A. Vlasov, and I. I. Evtichiev, eds., *Sovetskoe administrativnoe pravo* [Soviet administrative law] (Moscow, 1950), p. 126 ff.; Iu. M. Kozlov, ed., *Sovetskoe administrativnoe pravo* [Soviet administrative law] (Moscow, 1962), p. 141. The fixed character of the office and the continuous execution of official duties is the factor that distinguishes state service from the occasional exercise of official responsibilities. The officeholder assumes civil service status as soon as he is appointed. Among those in state service one can distinguish between representatives of state power (*predstaviteli vlasti*) and those who perform customary functions (*funktsional'nye rabotniki*). These differences are not satisfactorily dealt with by Hofmann, *op. cit.*, p. 494 ff.

241. See B. Lewytzkij, "Die Nomenklatur: Ein Wichtiges Instrument sowjetischer Kaderpolitik," *Osteuropa* 11 (1961), p. 409 ff.; Schultz, *op. cit.*, p. 226 ff. We have to distinguish between the basic nomenclature and the registration nomenclature. The basic nomenclature is a list of official positions exclusively under the control of the party. The registration nomenclature embraces ruling positions and leadership personnel that fall outside this basic nomenclature. Khrushchev's successors have not made any changes in the "nomenclature system." See Lewytzkij, "Warten auf einen neuen Lenin," p. 13 ff.

242. On the organization of the Department for Party Organs of the Central Committee of the CPSU see Meissner, *Russland unter Chruschtschow*, p. 189.

243. For an account of the main types of bureaucracy see Morstein-Marx, *op. cit.*, p. 70 ff.

244. For a discussion of social role and the difference between inter-role conflict and intra-role conflict see R. Dahrendorf, *Homo Sociologicus*, 4th ed. (Cologne-Opladen, 1964).

245. See F. Croner's *Die Angestellten in der modernen Gesellschaft* (Frankfurt a. M.-Vienna, 1954), p. 31 ff., and *Soziologie der Angestellten* (Cologne-Berlin, 1962), p. 112 ff. See, in addition, H. Hofbauer, *Zur sozialen Gliederung der Arbeitnehmerschaft* (Cologne-Opladen, 1965), p. 111 ff.

246. For a critique of Croner's theory of delegation see G. Hartfiel, *Angestellte und Angestelltengewerkschaften in Deutschland* (Berlin, 1961), p. 87 ff., and Hofbauer, *op. cit.*, p. 100 ff.

247. Thus Stammer holds that the line which separates workers from white-collar employees has little to do with whether the work is intellectual or not. See O. Stammer, ed., *Angestellte und Arbeiter in der Betriebspyramide* (Berlin, 1959), p. 42; Hofbauer, *op. cit.*, p. 111 ff. With regard to the reclassification of workers on the basis of the function they perform in various areas of industry see Hartfiel, *op. cit.*, p. 111 ff.

248. See Hofbauer, *op. cit.*, p. 154 ff.

249. This is overlooked by Hofmann, *op. cit.*, p. 192, who mistakenly concludes that Soviet society is to be regarded only as an achievement-oriented society since it would exhibit a "far-reaching rank ordering of the functions of work." There are currently Soviet ideologues who, contrary to Khrushchev, emphasize the primacy of the political over the economic, who are against basing the social leadership function of the party on concrete economic leadership and, by so doing, getting involved with the labor leadership function, which is within the sphere of economic managers. Lewytzkij, "Die Nomenklatur," p. 7 ff., overlooks the fact that this is the main reason which prompts them to refer to the social leadership function as "policy-making" (*napravliat'*) and not as "administration" (*upravliat'*).

250. See D. Granick, *The Red Executive* (New York, 1960).

251. Bialer, *op. cit.*, p. 49, also estimates that the number of principal official party functionaries—those who hold ruling positions—is around 200,000. Bauer-Inkeles-Kluckhohn, *op. cit.*, p. 158, estimate that 1.5 million persons belong to the "ruling elite," which may be exaggerated.

252. The figure of 2.1 million indicated in the table comprises only the top bureaucracy and economic managers. Together with 250,000 other official officeholders the number, as Semenov indicates, comes to 2.4 million, *op. cit.*, p. 418. In this figure he includes, in addition to top bureaucrats, 1 million directors and leading personnel involved in production and 1 million official "state employees," but not 800,000 directors of trade and supply organizations who doubtless belong to these top groups. If they are included the total number of "leading cadres" would amount to almost 3.2 million.

253. One is hardly entitled to describe the entire "intelligentsia" (15.6 million) or just the "specialists" (8 million) as upper-stratum. Mehnert's assumption (*Der Sowjetmensch*, p. 47) that the Soviet upper stratum (including family members) totaled around 25–30 million in 1958 does not stand up. The number calculated by Wädekin (*op. cit.*, pp. 326, 329), around 5.8 million (less 1.9 million family members), is closer to the mark. According to the author's calculations the upper stratum in 1959 contained 7.9 million including family members.

254. Of the 2.4 million "leading cadres" as many as 0.7 million (30 percent) might not have completed their university or advanced technical-school training. The "leading cadres," less the top bureaucracy and university graduates (1.7 million) but including the remaining specialists with advanced technical-school training (4.1 million) and half of the remaining functionaries with higher education (0.7 million), amounted to nearly 6.5 million persons.

255. Official figures indicate that the number of office clerks and petty "white-collar employees" comes to only 4.2 million, since Semenov obviously has counted them as a segment of the working class which exercises white-collar functions. The later account of the social classification of the employed population (Table 24) is based on official figures.

256. Berlinius, op. cit., p. 43.

257. See Glezerman, op. cit., p. 150 ff.; see also his "Moral'no-politiches-koe edinstvo sotsialisticheskogo obshchestva i stiranie grany mezhdu klass-ami" ["The Moral and political unity of socialist society and the inter-mingling of the classes"], Kommunist, 1956, no. 15; Ost-Probleme 9 (1957), p. 158 ff.

258. F. C. Schroeder, "Inhalt and Entwicklung von Staat und Recht nach dem neuen Parteiprogramm der Kommunistischen Partei der Sowjet-union," Part I, Jahrbuch für Ostrecht, III/1 (1962), p. 68.

259. See Glezerman, Ost-Probleme 9 (1957), p. 162 ff.; C. A. Stepanjan, "Die Widersprüche in der Entwicklung der sozialistischen Gesellschaft und die Wege zu ihrer Überwindung," Die Presse der Sowjetunion, 31 July 1955, no. 88.

260. P. Ch. Ludz, "Konflikttheoretische Ansätze im historischen Mate-rialismus," Kölner Zeitschrift für Soziologie und Socialpsychologie 13 (1961), p. 673 ff.; see also his "Widerspruchsprinzip und Soziologie" in Boettcher-Lieber-Meissner, op. cit., p. 307 ff. The Polish sociologist Stanis-law Ostowski, in his Klassenstrucktur im Sozialen Bewusstsien (Neuwied, 1962), p. 140, correctly points to the fact that for Marx and Lenin "non-antagonistic classes" are a contradicto in adiecto.

261. See Meissner, Das Parteiprogramm der KPdSR, p. 102 ff.

262. For a discussion of criteria for determining social stratification and the problems of empirically defining a social stratum see Th. Geiger, "Schichtung," in W. Bernsdorf and F. Bülow, eds., Wörterbuch der Soz-iologie (Stuttgart, 1955), p. 432 ff. See also K. V. Müller, Begabung und soziale Schichtung in der hochindustrialisierten Gesellschaft (Cologne-Opladen, 1956); see also R. Mayntz's Soziale Schichtung und sozialer Wandel in einer Industriegemeinde (Stuttgart, 1958); "Gedanken und Ergebnisse zur empirischen Feststellung sozialer Schichten" in R. König, ed., Soziologie der Gemeinde, 2nd ed., (Cologne-Opladen, 1962), and "Kritische Bermerkungen zur funcktionalistischen Schichtungestheorie," in D. V. Glass and R. König, eds., Soziale Schichtung und soziale Mobilität (Cologne-Opladen, 1961), p. 10 ff.; K. M. Bolte, Sozialer Aufstieg und Abstieg: Eine Untersuchung über Berufsprestige und Berufsmobilität (Stutt-gart, 1959); H. Kluth, Sozialprestige und sozialer Status (Stuttgart, 1957); E. Scheuch and H. Daheim, "Sozialprestige und soziale Schichtung," in D. V. Glass and R. König, Soziale Schichtung und soziale Mobilität, p. 65; Hofbauer, op. cit., p. ff.

263. The criticism that is directed at the theory of conflict developed by Ralf Dahrendorf is based in the final analysis on his equating institutional-ized power with social leadership. A look into the field of international rela-tions shows clearly that hegemony and imperium, i.e., absolute rulership, are not the same. See H. Triepel, Die Hegemonie: Ein Buch von führenden Staaten (new printing, Aalen, 1961). The same is true in another sense of social organizations and affairs within nations. It is hardly justified, there-

fore, to follow Dahrendorf and regard institutions that are not basically political in character—e.g., industrial plants—exclusively as power institutions. See Darhendorf's *Soziale Klassen und Klassenkonflikt in der industriellen Gesellschaft* (Stuttgart, 1957), p. 215 ff., and "Der soziale Konflikt," *Die Zeit*, 29 October 1965, no. 44, pp. 43–45. Hofmann's effort (*op. cit.*, pp. 226 ff. and 477 ff.) to eliminate institutionalized power in his consideration of Soviet society and simply to proceed on the basis of a society ordered by noninstitutionalized power, understanding it as social, is also an error. The one-party dictatorship means institutionalized power in every case. For this reason Hofmann has been unable to grasp the significance of the ruling structure for the class character of Soviet society.

264. The qualitative difference between state and society and, thus, between social and legal norms is not very satisfactorily treated by sociologists. The state is not only the most comprehensive social structure in given areas of activity. It is at the same time the only large social organization which is equipped with sovereignty, i.e., basic ruling power and the ability to enforce its decisions, and is hence justified in representing the people, society as a whole, in the performance of its varied public functions. The party or some other interest group with a pronounced power structure is capable of establishing itself as the most important holder of state sovereignty. However, it can never replace the whole. See H. Krüger, *Allgemeine Staatslehre* (Stuttgart, 1964), p. 185 ff.; U. Scheuner, "Das Wesen des Staates und der Begriff des Politischen in der neueren Staatslehre" in *Staatsverfassung und Kirchenordnung: Festgabe für Rudolf Smend* (Tübingen, 1962), p. 22 ff. The suggestion of H. Ehmke ("Tribute to Smend," *op. cit.*, p. 46) to think in terms of "political community" and "government" instead of "state" and "society" obscures the more correct view that the state is not only a power organization but also a community based on the solidarity of men. R. W. Füsslein pointed this out in his book *Die unwandelbaren Fundamente des Staates: Grundzüge einer wertgesetzlichen Staatslehre* (Hamburg, 1947).

265. See Krüger, *op. cit.*, pp. 365 ff. and 840 ff. It is interesting that Mihajlov (*op. cit.*, p. 58) speaks of a similar difference for the Soviet Union as he distinguished between a "commanding" and a "leading" role.

266. Dahrendorf, who does not differentiate social leadership from institutionalized power, describes all ruling positions as positions of "authority." In order to avoid confusion here a distinction is made, analytically, between positions of social leadership and institutionalized power and not between positions of authority and command.

267. See H. P. Dreitzel, *Elitebegriff und Sozialstruktur* (Stuttgart, 1962), p. 75 ff.

268. *Ibid.*, p. 92 ff.

269. *Ibid.*, p. 153.

270. *Ibid.*, p. 100 ff.

271. When Hofmann (*op. cit.*, p. 499) speaks of Soviet functionaries as a "service elite" whose individual advancement is regulated by the efficiency

principle, he overlooks completely the central role which the singular ability to get ahead and party patronage play in the Soviet system. Nor does
this distinction appear in Boettcher's work (*op. cit.*, p. 108 ff). On the
other hand Djilas (*op. cit.*, p. 92) is fully cognizant of the significance of
ability-to-get-ahead as a basic condition of membership in the "ruling class."

272. Thus social stratification, together with the inequality expressed by
it, cannot alone be traced back to the power structure, as R. Dahrendorf has
done in his inaugural lecture at Tübingen. See R. Dahrendorf, *Über den
Ursprung der Ungleichheit unter den Menschen* (Tübingen, 1961), p. 28
ff. Whereas he originally started by equating the theory of institutionalized
power and the theory of integration, he finally reached the conclusion that
stratification would proceed from power, integration from constraint, and
stability from change. Dahrendorf's theses have been sharply criticized by
Schelsky in his "Die Bedeutung des Klassenbegriffs für die Analyse unserer
Gesellschaft," *Jahrbuch für Sozialwissenschaft*, vol. 12 (1961), p. 237 ff.
Schelsky rejects the one-sided emphasis of the theory of institutionalized
power just as much as the complete separation of that theory and the theory
of integration. Admittedly, he does not set out to distinguish between social
leadership and institutionalized power, but rightly points out that a one-
sided interpretation of power as conflict and tension does not work, since a
power relationship also involves identification and cooperation between the
rulers and the ruled. His idea, however, that rulership should be understood
not only as power but also as justice hardly applies to totalitarian rule.

273. See also the informative report by Mihajlov, *Moskauer Sommer
1964* (Bern, 1965).

274. From a comparative study of professional prestige in individual
countries undertaken by American sociologists in 1956 it was reported that
doctors, scientists, and engineers were at the top of the ladder in the Soviet
Union. Following these were industrial managers and accountants, officers
and teachers. A skilled worker was rated higher than the chairman of a kolkhoz. The ordinary kolkhoz peasant was at the bottom of the scale. See A.
Inkeles and P. H. Rossi, "National Comparisons of Occupational Prestige,"
The American Journal of Sociology 61, no. 4 (1956), p. 336 ff.

275. See also V. B. Ol'shanskii "Lichnost' i sotsial'nye tsennosti" [Per-
sonality and social value], *Sotsiologiia v SSSR*, vol. I, pp. 491–530; Wagenlehner, "Die empirische Sozialforschung," p. 410 ff.

276. Opera and theater in the Soviet Union are very instrumental in pre-
serving this continuity.

277. Forty-seven percent of those questioned, who averaged 27 years of
age, said that their children were baptized; 18 percent side-stepped this question, which probably means that their children were also baptized. Only 35
percent indicated that their children were not baptized. Regarding the relation between church and state, the success of Christian sects, particularly
the Baptists, and the sharpening conflict between the atheistic regime and
religious communities see W. Kolarz, *Die Religion in der Sowjet-Union*

(Freiburg, 1963); Hindus, *op. cit.*, p. 108 ff. and 126 ff.; Mihajlov, *op. cit.*, p. 99 ff.; R. Dupine, "Die Sowjetunion in christlicher Sicht," *Die Orientierung*, October 1965, p. 26 ff.; "Methoden des Kirchenkampfes in der Sowjetunion," *Neue Zürcher Zeitung*, 13 November 1965.

278. The question was what the individual person would like to have if he had the money to buy it; 24.5 percent mentioned a better apartment or home furnishings, 12.3 percent mentioned cultural objects (books, musical instruments, etc.), 11.3 percent clothing and food, 10.5 percent motorized travel (9 percent of whom wanted their own auto); 17 percent expressed no desires. Nine percent declared that they had no excess wealth and never would have it.

279. A Leningrad survey taken in 1963, in connection with which 2,700 workers were questioned, shows 77 percent of the respondents declaring that they would regard the material advantages of work as the main thing. Only 23 percent would want to stay with a job that they would receive from the party. See H. Wagenlehner, "Die Entwicklung des Kommunismus in der Sowjetunion," supplement to weekly newspaper *Das Parlament*, 8 September 1965, p. 19.

280. Numerous examples can be found in Achminov's book.

281. See K. Olgin, "Zwischen Soziologie und Sowjetologie," *Sowjetstudien* June 1965, no. 18, p. 60 ff.

282. See "40 Millionen Minimalverdiener," *Ost-Probleme* 12 (1960), p. 367 ff. The analysis is based on the standard prior to the currency reform of 1 January 1961 that foresaw the exchange of the old money in a relation of 10 to 1. In order to make a comparison with the present, the salary amount has been converted into new rubles.

283. According to official statistics based on the income of all salaried and paid men, only a monthly average income of 95 rubles was reached in 1965 (according to the Soviet rate of exchange, $105). If one considers the social services of the state and all other incomes we have an average monthly gross income of 128 rubles ($142.25). See *Kölner Stadt-Anzeiger*, 3 February 1966, p. 8.

284. Figures are from *Vestnik Statistiki* [Statistical reports], 1961, no. 7, p. 94. Also *Deutsches Industrie-institut, Taschenbuch für die Wirtschaft* (Cologne, 1961), p. 565.

285. See Djilas, *op. cit.*, pp. 57, 64, 69, and 86. That only a part of the withheld social product is used for the personal benefits of rulers is not important in this connection. It is important to note that members of the power elite have incomes measurably higher than the general public, comparable to the situation in other industrial societies.

286. The exact level of the income of top functionaries is kept secret in the Soviet Union. In 1960 an academy member received a salary (in new rubles) of 800–1,500 rubles, an opera star about 500–2,000 rubles. See E. Nash, "Purchasing Power of Workers in the U.S.S.R", *Monthly Labor Review* (1960), no. 4; *Ost-Probleme* 12 (1960), p. 372.

287. According to Nash, *op. cit.*, p. 372, the average monthly earnings of a factory manager in 1960 was 300–1,000 rubles (new rubles), a full professor 600–1,000 rubles, a minister or head of a division in a ministry 700 rubles (less ministerial allowances, etc.), a lecturer 300–500 rubles, an engineer 100–300 rubles.

288. The average monthly salary in 1960 of a technician was 80–200 rubles, a qualified specialist worker 100–250 rubles, a physician 95–180 rubles, and a secondary school teacher 85–150 rubles. At the end of the middle-income scale come the ordinary skilled worker and the elementary schoolteacher with 60–90 rubles.

289. The average monthly salary of an unskilled laborer in 1960 amounted to 27–50 rubles, the kolkhoz peasant around 10 rubles.

290. Higher incomes are derived from greater turnover on the collective farm markets and from a sharp increase in the official buying price for agricultural products. More recently, from 1952 to 1964, the average price has gone up fifteen- and twenty-fold; potatoes have increased in price forty-fold. See Wagenlehner, "Die Entwicklung des Kommunismus in der Sowjetunion," p. 19.

291. See G. Specovius, *Die Russen sind anders* (Düsseldorf-Vienna, 1963).

292. A breakup of the upper stratum would, theoretically, be entirely defensible. With an upper-upper stratum of some 0.8 million, the top bureaucracy—with 0.4 million—would be about equal to the number of intellectuals in top positions requiring an academic background, while some 3 million persons would make up the lower-upper stratum. With the increasing number of university graduates an academic background might possibly lose the importance it has had up to now in dividing the upper stratum from the upper-middle stratum. In 1959 the number of university graduates who because of their professional function belonged to the upper-middle stratum corresponded almost to those outsiders without academic training, e.g. the writers, who constitute a part of the upper stratum.

293. Rutkevich, *Sotsiologiia v SSSR*, vol. I, p. 774.

294. See, for example, the play *Gosti* [The guests], by Leonid Sorin, which appeared in the winter of 1953–54 and was reprinted in *Osteuropa* 6 (1954), p. 4; see also the well-known books of Vladimir Dudintsev, *Not by Bread Alone* (New York, 1957); Valeriy Tarsis, *Bluebottle* (New York, 1963); Alexander Solzhenitzyn, *One Day in the Life of Ivan Denisovich* (New York, 1963). See also Mihajlov, *op. cit.*, p. 102.

295. Up to now the difficulties of constructing such a totalitarian model have stemmed from the lack of adequate generalization from an underestimation of the importance of mass terror, along with an underestimation of the effects of genuine social conflicts upon the ruling party. See P. Ch. Ludz "Entwurf einen soziologischen Theorie totalitär verfasster Gesellschaft," in Ludz, ed., *Studien und Materialien zur Soziologie der DDR* (Cologne-Opladen, 1964), p. 11. Regarding the question of research on totalitarianism see, in addition, the special edition of *Soziale Welt* 12, no. 2 (1961), which

includes contributions from O. Stammler, G. Schulz, and P. Ch. Ludz. Regarding the idea and nature of totalitarian rule see also O. Stammler "Politische Soziologie" in A. Gehlen and H. Schelsky, eds., *Soziologie*, 3rd ed. (Düsseldorf-Cologne, 1955), p. 290 ff.

296. This is true above all for authors such as Hannah Arendt, Carl C. Friedrich, and Zbigniew K. Brzezinski.

'297. For detailed arguments relative to the three basic elements of totalitarianism of the Soviet communist type see Meissner, "Wandlungen in Herrschaftssytem und Verfassungsrecht der Sowjetunion" in Boettcher-Lieber-Meissner, *op. cit.*, p. 142 ff.; "Party and Government Reforms in Russia since Khrushchev," *Survey*, July 1965, p. 31 ff.

298. In his introduction to E. Richert's book, *Macht ohne Mandat: Der Staatsapparat in der sowjetschen Besatzungszone Deutschlands* (Cologne-Opladen, 1958), Martin Draht described the attempt to establish a wholly new value system for the society as a "primary phenomenon" of totalitarianism, which he differentiates from authoritarianism. Certainly this aim, when linked to a system of total planning, is characteristic of totalitarianism. From a politico-sociological point of view, however, this can hardly be regarded as a "primary phenomenon." This is more in the nature of a transfer of totalitarian principles of organization from the party to the state and thus to the people, which underscores the unlimited character of the party dictatorship. Authoritarianism, on the other hand, is a type of dictatorship that contents itself with the centralization of political power and limited controls over certain sectors of society; planning is limited and independent of the question whether or not a completely new value system is attempted.

299. See Meissner, *Das Parteiprogramm der KPdSU*, p. 106.

300. Ludz, "Entwurf einer soziologischen Theorie," p. 18 ff.

301. See Sering (Löwenthal), *Jenseits des Kapitalismus*, 209 ff. and his "Totalitáre und demokratische Revolution," p. 40.

302. See Ludz, "Entwurf einer soziologischen Theorie, p. 19.

303. Also the further thesis of Ludz, *ibid.*, p. 21, that the Bolshevik system, under conditions of an industrial society, tends more toward an authoritarian than a totalitarian organization, may be overstated in this form. The question of where the Bolshevik system is going is still very much open.

304. In contradistinction to the decisions of parties in democratically organized societies, the decisions of the Bolshevik party are frequently in need of no official transformation but are to be regarded as binding orders.

305. Nikolai Berdyaev already insisted on this point in the 1930s. See *The Origin of Russian Communism* (Ann Arbor, 1960 [first published in 1937]), p. 128. He said: "This new Soviet bureaucracy is more powerful than that of the Tsarist regime. It is a new privileged class which can exploit the masses pitilessly. This is happening." A spirited discussion of the bureaucratic rulership can be found in the satirical drama *Sjena* [Shadows], authored by Evgeny Shvarts in 1940. See also Djilas, *op. cit.*, pp. 57, 64, 69, 86 ff. Hofmann, *op. cit.*, p. 500 ff., does not adequately consider that

under the conditions of an industrial society economic power depends primarily on de facto control of property, not alone on the right to property. Moreover, history has witnessed other power elites whose rule was not based on private ownership of the means of production. See the examples in K. A. Wittfogel, Oriental Despotism, 5th ed. (New Haven: Yale University Press, 1964). Also, Hofmann's objection (op. cit., p. 498) that the Soviet leading hierarchy possesses only delegated power, does not apply to the bureaucratic power elite, since the party apparatus is an essential element of the state apparatus. The holders of state offices and the sections of the party with direct functions in the state are representative of the state and thus are exerting more than control by delegated power. The whole power and organization of all power over government and administration is concentrated in the hands of the oligarchical top group within the ruling power elite.

306. Hofmann writes (op. cit., p. 505): "Every social ruling group in history has sought to provide its members, with the aid of the organization, with a greater measure of advantages than the individual members would have gotten without the organization." This is precisely the situation of the Soviet power elite. It is hard to understand why Hofmann, on the other hand, speaks only of a "service elite."

307. See Djilas, op. cit., pp. 64 and 73. The parasitical character of party functionaries has recently been stressed by some courageous Soviet writers. See Tarsis, op. cit., p. 39 ff.

308. See Dahrendorf, Soziale Klassen und Klassenkonflikt, p. 5 ff. For a critique of Marx's class theory see also Th. Geiger, Die Klassengesellschaft im Schmelztiegel (Cologne-Hagen, 1949).

309. See Dahrendorf, ibid., p. 139.

310. W. I. Lenin, Ausgewählte Werke, vol. II (East-Berlin, 1953), p. 570.

311. See Dahrendorf, Soziale Klassen und Klassenkonflikt, p. 159 ff.

312. See R. Dahrendorf, "Zu einer Theorie des sozialen Konflikts," Hamburger Jahrbuch für Wirtschafts- und Gesellschaftspolitik (Tübingen, 1958), p. 84 ff.

313. The holders of the actual ruling positions in the Soviet Union are named in "Predstavitili Vlasti" [Representatives of the state].

314. Djilas, op. cit., pp. 58, 62, 68, comes to a similar position. For him the "political bureaucracy," i.e., the party bureaucracy and the apparatus dependent on it, constitutes a "new class." He asserts that the establishment of the new ruling class has resulted in the weakening of the party. He writes, (op. cit., p. 65): "The party produces the class, but the result is that the class grows and uses the party as a basis. The class grows stronger, while the party becomes weaker; that is the unavoidable fate of the Communist Party."

315. The bureaucracy in the narrow sense can be regarded as belonging to the ruling class, but not to each and every officeholder, as Dahrendorf obviously assumes ("Zu einer Theorie des sozialen Konflikts," p. 84 ff.).

316. Membership in the party is not entirely decisive here. Of 7.5 million "specialists" in 1958, 2.3 million (30.7 percent) belonged to the party; 5.2 million (69.3 percent) were not members of the party. See Meissner, *Russland unter Chruschtschow*, p. 194.

317. Regarding the similarities between the workers and peasant proletariat see Bauer-Inkeles-Kluckhohn, *op. cit.*, p. 189.

318. See Bauer-Inkeles-Kluckhohn, *op. cit.*, p. 182.

319. Th. Geiger, in his work, *Aufgaben und Stellung der Intelilgenz in der Gesellschaft* (Stuttgart, 1949), has characterized the intelligentsia as the totality of creators and guardians of the essentials of the representative culture in an ideal and material sense, i.e., intellectual culture and civilization. The process of intellectual emancipation in the Soviet Union shows that the Soviet intelligentsia, strictly speaking, will gradually be accorded the status of an elite in the cultural-sociological sense. Besides the unlimited paternalism of the party, to which Mihajlov (*op. cit.*, p. 91 ff.) refers, there is above all the far too narrow professional education which inhibits this development.

320. See Schelsky, *op. cit.*, p. 262. For Dahrendorf the power conflict is the dominant social conflict. It is for him not the only source of social change.

321. Dahrendorf, "Zu einer Theorie des sozialen Konflikts," p. 90 ff.

322. This omission is typical of all representatives of "Machiavellian" power theories (Mosca, Pareto, Michels, etc.) and not only of the sociological interpreters of historical materialism.

323. See Bialer, *op. cit.*, p. 47 ff. This statement is corroborated by the on-going power conflicts in the Kremlin. Consider, for example, the liquidation of Beria, the dismissal of Malenkov, the exchange between Khrushchev and the "anti-party" group, the downfall of Marshall Zhukov, the "palace revolution" against Khrushchev, etc. The author has dealt with all these conflicts within the power elite in his book *Russland unter Chruschtchow*, as well as in several essays and reports in *Osteuropa*.

324. On the development of these power institutions under Lenin and Stalin see B. Meissner, *Russland im Umbruch* (Frankfort a.M., 1961); see also his "Die sowjetischen Gewerkschaften als Instrument des sozialistischen Staates" in *Auslandsforschung*, no. 2 (Darmstadt, 1953), pp. 19–33.

325. Research here would involve an investigation primarily of the Soviet power elite's origin, recruitment, socialization, cohesiveness, and circulation. Party activity would be particularly significant. The same aspects would be studied in an investigation of economic managers and the prestige elite. Research on the German elite was recently carried out by one of Dahrendorf's students. See W. Zapf, *Wandlungen der deutschen Elite: Ein Zirkulationsmodell deutscher Fuhrüngsgruppen 1919–1961* (Munich, 1965). For a treatment of the American elite see F. Hunter, *Top Leadership U.S.A.* (Chapel Hill, 1959) and C. W. Mills, *The Power Elite* (New York, 1956).

326. Tensions exist also between the technico-economic and the scientific-cultural intelligentsia. Mihajlov, *op. cit.*, p. 101 ff., even holds that coming conflicts in the Soviet Union will be directed less against the party bureaucracy, which is being driven back more and more, and much more against the technocracy. These conflicts are most likely to be carried out at the intellectual and not at the material level. Their solution would require a "third revolution" in the form of a "revolution of the spirit," which would lead to a renewal of social life in Russia.

EDUCATIONAL POLICY AND SOCIAL STRUCTURE IN THE SOVIET UNION

The close relationship between educational policy and social change has become manifest in the second half of this century, despite the failure of many tradition-bound countries of Europe until recently to recognize this when planning their own school systems and the future of education. Consider by way of contrast those countries undergoing rapid socioeconomic transformation that have committed themselves to revolutionary social change; here we find that economic, social, and educational policies are not regarded as autonomous fields but as closely related areas of concern.

This is particularly true of the Soviet Union, where the linkage between these policy areas has been recognized for decades. The notion of a "socialist cultural revolution," coined as such by Lenin and adopted by Stalin, embodies revolutionary socioeducational aims; it is also a shorthand way of describing the nature of the main socio-structural change that marks twentieth-century Russian history, namely the transformation of Russia from a basically agrarian to an industrial country.

The following considerations are based on this linkage between economic, social, and educational policy. This does not mean, however, that the three factors were always so closely linked in Russian history or that each factor had an invariable relationship to the other. Our inquiry here is to determine what role educational policy played in the social transformation of Russia since the 1917 Revolution, along with its current role in the evolution of Soviet society. Given the scope of this chapter we will not consider such aspects of Soviet educational policy as curriculum reform and teaching methods, or the intellectual reorientation that has taken place since the revolution and the changes that have been made in the content of Soviet education. We are interested primarily in the following sociological questions that loom in the background of these matters: How have schools contributed to social advances in the Soviet Union? How does the Soviet population break down according to the degree of educational attainment? What plans are being formulated by the communist leadership with respect to the educational level of Soviet society?

For a more precise analysis of the impact of educational policy the following queries should also be probed: Does equality of educational opportunity really exist in the Soviet Union? How do the very considerable differences between urban and rural environments, along with those between provincial cities, central republics, and large cities, affect the education that young people receive in those areas? What is the social background of students attending various types of schools such as boarding schools or schools with extended programs of foreign-language instruction? Into what professions do the graduates of the eleven-year Soviet secondary schools enter? Is there any connection between nationality, educational opportunity, and the subsequent social status of people living in the non-Russian republics of the USSR? From what classes are Soviet teachers recruited for the various levels of education today, in view of the fact that up to the 1930s they were drawn mainly from the peasantry and the petty bourgeoisie?

1. A Sociological Analysis of Soviet Education

An attempt to answer these and similar questions is hampered by an almost total lack of any existing sociology of Soviet education. Such studies did appear in the 1920s, but were not carried out during the Stalin era.[1] It was not until after 1956, with the advent of destalinization, that Soviet scholars sought to substitute "hard sociological research" for the dogmatism that characterized their earlier work; during this time sociological studies of Soviet education began sporadically to appear.[2] They dealt mainly with problems connected with the rise of the cultural-technical level of the working population, the structure of the family, and the uses of leisure—matters that played a considerable role in social planning. Hence we cannot exclude the possibility that the Soviet Union will develop a working sociology of education, marked by methods of empirical research, and will eventually catch up with American and West European scholarship. The extent to which this research withstands critical examination will not in the final analysis depend on whether Soviet social scientists succeed in actually assembling and publishing hard sociological data that satisfy empirical tests of reliability. But party and state leaders do need access to the results of this research because of its utility for economic and social planning. There are severe limitations, however, on the publication of those research findings that do not fit into the developing scheme of Soviet society; these restrictions are imposed for ideological reasons and in the interest of the party.

So long as such publications remain scarce Western scholars engaged in the sociological study of Soviet education can leave no stone unturned in their attempt to uncover other reliable sources of information. Among these, for example, are published Soviet statistical data, the research of scholars laboring in other disciplines, sporadic eyewitness reports of Western observers, and, last but not least, various official statements on educational policy that are susceptible to sociological analysis. Such inquiries

are more valuable than attempts to undertake pedagogical
field research in a system that is still highly unlikely to open its
doors to strangers.[3] Although some of the questions raised above
have already been the subject of study[4] most of them remain
unanswered. Hence the following discussion of the relationship
between educational policy and social change in Soviet Russia
must remain wholly tentative; especially is this true of questions
dealt with here for the first time. Nevertheless, such a study
may not be unwelcome as a stimulus to further inquiry and as
an important aspect of social change in Russia.

2. Soviet Education after 1917: Its Egalitarian-Democratic and Proletarian-Revolutionary Phase

A commonplace of modern Russian social history is that the
population in old Russia was divided between a thin upper-class
layer of highly educated men at the top, very European in their
style of life, and a mass of uneducated and simple people below.
In the field of education this cleavage corresponds to the large
gap—narrowed somewhat only in the last years of the tsarist
regime—that existed between ordinary elementary schools and
the gymnasium. This situation largely prevailed up to the time
of the revolution, since the manner of social living was conditioned by social ranks developed by the state bureaucracy since
Peter I.

Nevertheless, the steady democratization of education that
took place in Europe, including Russia, since the end of the
nineteenth century should not be overlooked. Because of efforts
of the Russian intelligentsia to enlighten the people, to extend
adult education, and to distribute popular literature in the villages, the Russian populace—until then wholly uneducated—
was slowly being emancipated. This democratizing tendency
was expressed also by the growing number of children from the
"lower estates" who were attending the gymnasium, ordinary
secondary schools, universities, and higher technical institutes.[5]

After Russia embarked upon a program of state-supported capitalism in the 1890s powerful forces emerged to demand new forms of vocational training which undermined the old class structure upon which the educational system was built. The comprehensive school reform plan of 1915–16, drafted by the last great Minister of Education, Count P. Ignatiev, was the culmination of this development; the plan provided for a three-level system of general education as well as a system of professional and technical schools, all of which Ignatiev felt was necessary to meet the modern needs of an emerging modern industrial state. While formal education was only one of many factors in old Russia that determined the social rank of the individual—aristocratic birth and ownership of property were much more important—it, along with vocational training, began rapidly to replace traditional status symbols. The evolving Russian middle class created its own schools; there privileges were no longer conferred as a matter of birth and everyone had the formal right to receive an education—a development that Lenin greeted as "a step in the process of the general and comprehensive Europeanization of Russia."[6]

The Bolshevik Revolution, in its sociopolitical impact, influenced education in two ways. On the one hand, several policies pursued during the first years of the Soviet regime could be regarded as a logical and radical continuation of the democratization process mentioned earlier; on the other hand, proletarian class ideology intervened to militate once again against the democratic principle of equal educational opportunity for all. Just as opposing models of democratic and socialist education were reflected in the grand educational schemes of Condorcet and Lepeletier during the French Revolution, the political manifestoes of Lenin, Lunacharskii, and Krupskaias between 1917 and 1919 also offered a clear and obvious contrast between egalitarian-democratic and proletarian-revolutionary aims. In August 1918 a policy of open admissions was adopted for the universities; preparatory training and social origin were no longer

of any importance. Gradually, however, political and social
norms were more stringently applied and efficiently administered
in the selection of students for secondary schools, technical
schools, and the universities. With the express purpose of proletarianizing the universities (both in a social and partisan political sense) along with the nine-year labor schools, workers'
faculties were set up in 1919 to serve as special preparatory
institutes whose graduates were entitled to receive the same
privileges as those of other schools.[7]

In 1917, 60 percent of the population was illiterate; this was
of course a critical problem during this early period of Soviet
education. Two decades later, largely because of adult education
programs and four years of compulsory education (since 1930),[8]
this problem was in great measure overcome. The democratization process which began in the nineteenth century was completed in the sense that every person was now required to have
at least an elementary knowledge of reading, writing, and arith-
metic. Responsible people in Soviet Russia were fully aware,
however, that these basic educational attainments would provide only for the minimal educational needs of a rapidly indus-
trializing society. It would be a long-term effort for the Soviet
Union to train a broad stratum of technicians, economists, and
scientists.

Before turning to this effort, which was the central objective
of the Stalin era, let us examine more closely the social results
of educational policy in the 1920s. Viewed historically one no-
tices that the Soviet school system had become far less a sociopolitical instrument than anyone might have expected under
communist educational policy. Despite all the restrictions and
demands dictated by this policy, the social composition of students in higher educational institutions, from the point of view
of a well-planned process of class-selection, remained unsatisfactory. Table 1 reveals the social composition of various schools in
the RSFSR, the largest Soviet republic, as of 1 December 1926;
it shows the percentage of the working population from each

TABLE 1

Schools	Workers	Farm laborers	Farmers	White-collar employees	Independent professions	Craftsmen	Nonworking population	Other
Level I schools (4 years)	8.4	1.7	78.9	5.5	0.5	2.4	0.9	1.7
Seven-year schools	35.3	--	25.8[a]	26.5	--	--	--	12.4[b]
Level II schools (5-9 years)	13.6	--	30.7[a]	34.0	--	--	--	21.7[b]
Vocational schools	28.3	1.0	32.2	27.9	0.9	2.5	0.8	6.4
Technical schools	20.8	0.9	33.6	34.7	0.9	2.5	0.7	5.9
Workers' faculties	53.4	3.5	35.3	5.4	--	--	--	2.4
Higher education	23.7	1.6	24.7	39.3	4.6	3.0	0.7	2.4
Social classes in the working population, less family members	17.0	[c]	64.4	12.3	0.4	3.8	0.9	1.2

Source: *Narodnoe prosveshchenie*, 1928, no. 12, pp. 72 ff.

[a] Includes farm laborers.

[b] Includes independent professions, nonworking population, and craftsmen.

[c] Precise figures are not available. They are probably included within the total number of farmers or workers.

stratum represented in these schools, thus mirroring the actual significance of social class in the educational system.

What is most striking about this table is the disproportionately high number of children from both white-collar and professional categories who attended these schools, particularly upper-level institutions. Moreover, other data[9] show that the number of working-class children drops off considerably from grade to grade, particularly after the fourth primary school year; hence, those classes which were defined as bourgeois or petty bourgeois had an absolute advantage on the upper level.[10] Regarding the social composition of students in secondary schools the director of the main city school administration in Moscow observed that "in the proletarian hub of the country, eleven years after the Revolution, level II schools still predominately serve the middle class and that it was high time that they be proletarianized."[11]

There are many reasons for this astonishing situation, which so clearly contradicted the sociopolitical aims of the Soviet government at this time. The most important reason is doubtless to be found in the defective structure of the Soviet educational system itself. Soviet leaders simply could not overcome the existing inequality of the educational system given the disparity between the number of basic four-year schools and the further institution of secondary education, a situation that still prevailed at the close of the NEP period.[12] From the very beginning the rural population especially was greatly disadvantaged in terms of educational opportunities when compared to urban residents. In 1926 nearly 82 percent of the population resided in rural areas, yet only 12,224 children were enrolled in the eighth and ninth grades during the 1927–28 school year; by comparison, urban schools enrolled 114,401 children in these grades.[13] In the cities the children of urban workers were formally privileged to attend these schools, but they could not take full advantage of this opportunity. Income was not the main reason for this, for the industrial worker actually earned more than a teacher or an office employee. Far more important was the traditional unfamiliarity of the working class with the gymnasium; such children could not be enticed into the secondary school by renaming the *gymnasium* a "unified workers' school." On the other hand, the old educated class, together with those white-collar employees whose status was not yet wholly recognized by the Soviet regime, made considerable sacrifices in order to give their children a well-rounded education; in this way they were able to compensate for their inferior social status under the Soviet regime. So long as attendance at school beyond the fourth grade remained a matter of parental decision the children of these classes, because of the motivation of their parents, had the advantage, whereas quite often the worker failed to manifest any interest in higher education until his later years.

By the end of the NEP period the policy of recruiting students to various levels of education on the basis of their class affiliation did not fulfill the expectations of the Communist Party; thus, a second effort to proletarianize the schools, particularly universities and technical schools, was launched in 1928 within the framework of the Five-Year Plan. The party consecrated itself to the task of training a proletarian intelligentsia that would be made up of politically reliable "Red specialists." Just as the revolutionary proletariat had sought to alter the character of the universities with the help of workers' faculties back in 1919, party leaders, beginning in the summer of 1928, initiated a whole series of measures designed to change the social profile of both universities and technical schools. Students of working-class origin who were newly admitted to the higher technical institutes reached first 65 and later 70 percent of enrollment;[14] their representation in other higher institutions and technical schools was similarly high. Since there was some doubt that these measures would actually change very much the social composition of the student body, requirements for admission to universities and technical schools were substantially lowered as well.[15]

Another important measure was the policy, initiated in 1928 and carried out gradually until 1931, of appointing members of the party, trade unions, and the Komsomol for study at universities and technical schools; these groups supported those politically active elements in the institutes who were trying to eliminate opponents of Marxist ideology. Because of these efforts the number of those studying at worker faculties reached 70,000 in 1929 and 339,000 in 1932.[16] At the end of the First Five-Year Plan the proletarian representation in higher education amounted to over one-half of all students, while it made up nearly two-thirds of all students attending institutes for engineering training.[17] The social composition of students in all establishments of higher education underwent the following changes from 1928 to 1938 (figures are in percentages):

TABLE 2

	1928	1929	1930	1931	1932	1933	1934	1935	1938
Workers	25.4	30.3	35.2	46.4	58.0	50.3	47.9	45.0	33.9
Farmers	23.9	22.4	20.9	19.3	14.1	16.9	14.6	16.2	21.6
Other	50.7	47.3	43.9	34.3	27.9	32.8	37.5	38.8	44.5

Source: DeWitt, *Education and Professional Employment in the USSR* (Washington, 1961), p. 655.

As a result of all these measures the nature of the Russian intelligentsia had changed radically. A new class of technical and administrative experts emerged—a Soviet semi-intelligentsia, in effect[18]—while the old Russian intelligentsia, a class educated in the classical mould, began to fade away. A substantial part of this new "technical intelligentsia" originated in the working class; official statistics on this matter, however, are not entirely accurate since persons who were not of working-class origin were frequently able to acquire proletarian identification credentials on the basis of which they were admitted to study.

Perhaps more important than the social effects of these measures was the fact that the Communist Party was able to establish thereby a cadre of intellectuals politically loyal to it; after all, those people emerging from universities and technical schools during the course of the First and Second Five-Year Plans owed their status as members of the official elite in large measure to the party. But the cost of all this was a loss of the "critical thought" that so distinguished the old Russian intelligentsia: such attitudes had no chance whatsoever of surviving, much less flourishing, under Stalin.

3. Social Differentiation under Stalin's Cadre Policy

This alteration in the social basis of the Russian intelligentsia was a by-product of the state's cadre policy. The training of cadres has been an important aspect of Soviet economic planning since the Central Committee of the CPSU adopted the 12 July 1928 resolution that scored the large gap between the demand for qualified personnel and job preparation. Backed by a systematic program of instruction and centralized job assignment, cadres were organized to meet the Soviet economy's need for trained personnel. The aims, structure, and course of study in the various educational institutions were substantially influenced by Soviet labor policy. One is justified actually in describing the whole educational system as a means to produce and reproduce a skilled labor force, for the training of cadres has been the vital center of Soviet educational policy since 1928.

Our interest here is in the sociological impact of Stalin's educational policies. Aspects of these policies that were of particular significance between 1931 and 1940 are: (1) the extension and "stabilization" of the school system as a whole; (2) the abolition in 1935 of socio-political criteria for admission to universities and technical schools, followed some five years later by the introduction of fees for study in institutions of higher learning; and (3) the "mobilization" (since 1940) of young people from rural and urban areas for the purpose of training them as labor reserves.

After the initial phase of educational experimentation the Soviet school system, around 1934, assumed a character that was to last for the next quarter-century. The structure of the general school system—the four-year elementary schools along with seven- and ten-year secondary schools—had to provide training for different occupational groups and to channel students into areas of the economy specified by the state. That this was the principal purpose of these schools is manifest when examining more closely their specific functions. On the basis of the compulsory primary school, which later evolved into a seven-year school, vocational schools and courses for lower working-class groups have been organized. Those attending school less than seven years turned out to be either kolkhoz peasants or semiskilled industrial laborers; after seven years of school one could qualify for a job as a skilled worker or a low-level office employee. Next came the technical schools, which placed their graduates in various middle positions in industry, agriculture, administration, and public education. The ten-year secondary school was more or less a prerequisite for study in the university or a higher technical school.[19] Graduates of the latter were among those "specialists of higher education," who by definition belong to the new Soviet intelligentsia.

Since the mid-1930s there has been, on the whole, a rather clear and distinct tendency on the part of various types of educational institutions to place people in professional jobs strictly on the basis of their training or education. Previous criteria of selection and placement, such as a person's peasant or proletarian origin or political fidelity, lost their significance. This switch from the application of social and partisan political criteria to those of academic background and professional ability was expressed in new admission requirements, adopted in December of 1935 for study at universities and higher technical schools. Admission to these institutions now depended solely on the results of an examination and no longer upon social origin. The importance of intellectual ability and knowledge was clearly underlined by the introduction of gold and silver medals conferred upon superior secondary-school graduates, who, as a result, were privileged in enrollment to higher institutions of learning.[20]

While the measures just mentioned are by themselves understandable as means to improve the academic quality of advanced schools, the changes introduced on September 1, 1940[21] for attending secondary schools (grades eight to ten), technical schools, and universities raise the question whether the intent was to restrict admission along sociopolitical lines or to maximize the potential labor force. This has received very little clarification.[22] Even if one is not inclined to regard these regulations, which remained in force until 1956, as clear evidence of a conscious plan to install a new Soviet upper class, the fee requirement alone implied that the size of a family's income would henceforth very largely determine who would attend higher institutions of learning, and suggested the abandonment of the egalitarian principles of 1918 as well as a serious breach in the ideology of socialist equality.

The children of the intelligentsia, because of the intellectual climate and respect for educational achievement found in their homes, were favored by this renewed stress on academic ability as the basis of continuing one's formal education. By the same token a decree on labor reserves[23] issued 2 October 1940—the same day that the fee requirement went into effect—confined large numbers of young workers and kolkhoz peasants to the material sphere of production. Around 800,000 to 1,000,000 male youths between fourteen and seventeen years of age were gradually "mobilized" and trained in various vocational "Labor Reserve Schools" as a corps of labor reserves. After completion of their training they were ordered to stay at least four years on the job.

Educational policy under Stalin, in contrast to the earlier egalitarian-democratic and proletarian-revolutionary phase of

Soviet education, tended to stabilize the emerging and differentiated social order that was evolving in part out of the educational system. By virtue of their formal education peasants and
workers could still move upward into the intelligentsia, as
before, but this became much more difficult to accomplish after
the state had stopped its policy of formally recruiting these
groups on socio-political grounds. No really equal educational
opportunity could exist in circumstances where, despite the
construction of secondary schools in rural areas, the quality of
rural education lagged so far behind that of urban areas. This
situation still obtains today in the Soviet Union.[24] Even in
cities, as mentioned earlier, children from upper social strata
enjoyed superior educational opportunities. One indication of
the "deproletarianization" of advanced education—a process
that had begun at the end of the 1930s—is the Soviet failure,
since 1938, to publish statistics on the social makeup of students. In 1958 Khrushchev spoke of the "clearly anomalous
situation" in Moscow's higher educational institutions where
only 30 to 40 percent of the students were children of workers
and kolkhoz peasants, while the majority of them came from
families of the intelligentsia or white-collar employees. "And I
don't have to mention," he added, "that we can literally count
on our fingers the number of workers and peasants who are
studying as regular students while interrupting their working
lives."[25]

4. The Educational Level and Social Structure of the Soviet Population

The Soviet Union's elimination of illiteracy along with its
imposition of minimal educational standards have produced a
population marked by significant differences in educational
achievement. The Soviets distinguish between the following
education stages:

1. Incomplete secondary education: seven years of schooling; since the law of 1958, eight years.
2. Complete secondary education: ten years of schooling; since 1964 eleven years.
3. Secondary specialized education: a full course of study in a technical school or some other secondary vocational school.
4. Higher education: a full course of study in a university or higher technical school.[26]

Besides these there are lower vocational schools—after the incomplete secondary schools—along with adult education programs, neither of which qualifies students to continue their education at higher levels.

The January 1959 census for the first time provided accurate figures on the education of the Soviet population. They are presented in Table 3.[27]

According to the figures in Table 3 barely half the USSR adult population in 1959 has attended school for more than four years; about 40 percent received at least seven years of schooling, 16 percent at least ten, while 2.5 percent had a full higher education.[28]

The census further revealed that the educational differences between urban and rural inhabitants are still great. Compared to 1939 the number of urban residents with a higher education increased by around 331 percent, in rural districts by around 275 percent. Nearly every fifth rural resident has a minimum of seven years of schooling, compared to every third urban dweller. What is noteworthy here are the relatively equal levels of education on the part of both sexes and the large number of women with an advanced education. Women constitute 49 percent of those with higher education and actually 56.6 percent of those with secondary professional training, a finding attributable mainly to the large numbers of women who enter the teaching and medical professions.

The number of people with higher education in the different

TABLE 3

Population over 15 years of age	Thousands 148.186	Percent 100.
Level of Education		
Four years of school or less	76.978	51.7
Less than seven years of school	12.500	8.4
Incomplete secondary education (between seven and nine years of schooling)	35.386	23.9
Ten years of general education	9.936	
Specialized secondary education	7.870	
Total with complete secondary education	17.806	12.0
Incomplete higher education	1.738	1.5
Complete higher education	3.778	2.5

Source: *Narodnoe khoziaistvo SSSR v 1959 godu* (Moscow, 1960), p. 21.

union republics is also interesting. An average of 18 out of every 1,000 persons in the USSR has a higher education. Well above this are the Georgian SSR with 38, the Armenian with 28, the Azerbaidzhani with 21, the Latvian with 21, and the Estonian with 21; far below the USSR average are the Moldavian SSR with 10, the Tadzhik with 10, the Kasakh with 12, and the Belorussian with 12 out of every 1,000 inhabitants in possession of a higher education. Here the impact of varying cultural traditions seems clearly evident.

It is much more difficult to identify the levels of education within the various social classes. Soviet statistics are not broken down in this way, due largely to the Soviet theory of social stratification which postulates the existence of only three major

TABLE 4

	Number per Thousand			
	Higher education (complete and incomplete) and secondary specialized education	General secondary education	Incomplete secondary education	Primary school or less than seven years of education
Urban Population				
Workers	17	49	209	290
Employees	286	128	190	132
Kolkhoz peasants	32	92	190	222
Rural Population				
Workers	7	21	154	279
Employees	251	77	176	129
Kolkhoz peasants	5	15	124	242
Rural and Urban Population				
Workers	14	39	190	286
Employees	276	114	186	131
Kolkhoz peasants	7	19	127	241

Source: *Itogi vsesoiuznoi perepisi naseleniia 1959 goda,
SSSR (svodnyi tom)*, (Moscow, 1962), p. 111.

social categories, namely workers, farmers, and white-collar employees; this poses difficulties for Soviet theorists when they are called upon to isolate and define various social groupings, particularly within the intelligentsia.[29] Here too Soviet statistics are not very helpful.

With these reservations in mind Table 4, which is also based on the 1959 census, shows us the general educational level of individual social classes and occupational groups.

TABLE 5

	Higher education (complete and incomplete) and secondary spe- cialized education	General secondary education	Incomplete secondary education	Primary school or less than seven years of education
	Number per Thousand			
Urban Population				
Workers	24	71	329	408
Employees	491	151	256	88
Kolkhoz peasants	19	30	192	357
Rural Population				
Workers	12	35	264	435
Employees	487	127	265	104
Kolkhoz peasants	9	23	194	355
Rural and Urban Population				
Workers	20	59	307	418
Employees	490	145	258	92
Kolkhoz peasants	9	23	194	355

Source: *Itogi vsesoiuznoi perepisi naseleniia 1959 goda,*
p. 15.

Table 4 represents the entire population. Table 5, on the other hand, discloses the educational level of the employed population.

The education of those professionally trained persons employed by particular branches of industry is presented in Table 6. These tables do not distinguish between those persons engaged in nonmanual and manual labor or between executive and man-

TABLE 6

	Higher education	Secondary special-ized education and unfinished higher education	General secondary (including incomplete secondary) education	Primary education and less than seven years of education
		Out of 1000 Employed Persons		
Entire Economy	33	76	324	331
Industry	20	63	426	364
Construction	30	63	378	405
Agriculture	3	15	226	359
Transportation	13	63	415	380
Trade and public supply	16	87	467	278
Health and social welfare	108	309	242	197
Education	213	350	217	114
Science (including auxiliary service)	213	163	346	201
Art	81	135	517	206
Administration	130	153	456	177
Party, Komsomol, trade unions, cooperatives, and other social organizations	152	242	426	107

Source: *Itogi vsesoiuznoi perepisi naseleniia 1959 goda,* pp. 123 ff.

agerial personnel; Table 7, however, which presents data on the educational level of persons engaged in physical and nonphysical labor, give us important insights into the social structure as well as the evolution of Soviet society itself.[30]

TABLE 7

	1939	1959
Total Employed Personnel	78.8 million	99.1 million
Those mainly involved in physical labor	65.0 million (= 82.5%)	78.6 million (= 79.3%)
Those mainly involved in nonphysical labor	13.8 million (= 17.5%)	20.5 million (= 20.7%)

Source: *Itogi vsesoiuznoi perepisi naseleniia 1959 goda,*
p. 130.

In the individual branches of industry the number of persons with at least seven years of schooling per 1,000 employed is presented in Table 8.

The tables clearly manifest two current and parallel trends:

1. The general educational level of workers and kolkhoz peasants employed in industry and agriculture has improved constantly since the 1940s when seven years of compulsory schooling were required of everyone. In 1959, 302 out of every 1,000 manual laborers had attended school from seven to ten years— only 14, however, had gone on to a technical school or a higher institution of learning. These results would not be surprising even if the Communist Party had not sought consciously to eliminate inequities based on educational background and— according to the official party line—to elevate the "cultural-technical level of the working masses" up to that of the intelligentsia.

2. The data make equally plain that the education of persons engaged mainly in nonphysical labor has risen appreciably. Out of every 1,000 persons falling into this category 476 have higher or specialized secondary education (in contrast to 14 among manual laborers) while another 408 have from seven to ten years

TABLE 8

	1939	1959
Total Employed Population	123	433
Those engaged mainly in physical labor	43	316
Industry		
Metal	176	535
Chemical	113	514
Railroads	71	408
Textile	60	478
Mining	55	407
Construction	30	318
Agriculture	13	220
Those engaged mainly in nonphysical labor	498	884
Scientists, teachers, and educators	892	991
Writers, journalists, and publishing personnel	818	989
Jurists	684	987
Doctors and other medical personnel	674	969
Artists	644	894
Engineers and technicians	630	910
Agronomists, veterinarians, and foresters	622	936
Economists, accountants, and related personnel	515	900
Leading personnel of state, party, Komsomol, union, and other social organizations	359	908
Directors of industrial enterprises and collective farms	285	853

Source: *Itogi vsesoiuznoi perepisi naseleniia 1959 goda,* p. 177.

of general education. The importance of specialized training as
a condition for membership in the intelligentsia is clear; but the
difficulty involved in implementing a truly egalitarian educational policy, which has been tried since 1958, is equally
manifest.

5. Sociological Aspects of Khrushchev's Educational Reforms

Sociopolitical considerations were among the reasons that
moved Soviet party and state leaders to begin in 1958, after
some two years of deliberation, far-reaching educational reforms.[31] We have already indicated that after two decades
of Stalin's cadre policy the social cleavage between the new
upper class and the mass of workers and peasants had widened,
a fact attributable mainly to the higher educational background
of Soviet specialists, which assured them membership in the
Soviet intelligentsia. And the fact that students were being
recruited more and more from the intelligentsia increased the
prospect of their isolation from the masses. Khrushchev doubtless saw this as the principal stumbling block in his plan of
"Transition to Communism," to homogenize Soviet society.
His trenchant criticism of education merely for the sake of
the social status it would confer, the pretensions of entrance
examinations, and the superiority complex of the new upper
class exposed the crucial points of the Soviet educational system,
especially when measured by the communist ideal of a society
of equals.

The reshaping of communist educational policy along egalitarian lines, concerning which more will be said later, was
generated chiefly by acute economic and labor problems that
originated in the growing disparity between the number of students graduating from secondary schools and the number of
those accepted by the universities; the disparity resulted in increasing numbers of young people unwilling to go to work.
While up to about 1952 nearly all graduates of the ten-year

school could count on further study, four years later the ratio of secondary-school graduates to openings in Soviet higher education was 5 to 1. In 1958 Khrushchev announced that around 2.5 million secondary-school graduates were unable to matriculate at a higher or specialized secondary institute between 1954 and 1957 alone; "upon receiving their school certificates," he said, "the majority of these students were unprepared for life and had no notion of what career they wanted to follow."[32]

The educational reforms that were implemented by the law of 24 December 1958, and in the following year by numerous decrees of the Soviet government,[33] have two sociological aspects:

1. The reform sought to raise the general educational level of the population even higher than it was in order to narrow the educational gap between various social groups.
2. In addition to intellectual achievement it reintroduced social criteria into the selection of the upcoming generation of students to be trained.

Soviet census data presented earlier showed that only 40 percent of the USSR adult population had more than seven years of schooling. Khrushchev's educational reforms, together with the long-term reforms mentioned in the 1961 program of the CPSU, were thus designed to raise the general educational level of the population and were to be implemented in two stages: With the commencement of the 1963–64 school year eight years of compulsory education were to be required of all school-age children (the plan, however, was not implemented in all school districts); by 1970 these children should receive, in both day and evening schools, eleven years of compulsory education. Parallel to this and by 1970 also, according to the party program, "those youths who were early absorbed into the economy and as a consequence did not receive equivalent schooling were to complete eight years of education; by the following decade every person would be granted the opportunity to receive a full secondary education."[34]

Thus it was hoped that by extending the period of formal education for young people, together with setting up adult-education programs of a general and vocational kind, the "cultural-technical level" of the entire population would be raised. The above-mentioned requirement of eleven years of compulsory schooling for all young people up to the age of eighteen was expected to increase the number of students in general schools, vocational schools, and secondary technical schools to some 60 million by 1970, as compared to 36.6 million in 1960. What all this implied in terms of school building and teacher education was, of course, clear for all to see. These aims have been approved by the Twenty-third Party Congress in 1966.

No less important, though far more difficult to achieve actually, are the proclaimed efforts to raise the educational level of the working population. Sociological studies by Soviet scholars have shown that the educational level of workers is highly correlated with productive output; these studies have also specified the kind of sociopolitical results that might be expected from raising the workers' level of education.[35] Investigations of several Ural industries between 1957 and 1959 showed that while workers with longer periods of schooling were increasing in number they still experienced considerable difficulty in adjusting to the novel technical procedures that had been installed in these factories. This was attributed to a general lack of basic knowledge along with an inadequate level of technical training. It became clear that cultural-technical standards in the Soviet Union would have to be raised substantially if further technical progress was to be made. Hopefully this would be accomplished by exposing the population to a well-rounded basic education, supplementary technical training, instruction in vocational skills, and a socialist attitude toward work.

For this reason Soviet educational plans provided for the organization of evening and correspondence schools. With regard to adult education the evening secondary schools, the correspondence or evening courses in the technical schools, and similar programs at the universities have three major functions: First, a substantial part of the working population still lack the minimum requirement of eight years of schooling, not to mention the attempt to raise this minimum to ten or eleven years by 1980; the long-range task of achieving this goal within this sector of the population is assigned to evening and correspondence schools. Second, these schools are helping to insure that vocational knowledge and skills will keep pace with the changing needs of Soviet society. This was actually the state's principal reason for setting up these programs in the first place. A third function of these schools is simply to provide people with an opportunity to acquire a liberal education over and above the need for vocational training or continuing education in a specific field of endeavor, where, in effect, education would become an end in itself—a luxury—and not simply a means to augment the nation's industrial capacity. Here various programs of popular education carried out by social institutions such as "cultural universities" are playing an increasing role.[36]

Thus, if Soviet education is designed primarily to serve the economy, yet at the same time permits people to indulge in the luxury of study for the sake of study, then educational policymakers will have to consider the impact of an evolving society whose members, as they secure more individual freedom, are not likely to regard their freedom merely as a means for increasing productivity. It is possible ideologically to justify this development, however, by invoking the vision of a future communist culture inspired by the spirit of utopian socialism and communism as represented, for example, by Strumilin; his long-range view of things includes, at the very most, a four-hour working day, which will afford every person the leisure to plan his life in such a way as to provide for the complete development of the human personality.[37]

Communist leaders expect that these efforts to elevate the cultural-technical level of workers and farmers will eliminate the distinctions which currently exist between the Soviet intelligentsia and the working masses. Although Soviet political and social scientists have long denied the existence of social classes, substantial differences in the living conditions of individual social groups in the Soviet Union are obvious. These distinctions are rooted in the educational gap that exists between those academically trained professional groups who govern and manage the society and those groups engaged mainly in the performance of manual labor and ordinary administrative functions.

It has been suggested that this dualism, rooted as it is in a capitalist past, could be minimized if not altogether eliminated. Two points of view have been expressed in this connection. It is asserted that "in the transition from socialism to communism, laborers and peasants must be trained as technicians from the start and qualify eventually for engineering and other higher technical posts;"[38] this is supposed to be accomplished by general educational programs as well as the continuing education of a vocational nature that we have already mentioned. Secondly, a new type of so-called "worker intellectual" is supposed to emerge from an educational system that combines theoretical study and practical work; in this way, too, the increasing intellectual demands of a modern industrial society will be met. Thus, gradually, social distinctions rooted in educational differences should disappear, after which men would be differentiated only by the necessary and specific functions they perform in society.

The nature and problems of a "classless society" as perceived by Marx and his Russian disciples, and raised by the above remarks, cannot be treated here. Let us turn our attention instead to certain realities of the Soviet system and the sociological impact of recent educational reforms as they relate to the tension we have observed between equalitarian ideology and elite tendencies of current educational policy. One can describe the Soviet dilemma as that of an educational policy oriented toward the ideal of a classless society but which is simultaneously dictated by the imperatives of a planned economy. Contradictions inherent in the numerous reforms implemented since the 1958 law concerning educational reform emerged out of this conflict of goals.

Three complex issues are involved here: university admission policies, the role of various special schools, and the integrative functions of Soviet education. Let us look more closely at each of them.

For twenty years, from 1935 to 1954, intellectual ability was the sole criterion of admission to higher education, whereby gold and silver medal winners among the graduates of the ten-year school, along with top technical-school graduates, did not have to take an entrance examination. From 1955 on, admission policy underwent steady change.[39] For one thing, the *otlitchniki*, i.e., applicants with high scholastic grades, were no longer preferred and almost wholly ignored; for another—and more importantly—since 1957 persons with two years of job experience have been favored for admission to the university.[40] Between 1957 and 1961 the number of students admitted to higher education who could claim practical working experience skyrocketed from 28 to 60 percent of student enrollment.[41] A further innovation, introduced in 1959, permitted industries, collective farms, and state administrative agencies to delegate experienced men for study at the university.[42] In these cases applicants for advanced study were required to have positive recommendations from the party, union, Komsomol, or manager of an industrial plant or collective farm.

Clearly, the injection of social criteria (working experience and socioeconomic status) into university admission standards, together with the increasing importance of vocational evening training and correspondence study, with their partiality toward practical study,[43] were designed substantially to alter the social composition of university students and, thus, the coming generation of intellectuals. The introduction of polytechnical education and professional training in the upper grades of the general secondary school had the same purpose. Every future specialist would be a person who started at the bottom of the ladder and climbed his way steadily upward, as a worker, into his final occupation. "By working and going to school at the same time a young man will be much more capable of finding his place in society," said Khrushchev,[44] who incessantly underscored the necessity of overcoming the alienation that existed between the working masses and the intellectuals. It was hoped that during their obligatory working periods students (among whom would be the sons and daughters of the intelligentsia itself) would find their place in society either as workers, farmers, or white-collar employees, and by undergoing such experience acquire a "worker's conscience" that would manifest itself in later life.

It was highly questionable, however, whether these expectations would ever materialize. Though until 1965 about 60 percent of the students passed an obligatory period of on-the-job experience there were numerous ways for the offspring of the upper strata to circumvent this requirement; for example, they could easily procure a formal certificate showing that they had work experience. Because of the security and material support that their families were able to provide, these students were at an advantage because they could more easily avoid the work-study experience and thus gain admission to the university. Moreover, those students whose social status impeded their future education often had to make great efforts to gain admission to advanced study. A rigid screening process for selecting a new generation of university students has been installed by the new regulations, but it is doubtful whether such controls could actually transform the social character of the population by "reproletarianizing" it. Developments since Khrushchev's dismissal in 1964 and subsequent revisions of most of his educational reforms have confirmed our skepticism.

Up to now we have discussed the social impact of various higher education admission policies. But there is no longer any doubt that these policies, for which Khrushchev fought so ardently, predominately served the state's economic goals. The educational reforms of 1958 were designed to improve labor policy by closely linking the educational system to the needs of the economy. For example, the inclusion of specialized vocational training in the curricula of general secondary schools—in contrast to original proposals for broad polytechnical training—stemmed from the need both to reduce the backlog of applications for advanced study and to funnel students more systematically into industry and agriculture.

Between 1960 and 1965 educational policy increasingly sought to exert tighter control over job allocation by channeling youths into occupations and areas of production—especially agriculture, which had suffered acute labor shortages—where they were needed. Thus, the individual's freedom to choose a field of study was further limited; previously these limitations had been defined mainly by restrictions on the number of openings available in vocational schools, technical schools, and universities. However, as indicated by reports of Soviet newspapers and trade journals, vocational orientation and guidance lagged behind the expectations of economic planners. Only a relatively small number of secondary school graduates actually took up the vocation in which they were trained through work-study programs; most of them attempted to enter other occupations more to their liking.

These educational policies actually hindered a substantial number of Soviet youths, particularly those living in rural areas, from going on directly to advanced study. The emphasis laid on evening and correspondence courses as "the main road to higher education" on the one hand opened the door to further training and thus greater professional advancement for those who were already employed; on the other hand—with respect to the young particularly—such training did not constitute a sufficient basis for continuing one's education all the way to a university degree.

We have discussed the conflict that exists between the egalitarian goals of communist leaders and the contrary tendencies of Soviet society as they are expressed in the positions of power and influence reached by the upper strata. This situation arises from the pressing need for highly qualified personnel in science, technology, and an economy that is becoming increasingly complex; as a result educational policy has to be oriented toward the selection and recruitment of talents. Herein lies the Soviet dilemma. An "elite education" based on ability rather than on political considerations is essential and is in conflict with the egalitarian ideology.

Soviet educational policy has recognized since the 1920s the special needs of artistically talented children, particularly those who were encouraged at an early age to attend schools of art, music, and dance. Special schools were established during World War II to accommodate the offspring of military officers (the Suvorov and Nachimov schools). A person who attended any one of them was as a rule assured of membership in the Soviet upper strata. When educational reform was being debated in 1958, various groups, scientists especially, underscored the importance of setting up special schools for children who early manifest mathematical and scientific aptitudes; Khrushchev, along with the Central Committee of the party, also endorsed the legitimacy of such schools. The Educational Reform Act of 24 December 1958, however, did not make express reference to these schools because of emerging ideological doubts about breaking down the unified school system.

In the following years, however, in addition to extracurricular circles of pupils, so-called "schools of mathematics" for the young were introduced to give supplementary instruction on a voluntary basis,[45] and special secondary boarding schools of physics and mathematics have been created, four of which were in existence by the end of 1963 (the best known among them was organized by the branch of the Academy of Science in Novosibirsk). Soviet scientists obviously succeeded in convincing both party and state leaders that the training of young talent, though it reduced the amount of time that the student could spend in work-study programs, was indispensable for the education of future scientists in highly demanding theoretical areas.

Similar schools, though not so highly selective, for expanded foreign-language instruction appeared after 1957; by 1965 they were to have numbered around 700.[46] These schools, in which children from the second grade up receive intensive instruction in a modern language, are designed to train systematically a strata of the Soviet intelligentsia in the use of a foreign language. Since the Soviet Union is a world power her agents in the fields of diplomacy, international trade, and scientific research need, to a much greater degree than before, to master at least one foreign language. That these advanced language schools open the gate to membership in the Soviet upper strata is clear. The state seems to recognize the social status involved in language study by allowing foreign-language instruction to be taught in kindergarten and in the early elementary-school grades; but parents must pay a fee for this service. Thus, the principle of paying fees on a voluntary basis was introduced at a very crucial stage of Soviet education.

Obviously, the Communist Party was willing to risk, for the economic reason mentioned above, the elitism that might be generated by such privileges. For there is little doubt that these educational reforms did help the Soviet upper strata to retain their superior status insofar as educational background is concerned. Not all children whose parents send them to a "better" school are more gifted than children in ordinary schools. But the children of the upper strata have a head start because their parents have more appreciation for the significance of an education and because they themselves are part of the intelligentsia.[47]

An interesting contrast to the above reforms was the organization in 1956 of boarding schools which were not established for purposes of selective admission. In 1965 the number of pupils in these schools totaled almost a million.[48] These schools were formerly linked to social welfare homes and orphanages, particularly those for needy children. Indeed, some quality boarding schools do exist to serve some of the specialized purposes we have just discussed. Most of them, however, are intended to be models of collectivized education under a developed communist system, much like the new integrated "pre-

school childrens' institutions" (creches and kindergartens),
which have experienced a rapid growth. The party program of
1961 mentioned that "in the immediate years ahead the need
for preschool facilities should be fully met" and "by 1980 it
should be possible for all families, if they wish, to place their
children, through their teens, in these schools without charge."
Unofficial figures in 1962 estimated that by 1980 there would be
around 40 million children in these preschool institutions and
from 55 to 60 million students in boarding and extended day
schools, which would include nearly 80 percent of all school-age
youths under eighteen.[49] As it appeared since the middle of the
sixties these plans were rather utopian and had to be cut back.

The long-range goal of a fully socialized educational system,
which for ideological reasons is uppermost in the minds of communist leaders, should not be underestimated as a means of
countering the differentiation we find to exist in Soviet education. It is important to emphasize in this regard that Soviet
schools play an important integrative role by creating a civic
consciousness which transcends all social and educational differences. Schools serve this function in all modern democratic
societies, but in the Soviet communist system it is of special
significance because of the politico-ideological uniformity that
party leaders insist upon. By teaching youth that they live in a
homogeneous nonantagonistic society in the process of abolishing all class distinctions, attention is deflected from the pressing
problems of political conflict and power. An ideology that
teaches social harmony in all schools—elementary through the
university—cannot fail to have some effect; yet expectations in
this regard have not been fully realized. The disparity between
consciousness and reality, together with the veiled role of ideology about which Marx wrote, applies equally to Soviet society.

6. Education in Modern Society: The Soviet Variant

This discussion has made clear that there is a close link, at all
stages in the development of Soviet educational policy, between

communist social ideas, the economic goals of the Soviet government, and educational policy. To understand the significance of this study for the present and the future we must realize that the Soviet Union—despite its unique characteristics—is a variant of modern industrial society and is exhibiting features that are common to Western countries in the second half of this century.

One such feature is the democratization of education, where all citizens, regardless of socioeconomic status, have the opportunity, through compulsory school-attendance laws, to advance their education. Education, however, has not yet been fully democratized in the Soviet Union, since equal educational opportunities beyond the lower levels have still not been fully realized; obstacles to such opportunities are different from those to be found in some West European countries. This situation is attributable to official education policy itself, quite apart from other kinds of disadvantages, such as those suffered by rural youths.

It is important to look at both sides of recent Soviet education policy. While on the one hand an effort was made to institute a wide choice of schools (e.g., the various evening and correspondence courses)—much more so than was the case under Stalin—the educational system for all practical purposes became the handmaiden of the economy where state interests took precedence over individual aspirations. The conflict between the concept of democratic education in the sense of equal opportunity for all and state control over educational channels is inherent to the Soviet system. In other words, admission to higher levels of education is much broader in the Soviet Union than in West Germany; but the possibility of choosing the field of study one likes is much more limited in the former. The idea of educational planning—not only in the sense of projecting future needs and costs—is gaining prominence in Western democracies, and it is essential that we bear in mind the possible threats that this poses to individual freedom, as the Soviet example demonstrates.

Another problem of major importance involves the phenomenon of "life-long learning," which is becoming ever more popular in industrially developed nations. Since vocational needs and demands expand as well as change, it is no longer possible for a person to divide his life into a period of formal education terminating upon graduation and a period of professional work-experience which begins immediately thereafter, as it was possible to do up to a few decades ago. Hence more and more people are continuing their education after graduation from school, a phenomenon that contributes both to industrial growth and social mobility. Continuing education has experienced its greatest growth, in the form of vocational as well as nonvocational schools and courses in the Soviet Union and the United States. In growing measure, too, along with this development, Soviet society is wrestling with the problem of leisure that was mentioned earlier. Leisure provides men with time to learn, and it appears that here the political will of the state with respect to education may possibly coincide with the educational wishes of citizens. On the one hand, men's leisure affords the state an opportunity to generate a uniform consciousness through its programs of adult education; on the other hand, one should not underestimate the inclination of men to use study as a means of liberating themselves intellectually.

These observations, however, exceed the limits of our inquiry. Whether higher education produces more freedom, whether the latter can be used for socially relevant purposes, whether possibilities exist for the development of an intellectual pluralism, and whether there are limits to the influence of party ideology over education are questions we cannot assay here; yet they constitute serious problems within Soviet society, the significance of which should not be overlooked in future studies of this kind.[50]

NOTES

1. Up to about 1931 research reports and statistical data dealing with the social origin of students, their religious identification, their occupational objectives, and the relationship between income and occupational qualifications appeared in the periodical literature. In view of the fact that education at this time was regarded as a socially determined process, such research was common, but it failed to produce systematic theoretical generalizations.

2. See Rene Ahlberg, "Die sowjetische Gesellschaftswissenschaft und die empirische Sozialforschung," *Osteuropa* 13 (1963), pp. 679–694. [Since the completion of this study in 1966 some Soviet research on current sociological problems in education based on empirical investigations carried out in a few cities and rural districts has appeared. See M. N. Rutkevich, "Zhiznennye Plany molodezhe," *Sotsiologicheskie issledovaniia*, volume II (Sverdlovsk, 1966) and "Sotsiologicheskie problemy narodnogo obrazovaniia," *Uchenye zapiski, Sbornik* 56 (Sverdlovsk, 1967). See also M. Yanowitch and N. Dodge, "Social Class and Education: Soviet Findings and Reactions" *Comparative Education Review*, 1968, pp. 248–267.—ed.]

3. An example of this is the collective work of about 70 American students and teachers who studied in the Soviet Union for several weeks. See G. Z. F. Bereday, W. W. Brickman, and G. H. Read, *The Changing Soviet School* (Cambridge, 1960). It is not based simply on sporadic observations of the Soviet school in operation but on systematic analysis of hard data.

4. See Erik Boettcher, "Offene Bildungswege in der Sowjetunion," in R. Dahrendorf and H. D. Ortlieb, *Der Zweite Bildungsweg im sozialen und kulturellen Leben der Gegenwart* (Heidelberg, 1959), pp. 152–173; Nicholas DeWitt, *Education and Professional Employment in the USSR* (Washington, 1961). (Although DeWitt's book deals primarily with the organization of the educational system, it is rich in sociological data.) See also Robert A. Feldmesser, "Social Status and Access to Higher Education, A Comparison of the United States and the Soviet Union" in *Harvard Educational Review* 27 (1957), pp. 92–106; Mark G. Field, "Some Sociological Perspectives on Soviet Education: Selection and Training for Advanced Studies" in George Z. F. Bereday and Jaan Pennar, eds., *The Politics of Soviet Education* (New York, 1960), pp. 175–191.

5. Students of aristocratic origin who attended the boy's gymnasium dropped from 73 percent of enrollment in 1863 to 32 percent in 1914, while students from urban classes and the peasantry rose, respectively, from 24 to 57 percent. In ordinary secondary schools the ratio between these groups was even more "democratic." Out of every 100 students who attended the university in 1914 36 came from the aristocracy and civil-service families, 39 percent from the middle class, the petty bourgeois, and the working class,

and 14 from villages. See Nicholas Hans, *History of Russian Educational Policy, 1701–1917* (London, 1931), p. 239.

6. *Lenin o narodnom obrazovanii, Stat'i i rechi* (Moscow, 1957), p. 21.

7. See the relevant documents in Oskar Anweiler and Klaus Meyer, *Die sowjetische Bildungspolitik seit 1917: Dokumente und Texte* (Heidelberg, 1961).

8. According to the census of 17 January 1939, 81.2 percent of the population over 9 years of age and 89.1 percent between 9 and 49 could read and write. See DeWitt, *op. cit.,* p. 72.

9. See V. Kasatkin, "Kak obsluzhivaiutsia nashei shkoloi deti rabochikh?" in *Narodnoe prosveshchenie*, 1928, no. 10, pp. 26–36, and Sergius Hessen and Nikolaus Hans, *Fünfzehn Jahre Sowjetschulwesen* (Langensalza, 1933), p. 80 ff.

10. In the ninth year of school the proportion of working-class children dropped from 37.3 to 17.9 percent, whereas children of white-collar employees went from 31.8 to 54.2 percent of enrollment at that stage. Kasatkin, *op. cit.*

11. M . Aleksinskii, "Voprosy obshcheobrazovatel'noi shkoly" *Vestnik prosveshcheniia*, 1928, no. 5–6, p. 7.

12. At the start of the 1927–28 school year, 9,910 million children in the USSR were in grades one through four; 1,332 million in grades five through seven; and only 126,625 in grades eight and nine. See *Kul'turnoe stroitel'stvo SSSR* (Moscow, 1956), p. 122.

13. *Ibid.,* p. 123.

14. See the CK decisions of 12 July 1928 and 16 November 1929 in *Die sowjetische Bildungspolitik seit 1917*, Documents 46 and 49.

15. See the decision of the Central Committee, CPSU (B) of 26 July 1929 in *Direktivy VKP (b) po voprosam prosveshcheniia*, 2nd ed. (Moscow-Leningrad, 1930), pp. 171 ff.

16. DeWitt, *op. cit.,* p. 577.

17. See A. V. Kol'cov, *Kul'turnoe stroitel'stvo v RSFSR v gody pervoi piatiletki (1928–1932)* (Moscow-Leningrad, 1960), p. 158; statistics concerning some universities are included.

18. I am employing the designation used by Richard Pipes in his article, "The Historical Evolution of the Russian Intelligentsia," which appears in his book *The Russian Intelligentsia* (New York, 1961), pp. 32–46.

19. The workers' faculties ceased functioning in 1940, while evening schools around this time hardly amounted to anything.

20. See the Decree of the CEC and the Council of People's Commissars of the USSR of 29 December 1935, "Concerning University and Technical School Admission Policy" in *Direktivy VKP (b) i postanovleniia sovetskogo pravitel'stva o narodnom obrazovanii: sbornik dokumentov za 1917–1947 gg.*, II (Moscow-Leningrad, 1947), p. 89, and VO of the Council of People's Commissars of USSR of 21 June 1944, "Concerning Measures for Im-

proving the Quality of Instruction in the Schools" in *Die sowjetische Bildungspolitik seit 1917*, Document 91.

21. *Die sowjetische Bildungspolitik seit 1917*, Document 83.

22. Compare DeWitt, *op. cit.*, p. 64 ff.

23. *Die sowjetische Bildungspolitik seit 1917*, Document 82 and notes.

24. In 1958, 46.2 percent of all students in grades one through ten were in urban schools, while 53.8 percent were in rural schools. In the upper grades (eight through ten), however, 55.9 percent were in urban schools, 44.1 in rural schools. See DeWitt, *op. cit.*, p. 142.

25. Memorandum "On Strengthening Ties Between School and Life and on the Further Development of the Public Educational System in the Country" of 21 September 1958 in *Die sowjetische Bildungspolitik seit 1917*, Document 102. (Russian Original: *Pravda*, March 21, 1958.)

26. The corresponding Russian designations are: (1) *Nepolnoe srednee obrazovanie*; (2) *polnoe srednee obrazovanie*; (3) *srednee special'noe obrazovanie*; (4) *vysshee obrazovanie*. In Anglo-Saxon usage groups 1 and 2 correspond to primary and secondary schools, group 3 to specialized secondary or semiprofessional schools, group 4 to colleges and universities.

27. Compare DeWitt, *op. cit.*, p. 439 ff.

28. It may be of interest to compare these figures with those in the USA (1959), if only because the Soviet Union likes to engage in such comparisons when it is to their advantage to do so. In the USA, of the 122.8 million inhabitants over fourteen years of age 79.8 percent had at least seven years of school, 41.3 percent had graduated from a high school (twelve years of school), a college, or a university, and 6.8 percent had finished at least four years of college education. See DeWitt, *op. cit.*, p. 440.

29. See Leopold Labedz, "The Structure of the Soviet Intelligentsia," in Richard Pipes, ed., *op. cit.*, pp. 63–79.

30. The division between these groups in many cases is somewhat arbitrary. For example, how does one classify shop clerks or laboratory assistants? For information regarding the basis of the census classification see *Itogi Vsesiouznoi perepisi naseleniia 1959 goda, SSSR* (Moscow, 1962), p. 11.

31. See the author's "Die Reform des sowjetischen Bildungswesens" in *Osteuropa* 9 (1959), pp. 128–143, and "Zwischenbilanz der sowjetischen Schulreform" in *Osteuropa* 11 (1961), pp. 285–301.

32. *Die sowjetische Bildungspolitik seit 1917*, Document 102.

33. In addition to my articles cited in note 31 compare Arnold Buchholz, *Neue Wege sowjetischer Bildung und Wissenschaft* (Cologne, 1963).

34. *Pravda*, 2 November 1961.

35. See M. T. Iovchuk, "Kul'turno-tekhnicheskii rost rabochego klassa SSSR" in *Voprosy filosofii*, 1960, no. 7, pp. 34–49. (Under the same title there appears a multi-authored volume by Iovchuk *et al.* which gives the research results in detail.) See also *Sotsial'no-ekonomicheskie problemy tekhnicheskogo progressa* (Moscow, 1961); *Tekhnicheskii progress i voprosy*

truda pri perekhode k kommunizmu (Moscow, 1962).

36. See Hartmut Vogt, "Die Erwachsenenbildung in der Sowjetunion" in *Berliner Arbeitsblätter für die deutsche Volkshochschule* 19 (1963), pp. 1–56.

37. S. G. Strumilin, *Problemy socializma i kommunizma v SSSR* (Moscow, 1961), pp. 369–396.

38. M. T. Iovchuk, "Nepreryvnyi pod'em kul'turno-tekhnicheskogo urovnia rabochikh—zakonomernost' razvitiia sotsialisticheskogo obshchestva," in *Sotsial'no-ekonomicheskie problemy tekhnicheskogo progressa* (Moscow, 1961), p. 194.

39. See DeWitt, *op. cit.*, pp. 248–251.

40. See the announcement regarding new admission standards for universities that appeared in *Pravda*, 4 June 1958, in *Die sowjetische Bildungspolitik seit 1917*, Document 101.

41. *SSSR v tsifrakh v 1961 godu* (Moscow, 1962), p. 324.

42. Decree of the Council of Ministers of the USSR of 18 September 1959 in *Srednee special'noe obrazovanie v SSSR* (Moscow, 1962), p. 218 ff.

43. During academic year 1961–1962 54.5 percent of all Soviet students in higher education and 49.2 of all students in specialized secondary education were taking evening or correspondence courses, most of them continuing their education in their present profession or in the specialized area for which they were trained.

44. *Die Sowjetische Bildungspolitik seit 1917*, Document 102.

45. See Eugene Lemberg, "Begabtenauslese und Begabungspflege im sowjetischen Bildungswesen" in *Recht und Wirtschaft der Schule* 2 (1961), pp. 65–69.

46. See Bernhard Schiff, "Fremdsprachenunterricht in der Sowjetunion" in *Osteuropa* 13 (1963), pp. 810–817. Text of Decree of the Council of Ministers of the USSR of 27 May 1961 is to be found in *Pravda*, 4 June 1961.

47. A sociological analysis of the student body in such schools would certainly confirm the impression of various people who have visited these institutions that they are "elite schools" for the urban intelligentsia.

48. Since 1961, when it was disclosed that there were not going to be 2.5 million boarding school students by 1965 as originally planned, Soviet statistics combined the figures relating to pupils in boarding schools and extended day schools.

49. A. M. Arsen'ev, "Edinstvo tekushchikh zadach perestroiki Sovetskoi shkoly i perspektiv sozdaniia kommunisticheskoi sistemy narodnogo obrazovaniia SSSR" in *Doklady Akademii pedagogicheskikh nauk RSFSR* (1962), no. 1, pp. 5–11.

50. See Arnold Buchholz, *Der Kampf um die bessere Welt*, 2nd edition (Stuttgart, 1962) and Georg Paloczi-Horvath, *Rebellion der Tatsachen* (Frankfurt a.M., 1963).

THE SOCIOLOGICAL IMPACT OF SOVIET ECONOMIC POLICY

KARL C. THALHEIM

Karl Marx has very sharply underlined the close link that exists between society and the economy. By stressing the interrelationship between social and economic variables, a relationship that is only marginally considered in classical economic teaching, he gave us a new perspective for viewing socioeconomic phenomena. It is truly amazing to observe, particularly when we remind ourselves that the Soviet system has always regarded Marx as its spiritual forefather, that Soviet science today has almost totally ignored the links between social and economic forces, as far as research on the state of affairs in the Soviet Union itself is concerned. With regard to the "capitalistic" world Soviet scholars have described these links in an extremely biased way; with regard to their own country they are only now beginning to inquire into current social realities.[1] This appears astonishing at first glance; a closer look soon discloses the great discrepancy that exists between social reality under Soviet communism today and the objectives of classical Marxism. This discrepancy between current reality and the ultimate goals of the Soviet Union's.spiritual forefather was largely the result of Soviet economic policy, particularly during the Stalin era.

211

The evolution of Russia gives us many examples of the inter-relationship between social and economic forces. We should remind ourselves here of the four unresolved social problems that afflicted old Russia: (1) the terrible condition of the large mass of Russian peasants, (2) the gloomy outlook for the rapidly growing industrial proletariat, (3) the lack of a strong middle class, and (4) the emerging attitude—partly due to economic reasons—of the Russian intelligentsia. The convergence of these four unresolved problems created a potentially revolutionary situation that laid the basis for the Bolshevik victory in the October Revolution. It was this revolution that would enable Russia to reach the ideal of a socialist-communist economic order, the basic features of which are described in classical Marxist thought.

The extent to which Bolshevik leaders really depended upon Karl Marx's conception of the future socioeconomic order in the formulation of their own plans is a debatable question. Many people maintain that Marx's teachings were not very important. I am essentially in disagreement with this contention and would prefer to state—perhaps a little too vigorously—the opposite view: that it was precisely the objective of the Bolshevik Revolution to realize his ideas in the reconstruction of the socioeconomic order. The fact of the matter is, in any case, that the Bolshevik Revolution triggered a revolutionary transformation of both the economic and social orders.

I regard as critical the fact that in West and Central Europe the industrial revolution generated by capitalism was caused primarily by natural social forces even though it was hastened by economic, political, and legal decisions rooted in economic liberalism; on the other hand, in tsarist Russia, but even more so in Soviet Russia, it occurred as a result of conscious state planning; during the Bolshevik period, however, we must bear in mind that the Communist Party was naturally always the representative of the state's will. And we must also bear in mind that in the various countries of the Soviet empire, in East-

Central Europe, in Southeast Europe, just as in the Communist countries of Asia, the revolution has been imposed from above with extreme force.

In order to transform the socioeconomic order from stem to stern in accordance with the revolutionary goals of Marx, the Bolsheviks have resorted, directly and indirectly, to a whole series of drastic measures. The indirect methods used were politico-economic and fiscal in nature. There was no room, of course, for the operation of an independent economy in the Soviet system—for the economy was an essential part of what was to be a totally planned and centrally directed social system; by the same token, measures that by traditional Western standards would be regarded as political and economic in nature were carried out in the Soviet Union for sociopolitical and not for economic reasons. In the course of the last decade the harnessing of economic policy in the Western world for essentially sociopolitical purposes has also grown in importance; I think here of the nonfiscal goals which fiscal policy, in almost every country of the Western world, seeks increasingly to achieve.

In addition to direct methods of nationalizing or collectivizing the political economy I would like to offer a few examples of the various ways in which policies fundamentally politico-economic and fiscal in nature were designed for sociopolitical purposes. Chief among them is tax policy. After the end of the NEP period those small private enterprises that were allowed to survive or to start up during the NEP were quietly done away with by means mainly of a confiscatory tax policy which rendered the continuance of these concerns impossible. Those aware of conditions in the Soviet zone of Germany are also familiar with the cold and calculated policy of socialization that was instituted after the first great wave of nationalization had taken place, almost paralleling the methods used by the Soviet Union after the termination of the NEP. We find, too, that the Soviet Union has used tax policy for sociopolitical purposes in the most recent past. For when Khrushchev so modified the

income tax, the abolition of which meanwhile was stopped, that
the full effect of the tax relief would favor only those with small
incomes, but also reduce the salaries of those employees in middle and high income categories in part or equal to the amount
of the abolished income tax, a measure that was primarily financial in character became socially relevant. This was part and
parcel of a whole series of measures by which Khrushchev
attempted to reduce the income gaps that developed during the
Stalin era.

Another example was the use made of credit policy; at the
end of the NEP period credit policy in the Soviet Union varied,
as it did later in the Soviet zone of Germany, depending on
whether government enterprises, producers' cooperatives, or
private businesses were involved. The policy was designed to
discriminate against certain kinds of enterprises, which for sociopolitical reasons were to be eliminated. A final example is the
varying delivery rates charged for shipping goods from large,
medium, and small farm enterprises; these rate differentials had
little to do with the efficiency of these farm operations and
were intended actually to eliminate large farmers. Here again
the same policy was followed in the Soviet zone of Germany.

The basic outline of the change in social structure which
emerged from the reorganization of the economic system is well
known. Unfortunately, however, we have little specific information about these changes in the social structure and men's place
in that structure. At least we are unable to identify the changes
which have been introduced by using ordinary standards of scientific research. I have already mentioned that empirical research on social processes is just beginning in the Soviet Union.
Nevertheless, it is important that we look closely at these original research efforts, if only for the reason that Soviet statistics
relative to social processes are extremely fragmentary. This is
particularly the case with respect to the growth and distribution
of income. As a consequence this study will actually raise more
questions than it is able to answer.

What aspects of Soviet economic policy are sociologically relevant? Obviously one could produce a long list of such factors, but the limits of this study will permit us to emphasize only those policy matters that are critically important in terms of their sociological impact. In my view seven aspects of Soviet economic policy seem to be particularly relevant.

1. The general socialization, or collectivization, of the means of production.
2. The Communist Party's domination of the state apparatus and its accompanying influence, through its corps of functionaries, upon the organization of the economy.
3. Central planning, important for two reasons: first, it necessitates a large apparatus in which men receive positions and jobs the social functions of which are highly specified; second, it defines the main goals of the economy, these goals being set by those who shape the political will of the state with no participation on the part of the masses.
4. The decision to maximize economic growth in order to "match and overtake that of the most developed capitalist countries."
5. An emphasis upon industrial growth.
6. The primacy of heavy industry.
7. A strong emphasis on the establishment of large and giant concerns, which is of special sociological significance.

Relevant also is the question: What sociological factors are important in determining the impact of these aspects of Soviet economic policy? First, and of fundamental importance, is the general problem of the individual's relationship to society. Second, the social structure raises the very important question—which I do not pretend to answer—of the extent to which it can really be understood with the use of Western sociological models and categories. Third, there is the income structure; fourth, there is the question of social mobility; fifth, there is the status of individual social groups, such as workers and white-collar employees, concerning whom we must distinguish between clerical and technical employees; sixth, there is the matter of the position and functions of social organizations, represented, for the most part, by trade unions; and finally, there is the social structure of economic enterprises.

Obviously this does not exhaust the relevant queries, for many other important questions could be asked. For example: what is the sociological impact of Soviet economic policy upon the family; what is the impact upon the family of employing women in such a wide area of the economy? Other important queries which do not fall within the scope of this inquiry concern the links between the ruling system and the economic system, not to mention questions of political sociology. In any case, at this stage of inquiry we can give only partial answers to the questions raised above.

With regard to the general relationship between the individual person and society it is quite clear to me that under Soviet communism, now as before, the individual is wholly subordinate to the collectivity or society. The question is whether this is an inevitable consequence of Soviet economic policy. In my view it clearly is, particularly where property relations are concerned; total socialization of society is the direct result of the primacy that is accorded to the collectivity. "Socialistic" property is incompatible with private property and is in opposition to the classical liberal notion that the individual is entitled to maximal freedom; this notion appears to have been wholly irrelevant to the proletariat's initial demand for liberation and the later demand to be free of class distinctions.

The idea of freedom did not wholly lose its vitality, but it was a far different notion than that implied in liberal theory. The concern here was not with individual freedom as such, but with class freedom, especially freedom from class domination. In the perennial conflict between freedom and equality, which the French Revolution mistakenly sought to resolve, the latter, namely equality, appeared to be considerably more important as the final goal of pure communism. It is paradoxical that on

the way to this final goal Soviet society today has realized neither freedom nor equality, but instead exhibits an extreme lack
of freedom along with a considerable measure of inequality. The
primacy of the society has been something of a political slogan
in the Soviet zone of Germany in recent years. The state's participation and entrance into producers' cooperatives was made
palatable for the few remaining private businessmen and craftsmen by the assertion that this would permit them to take the
"step from the I to the we" and thus enable them to avoid the
blemish of being capitalist exploiters.

The affirmation of the primacy of the collectivity resulted in
a general rejection of any private ownership of the means of
production and, thus, of any independent economic activity. I
emphasize: "the *general* rejection" of such activity. This is the
special feature that distinguishes communism, except for the
peasant agricultural economy in Poland and Yugoslavia, from
every other form of Western socialism today. This extreme radicalism was illustrated also by the original organization of the
smallest peasant and industrial enterprises into producers' cooperatives. For a long time these were officially and customarily
referred to as cooperative production enterprises. They enjoyed
some measure of autonomy, and were regarded as "lower" in
contrast to "higher" forms of socialist property—a value judgment if there ever was one—but later were taken over entirely
by the state. In recent years, too, most Soviet trade associations
have been transformed into state enterprises while the establishment of state farms—that is, state ownership of agricultural
property—goes forward irresistibly, as statistics show. The radicalism reflected in these goals, finally, is documented also by
the attempt to curtail the private economic pursuits of the
kolkhoz peasants. These private activities are referred to as
"auxiliary economic enterprises." Beyond this the government
is also seeking to stop the private raising of livestock. Khrushchev reduced considerably these small "farm estates," although
experience showed that here the economic situation required

exactly the opposite, namely the expansion of private enterprise, especially where livestock was concerned.[2] The goals for producing goods from livestock were not even remotely achieved, partly because this was the area of the private economy that had the best chance of reaching these goals, yet it was severely restricted —all of which seems to validate my thesis that ideology still today plays a decisive role in the Soviet Union.

Actually, central planners in the Soviet Union are forced to place the collective goals of the economy over private desires. They might, quite naturally, consider individual interests, but only if this appears desirable or necessary for psychological or political reasons.

The maximization of economic growth, being the central aim of the Soviet system, requires high rates of growth, which is impossible without high investment quotas. But this means a reduction in the amount of material goods available for individual consumption. The consequence of this, however, is to lower the standard of living.

To what extent actually are the main goals of Soviet economic policy—the general socialization of the means of production, central planning, and the maximization of economic growth— prescribed in classical Marxism? I believe that we have to distinguish between the relative importance of each in Marxist theory. Socialization of the means of production appears to be central to his teaching; this is indeed a necessary consequence of Marxist thought. But one might ask whether Marx actually intended to socialize property off which an individual secures his livelihood and where there are no additional hired hands; for example, the craftsman or small farmer working on property used for the support of himself and the immediate members of his family. Here there would seem to be no alienation since property is not being used to exploit workers. Apart from this it is nevertheless true that the socialization of the means of production is clearly the main supposition of classical Marxism.

Central planning is also a derivative of Marx's theory in view of its critique of the "anarchy of capitalist ways of production." Marx's basic critique inexorably leads to the conclusion that this "anarchy" must be replaced by central planning and direction of economic affairs. On the other hand, it is not at all certain how much Marx wanted to maximize economic growth. At the very least, one can say that this principle is not a necessary consequence of Marx's theory. Yet somehow all three factors are linked together in the following way: If an economic system claims to be superior—and Marxists make unquestionably clear that this is the case with regard to the economic order they seek to install—then this superiority would have to manifest itself in high managerial circles, since rapid economic growth is considered to be the result of managerial leadership. Thus, economic growth is accelerated, not only because it enhances a country militarily or because such growth is a useful propaganda weapon, particularly in developing countries, but also because it constitutes proof of the economic system's superiority.

Let us now consider the social structure. All seven aspects of Soviet economic policy mentioned earlier have somehow contributed to the change that has occurred in the social structure. This change, mainly economic, was brought about by industrialization and other measures designed to hasten this process. Industrialization is by far the most deep-seated kind of change, for it molds and transforms all spheres of human life. When the economy undergoes fundamental change through industrialization nothing remains untouched by it, neither the organization of society, political or cultural affairs, nor even the basic pattern of human existence.

To describe the depth of such changes that have taken place in the Soviet Union I would like to begin with the occupational structure, notwithstanding the dearth of available statistics on this matter. In 1928 agricultural workers constituted about 80 percent of all employed workers, which was actually somewhat more than the 1913 figure (around 75 percent). After the inauguration of the five-year plan the number of people employed by industry grew from one five-year period to the next, while agricultural workers declined to 55 percent of the work force in 1937 and to 37 percent in 1961. This drop in the number of agricultural workers to less than half of what it was in 1928 represented a fantastic rate of change. On the other hand, when comparing these figures to those of advanced Western countries, one finds that this development has not reached its final stage; only 8 percent of the population is employed in agriculture in the United States; in the Federal Republic of Germany the figure is around 11 percent. One can hardly assume that the Soviet Union will entirely catch up to these two countries, but the gap is still very considerable. On this point—and one that Eric Boettcher develops in his book *Die Sowjetische Wirtschaftpolitik am Scheidewege* [The Soviet economy at the crossroads] —it appears to me still very important that among this 37 percent are substantial reserves of men available for purposes other than agricultural work; indeed, they cannot immediately be assigned to other kinds of work, but over the long haul, as agriculture slowly mechanizes, they will be absorbed by other enterprises.

The decline in agricultural workers is in sharp contrast to the increasing number of men employed in industry and other non-agricultural areas of the economy. Men involved in industry and the construction trades increased from 8 to 33 percent between 1928 and 1961; those involved in ordinary commerce and the restaurant business went from 3 to 6 percent; in 1913, however, the latter was a little higher at 9 percent. The dip here was due to the long neglect of Soviet economic planners to develop retail trades. Transportation and the mail service increased their share of employees from 2 to 7 percent of the working force, a necessary by-product of industrialization. Finally—and this is important—those engaged in the field of education and health services shot up from 2 percent in 1928 to 12 percent in 1961.[3]

An occupational redistribution of this magnitude is obviously of great sociological significance, since the social climate of workers engaged in mining, industry, or railways is totally different from the agricultural setting from whence they came. In addition to the reordering of the occupational structure brought about by long-range economic planning, the respective policies of socialization and collectivization changed the status of various professions and occupations. The socialization and collectivization of the economy resulted in the complete elimination of certain social groups which in all Western countries have played a number of important roles, while other social groups have arisen in their stead. For example, those groups which no longer exist today in the Soviet Union are large landowners, "capitalist" contractors, together with the "independent middle class," that is, small entrepreneurs engaged in handicrafts (except for some wholly unimportant exceptions), in small businesses (these having existed during the NEP period), in commerce, and in transportation. In all Western countries these are precisely the areas where individuals have the best opportunity for independent entrepreneurship. A fourth group that has totally disappeared are the capital investors; a fifth group, with very few exceptions, are the independent farmers.[4] By contrast, cooperative farmers and cooperative craftsmen are two of the wholly new social categories that have sprung up in the Soviet Union; to be sure, the importance of cooperative craftsmen had declined with the conversion of commercial producers' cooperatives into state enterprises. The cooperative farmer, the kolkhoznik, has no counterpart in the West; a producers' cooperative of this type, if it exists at all, would be wholly unique in a Western country.

Workers today constitute, therefore, the principal component of the Soviet population. The Soviets have continued to retain the distinction between "workers" and "white-collar employees" although there is no longer any legal distinction between these two groups. This is also the case in the Soviet zone of Germany. In this connection the 1959 census gives us, for the first time, comprehensive figures on the composition of the Soviet population. According to these data a total of 99.1 million persons

were employed in 1959; 63 million of these were workers and
white-collar employees, while 32.2 million were kolkhoz peasants or laborers engaged in other cooperative agricultural enterprises; 0.3 million were individual peasants together with
"noncooperative" domestic workers who still exist in the Soviet
Union. Since individual peasants barely number 100,000 there
must be around 200,000 *kustari*, that is, commercial homeworkers or domestic tradespeople. Those in the army number about
3.6 million. Thus a good two-thirds of all those employed are
employees and workers; not included in these figures, of course,
are those family members of the agricultural population who
serve as helping hands on the premises. They number around
10 million.

The 63 million are, with very few exceptions, employees of
the state. So far as I am able to make out there are only three
exceptions: employees of consumer cooperatives who are not
part of producers' cooperatives, a few employees—but these are
rare—who actually do work for producers' cooperatives, and,
finally, a very small number of private domestic employees. The
fact that the state employs nearly everybody is, in terms of the
workers' social position, of utmost importance, particularly since
there are no counterbalancing influences flowing from independent trade unions or other representations of workers. The
state is both employer and labor-law giver, and it is because of
this that the worker's freedom is extremely limited.

This is the problem with a "socialized" economy. Ideologically,
socialism is supposed to give the worker maximum freedom after
having liberated him from capitalist exploitation; in reality,
however, the socialist system reduces him to a vassalage, the
severity of which is absolutely unimaginable within the framework of a market economy or a free sociopolitical order. We
might even ignore the fact that forced labor, although it has
diminished considerably since the Stalin era, still exists in the
Soviet Union[5] and constitutes not only the most extreme in-
fringement of human liberty but also the greatest debasement

of the original aims of classical Marxism; these laborers are nothing more, really, than "serfs of the state." But the fact that the individual worker, in the absence of the protection which autonomous union organization can give, also finds himself up against the power of a state that controls nearly all reproductive property means that his individual sphere of freedom is very limited.

One important result of industrialization was the deep-seated change that it brought in the population distribution in city and country. In 1926 the urban population was 23 million, and by 1959 it had soared very close to 100 million, constituting nearly one-half of the Soviet population. This overwhelming shift in the population balance was an inevitable by-product of the particular form that industrialization assumed in the Soviet Union; for the resettlement pattern was determined largely by the regime's preference for large-scale industrial enterprise, the demographic effect of which was to sharply curtail the birth rate and to effectively control population growth.

The following two factors are also of sociological significance. First, while a large number of unskilled workers were being replaced by machines, other parts of the labor force were receiving additional basic training. This training, however, was not always the equivalent of vocational training; automation demands new forms of highly skilled labor that does not necessitate vocational training as such; rather, it is training that seeks to communicate skills of precision judgment and capacity for decision going far beyond what was normally demanded of the trained worker in the past. The second factor is an increasing number of white-collar employees, owing not only to industrialization itself, but also to its secondary effects. Industrialization generates necessarily growing complexity in the social, political, and administrative structure; a large number of new job openings must be created as a consequence, way over and above that for which industry itself is directly responsible. In the Soviet system we must also consider the effects of central planning, mentioned earlier.

This demands a multitude of functionaries who perform white-collar responsibilities in both central offices of the state and in enterprises which have to handle an unending array of secretarial tasks, reports, statistical information, and so forth.

Thus rapid industrialization resulted in an enormous expansion of the white-collar working force. Between 1926 and 1959, according to Soviet statistics, the number of engineers, technicians, and agronomists increased from 267,000 to 4,683,000, teachers from 486,000 to 3,276,000, doctors and medical personnel from 199,000 to 1,702,000, while the number of scientists went from 14,000 to 316,000. We have no reason to doubt the veracity of these figures, since they correspond to the impression that we have otherwise acquired with respect to social development in the Soviet Union.

This leads me to mention what in my view constitutes the most important sociological effect of this entire process. That is the development of a broad middle class made up of a large group of men who, owing to their socioeconomic status, are at the very center of the social structure, even though in terms of income part of this group makes less money than top-level industrial workers. This is not unique to the Soviet system, however; the same is true in the Western world. By the same token, when measured in terms of their material well-being, many working men also belong to the middle class.

The growth of white-collar employees has still not reached its potential; in this respect the Soviet Union lags far behind Western countries, particularly in the area of service trades. In the United States today less than half of the employed are engaged in the production of material goods; it is precisely in the service trades that the number of employees is particularly high. The Soviet Union, however, is just now only at the start of such a development but is clearly headed toward the development of a social structure similar to that of Western countries.

Only a small part of those who are involved in industry actually belong to the upper class. These are the industrial managers, who are materially much better off than the mass of workers; on the other hand, though their social status is high, their future depends on the state and party respectively, on their capacity to fulfill state plans, and probably also on the degree of their popularity or unpopularity with existing party functionaries. Thus, they enjoy a good deal of prominence, yet are quite insecure.

But then we must ask: How much politico-economic influence does this group of "socialist managers" wield? When I think of the outcome of the Liberman discussions I am inclined to conclude that this influence is rather small. In these discussions the economic managers were almost wholly on the side of Liberman and those political economists in agreement with him; but the practical conclusions that political leaders drew from these discussions have been carried out only on a very limited basis up to now. This is one indication of the relatively small political and economic influence that has been exercised by this group.[6]

Regarding income structure the following six points seem to be of importance:

1. In the Soviet Union there is hardly any unearned income; unearned income that actually does exist (e.g., interest on savings, bank deposits, and government loans) is not very important to the social structure.

2. The amassing of wealth is strictly the business of the state —if we can disregard those durable consumer products such as houses—and not that of private persons. The rate by which the state has accumulated wealth is very high, but the general standard of living, as a consequence, is very low; there are no private property owners to whom this wealth accrues. I am convinced that both of these factors will play a very great role in any future contest with Soviet communism, particularly since the matter of unearned income has long been under fire.

3. The policy of economic growth and the effort to accelerate production at any price which was instituted in the Stalin era brought about major differentiation in income distribution.

4. High rates of growth forced the broad masses to reduce substantially their consumer demands. And still their income is far below that of developed industrial countries, and even below that which another economic policy—one that might not have sought to maximize economic growth at any cost—might have yielded in the Soviet Union.

5. In my opinion efforts made by the Soviets to exceed their planning goals—at least now as they seek to create the material-technical basis of communism, a movement that according to Khrushchev was not to culminate until 1980—is forcing them to maintain the principle of allocating rewards based on achievement and thus to generate very substantial differentiation in income.

6. Khrushchev tried to narrow these income gaps by raising incomes that were especially low and by making certain cutbacks in the salaries of "socialist managers" at the top.[7] I am convinced, however, that in the interest of increased economic output any effort to close the gap between income differentials will be confined to very limited areas. It is safe to say, in fact, that in regard to these income differentials, Khrushchev and, most notably, Stalin sacrificed the original Marxist ideology to the demands of reality.[8] Let us recall the thesis that Marx urged in his 1875 critique of the Gotha Program: Under socialism rewards would be distributed according to achievement; under communism according to needs. This is still the real justification for such wide income differences based on achievement in Soviet communism today. To be sure, I am convinced that Marx, when, in 1875, he announced the principle of distribution according to achievement under socialism, had not contemplated such wide gaps in income that developed in the Soviet Union during the Stalin era.

We must say a few words on the subject of social mobility.

Opportunities for measurable upward mobility, which for the broad masses of the population is independent of social origin and the material status of parents, has doubtless been one of the great attractive features of the Soviet system. Three things are extremely important in this connection: first, the need to compensate for the disappearance of the old leading class; second, the opportunities that a policy of economic growth has generated since 1928; third, educational policy. The social background changes of communist leaders seem to me to be particularly interesting. Bolshevik leaders—the "old guard"—were with very few exceptions men with nonproletarian origins; by contrast, today's leaders are in large measure of proletarian or peasant origin.

The following questions appear quite relevant here: Was the personnel need already satisfied in some leading occupations? Were there substantial cutbacks in projections for more personnel? What impact did the solidification of a new upper class —along with the hindrance to upward mobility that was caused by basing recruitment into the upper class as much as possible upon heredity—have upon opportunities for advancement?

With reference to the status of social groups two further points, in addition to the questions already discussed, are, in my view, of particular relevance. The first is social security. One can hardly argue that the Soviet economic system guarantees the individual a greater measure of social security than that which is possible in a market economy, if personal security is won at the cost of individual freedom; if this is the case, then the price is very high indeed. The other relevant point concerns social prestige. All propaganda is aimed at making the worker and peasant believe that they are living in a "worker-farmer state"; this belief is now really an ideology in the fullest sense of the word.[9] For the Soviet Union is no longer a worker-farmer state; rather, it has become a state of functionaries. Social prestige is now wholly a matter of titles, ranks, and medallions; one can point out, for example, that with reference to the value of particular occupational groups the social prestige of technicians is much higher than that of commercial white-collar employees, a fact that is heavily underlined by different levels of pay.

A few words, finally, should be said about the status and functions of social organizations. The unions come first to mind. During the initial phase of Bolshevik rule unions still retained their independence; but they completely lost it under Stalin, and the situation today seems hardly to have changed in this respect. Unions have no autonomy, for in actuality they are subordinate to the Communist Party. As a consequence, union objectives have also wholly changed; unions are no longer associations of workingmen whose first and virtually sole objective, at least in a market economy, is the betterment of the men represented by the union, together with the achievement of better working conditions. Soviet unions are primarily instruments for achieving the country's economic goals, fulfilling its plans, increasing its productivity, and lowering costs. It is not an exaggeration to say that unions constitute little more than the long arms of the state in the area of economic administration; I am mindful of Lenin's famous reference to a transmission belt here. With respect to these new functions, unions have received absolute powers of enormous significance; some of these powers have to do with the administration of the entire social security program, some with the functions of union operating committees, etc.

It appears to me that the social structure of industry has not at all changed in the post-Stalin era. Now, just as before, it is governed by the principle of *edinonachalie*, that is, exclusive control by an operating manager appointed by the state. To be sure, this operating manager finds himself up against two competing groups, namely the party organization and the union operating committee. They are not, however, competing groups in the sense that the union operating committee, for example, would have to represent primarily the social interests of the workers vis-à-vis planned economic goals. The new mechanisms created in the course of Khrushchev's economic reforms appear to have given merely the illusion of codetermination; we are mindful here of the "regular production conferences," the strengthening of rights of union operating committees, and also the production committees that Khrushchev referred to in his November 1962 speech before the CC of the CPSU. When all is said and done, however, the autocratic structure of industry has not been modified at all by these institutions; they have done little to increase the social status of workers.

Let me summarize. The social structure of the Soviet Union today is almost wholly determined by the collective ownership of the means of production and by the Communist Party and its economic goals, and particularly its attempt to maximize economic growth and productivity. The goal of maximizing economic growth is actually much more important to Soviet communism than the classical socialist imperative of doing away with social distinctions. A "society of equals" appears to be, according to the new party program, the hope and promise of the future; however, I believe that this is a utopian dream. Accordingly, despite many improvements and changes in the workingman's lot, social reality in the Soviet Union, even in the post-Stalin era, has gone way beyond that which the early socialist order was expected to yield; this discrepancy is usually justified by Marx's statement of 1875, which proclaimed that the first phase of socialism would be governed by the principle that rewards would be allocated on the basis of achievement. On the other hand, the policy of maximizing economic output—here one could speak simply of a genuine dialectical development— has permitted the growth of a modern industrial society which is far different from Russia under the tsars. And we can now take note of the demands that this maturing industrial society is beginning to make. For example, since the beginning of the Seven-Year Plan particularly, home construction has gone forward at a much greater pace than before; this would appear to be one effect of a changing social structure, especially the growth of a broad middle class for which satisfactory living space is a most important social need. Continuing attempts to improve the social situation, undertaken partly for formal and propagandistic purposes, appear to be an expression of the discrepancy between a modern industrial society, which Soviet economic policy has created, and styles of human living which are not appropriate to such a society. It is this factor that is of critical importance to the future of Soviet communism.

NOTES

1. Indeed, empirically oriented sociological research in the Soviet area has recently undergone a significant upsurge.

2. After Khrushchev's fall from power these restrictions have again been lifted; however, now as before, there is obviously no intention to expand the area of private plots.

3. It is indeed possible that the available statistics are misleading with respect to the size of this group because of their statistical definition.

4. After the 1959 census there were still 92,000 individual peasants.

5. See Boris Meissner's chapter "Social Change in Bolshevik Russia" in this volume.

6. On 4 October 1965 the Council of Ministers of the USSR passed an "ordinance Concerning Socialist State Production Firms." The uncommonly careful and cautious manner in which the suggestions of reformers were realized through this ordinance suggest, in the opinion of the author, that the influence of economic managers, who overwhelmingly approve of transferring greater decision-making authority to industries, could not have been very great.

7. See Meissner's chapter "Social Change in Bolshevik Russia."

8. This in no way corresponds to the image of Stalin, promoted in many Western countries, as an ideologue and of Khrushchev as a realist or pragmatist.

9. See Meissner's chapter "Social Change in Bolshevik Russia."

SOVIET SOCIETY UNDER KHRUSHCHEV'S SUCCESSORS

BORIS MEISSNER

Opposing tendencies have conditioned social development in the Soviet Union since Khrushchev's fall. On the one hand, with Stalin's partial upgrading, organizational structures characteristic of the Soviet ruling system have been restored. On the other hand, economic measures going beyond those of Khrushchev have been adopted. The changed style of leadership and shift in accent that have resulted from these developments are quite evident; indeed, they bear all the external signs of moving away from "Khrushchevism," yet signify no real departure from a system of "enlightened totalitarianism." It should be noted also that Khrushchevism was characterized by a continuous oscillation between a hard and soft line and by an attempt to play the forces of change and inertia against one another.

Under Brezhnev and Kosygin these contrasting tendencies have continued.[1] There was no retreat from "destalinization" at the Twenty-third Party Congress of the CPSU in March-April 1966. Too many social forces in the Soviet Union have a vested interest in sticking to the "destalinization" policy. Yet it has ebbed perceptibly. The new general line adopted by the Twenty-third Party Congress is a curious attempt economically to more effectively adjust to the demands of a modern industrial society but culturally to more rigidly tighten the reins.

The first aim was achieved by the limited economic reform that is associated with Kosygin's name and which went into effect in the fall of 1965.[2] This reform combined centralized planning and direction with more independence for state-owned enterprises. Economic planning was oriented somewhat more to market volume and earning capacity, hence to profit and not only to gross production. This was done in the consumer goods industries and in some other branches of the economy on the basis of careful orders by businesses and trade organizations. Thus, a better accommodation was struck between need and production, conforming to the well-known recommendation of Professor Liberman. By the summer of 1968 some 11,000 industrial enterprises were affected by the new economic policy.

This policy has been relatively successful and, more importantly, has led to the increased growth of the Soviet economy.[3] The extension of this policy to less efficient enterprises actually reduced its initial driving force. What is more, accelerated armaments production hindered the further construction of deficient branches of the economy, especially agriculture, and at the expense of long-range development (infra-structure, etc.).

The sociological significance of this economic reform is that it largely strengthens the power position of the state and the economic bureaucracy vis-à-vis the party bureaucracy, restoring conditions as they existed prior to the 1957 reform in economic administration. The primacy of the state and economic bureaucracy has actually limited the influence of "party organizers," who predominate in the party bureaucracy, to their supervisory function. At the same time the Twenty-third Party Congress seemed to approve the attempt of "party ideologues" to maintain the primacy of the party bureaucracy and to infuse into the main party apparatus a new self-consciousness. The new economic policy did bring about a better balance inside the top bureaucracy, but simultaneously it solidified the ruling position of the power elite as a whole.

Enterprise directors, the actual operating managers, have gained only minor benefits from these reforms, which currently provide them with no greater influence on policy than before. Kosygin has rightly resisted alien voices that have favored the introduction of a market-oriented economy in the Soviet Union and a "return to the path of capitalistic economic stewardship." He emphasized that the very nature of the economy depends on "the kind of people who control the state and means of production, and on the classes in whose interest production is developed and profits distributed."[4] Because of the current structure of Soviet society there is no doubt that the top bureaucracy, and particularly the party bureaucracy, which constitutes the former's political nucleus, can be characterized as a "ruling class."

While the party bureaucracy fears that these economic reforms, as they are currently operating, could undermine its totalitarian rule, they do not go far enough for the progressive elements of the technico-economic intelligentsia. Among economic managers and economists included in the prestige elite are forces which represent ideas very similar to those which have been espoused by Professor Ota Sik in Czechoslovakia. The chairman of the GOSPLAN, Baibakov, reported at the May 1968 "Economic Union Conference" that some progressive Soviet economists want more restrictions on central planning, greater autonomy for industry, and a stronger injection of competition into the market, along with a price system that is based solely on product value.[5] Present Soviet leaders have emphatically denied that a "socialist market economy" will be introduced and have reacted sharply against Sik's proposals for economic reform in Czechoslovakia. A much greater danger, in the eyes of the "collective leadership"—made up of the eleven full members of the Politburo—is the scientific-cultural intelligentsia's attraction for the liberal ideas of the Prague reformers.

The fear that these ideas of reform-oriented Communists would infect Soviet society was clearly the principal motive for the Soviet Union's military intervention in Czechoslovakia.

In the area of cultural affairs a freeze had already occurred prior to the Twenty-third Party Congress and meanwhile assumed the character of a "Kulturkampf."[6] The trial of the literati in Moscow together with the criminal prosecution of rebellious intellectuals in Leningrad and the Ukraine show that Soviet leaders of today will not shrink from using terroristic means to put down opposition forces.

The trial of Siniavskii and Daniel before the Moscow municipal court in January 1967[7] was followed by the trial of Ginsburg, Galanskov, Dobrovolskii, and Lashkova in January 1968.[8] Ginsburg had written a "White Paper on the Siniavskii-Daniel trial"[9] that he had forwarded to President Podgorny, while Galanskov had authored a study called "Russia's Road to Socialism," which was directed at the class dictatorship of the bureaucracy.[10] The trial against the young literati brought forth, as was the case with the earlier convictions of Siniavskii and Daniel, numerous protests from members of the prestige elite and other Soviet citizens.[11] Especially noteworthy was the letter of A. K. Efimovich—a kolkhoz chairman from Lettland—to Central Committee Secretary Suslov,[12] in which he characterized the prosecution of young dissenters in a country 50 percent of whose population is younger than thirty years of age "as an extremely dangerous policy, as adventurous." He appealed to party leaders to have the judgment against the literati reviewed and the mistake corrected, since workers and peasants have not yet involved themselves in this affair.

Opposition groups in Leningrad and the Ukraine must have occasioned even greater concern for Soviet leaders, for the former had committed themselves to the renewal of socialism.[13] With regard to events in the Ukraine the Lvov journalist, Chernovil, reported in a white paper what had followed from his conviction.[14]

It may be of crucial importance that the opposition within the scientific-cultural intelligentsia against totalitarian one-party rule and thus against the bureaucratic-class dictatorship is steadily expanding and that its progressive elements have developed a pronounced political consciousness. This has become very clear from the white papers of Ginsburg and Chernovil and particularly from the June 1968 memorandum of the atomic physicist, Professor Sakharov. Sakharov's basic conviction, which seems to be shared by wide circles within the Soviet intelligentsia and especially by the younger generation, is that intellectual freedom is indispensable to the Soviet industrial society if it expects to make any progress at all. This includes freedom of information, speech, and thought. Sakharov sees such intellectual freedom threatened mainly "by a calcified dogmatism of a bureaucratic minority and its favorite weapon, which is ideological censure." Intellectual freedom, he thinks, will be secured by the intelligentsia, whose subordination "to the will of the party or, more precisely, to the party apparatus and its functionaries" it rejects. Only the complete guarantee of intellectual freedom—resisted not only by the party bureaucracy but also in part by the managerial group, which has a vested interest in the existing system—can, according to Sakharov, return to the "public" and the "creative intelligentsia" their proper role in controlling the plans and decisions of the ruling group.

For liberal elements of the intelligentsia the progressive development of the Soviet Union depends basically on weeding out the last vestiges of Stalinism, abolishing censorship (in the broadest sense of the word), and doing away with the special privileges of the top bureaucracy and leading economic managers. Sakharov mercilessly attacks the inhuman character of Stalinism. The historical value of Khrushchev, regardless of his Stalinist past or the feebleness of his policies, lies mostly in the fact that he paved the way toward a confrontation with Stalinism.

Sakharov's conclusion about the real class structure of Soviet

society, based on his analysis of the Stalinist system, is similar
to the one arrived at in this book. He points out that Stalinism,
i.e., Soviet totalitarianism in its despotic form, "led to the
emergence of distinct classes in the Soviet Union, to a bureaucratic elite which occupied all key positions and whose members were rewarded with direct and indirect privileges." He saw
this as an important, even if not the only, reason for the "vitality
of neo-Stalinism."

The demands made in the Sakharov memorandum, which
would push Soviet society into a post-totalitarian phase of industrial development, coincide with the action program of the
Prague reformers to the extent that these demands are relevant
to the current situation.[15] They express the sharp clash between
Moscow's orthodoxy and the model of reform communists in
Czechoslovakia.

The present oligarchy in the Kremlin considers itself to a
greater extent than Khrushchev did as a representative of the
ruling bureaucratic class. It is much more dependent on the
party and state bureaucracy and also on a military organized
along national-conservative lines than was the case under the
leadership or despotic rule of one man. On the other hand, there
has never been for long a "boyar dictatorship" in Russia. History shows that the trend toward one-man rule is inherent in
autocratic-totalitarian systems. Moreover, the old Politburo
structure makes leadership changes inevitable. The current "collective leadership" has neither the power nor even the will
to carry out the comprehensive reforms that are necessary for a
new stage of Russian development. Only a strong personality
supported by the liberal forces of the entire intelligentsia could
bring about such a monumental change in direction. The future
of Soviet society is critically dependent upon whether such a
personality will emerge in the years ahead.

NOTES

1. See Boris Meissner, "Die KPdSU zwischen Reaktion und Fortschritt," *Osteuropa* 16 (1966), p. 416 ff., and "Die Sowjetunion vor und nach dem 50-Jahr-Jubiläum," *Osteuropa* 18 (1967).

2. See H. H. Höhmann, "Die Sowjetische Wirtschaftsreform vom Herbst 1965: Ausmass und Bedeutung der institutionellen Veränderungen," in K. C. Thalheim and H. H. Höhmann, eds., *Wirtschaftsreformen in Osteuropa* (Cologne, 1968), p. 41 ff.

3. See H. B. Sand, "Die sowjetische Wirtschaftsreform in der Praxis: Erste Ergebnisse und Probleme," in Thalheim and Höhmann, eds., *Wirtschaftsreformen in Osteuropa*, p. 68 ff., and K. Busch, "The Reforms: A Balance Sheet," *Problems of Communism*, July-August 1967, p. 30 ff.

4. A. Kosygin, "Referat auf dem Plenum des ZK der KPdSU am 27. September 1965" in *UdSSR: Neue Methoden der Leitung der Wirtschaft* (Moscow, 1965), p. 81.

5. Text of the Baibakov Report appears in *Ekonomicheskaia gazeta*, 1968, no. 21.

6. See Th. McClure, "The Problems of Soviet Culture 1964–1967," *Problems of Communism*, March-April 1967, p. 26 ff.

7. See E. Hayward, *On Trial: The Soviet State versus "Abram Tertz" and "Nikolaj Arzhak"* (New York, 1967).

8. See the report on the proceedings of the trial in *Neue Zürcher Zeitung*, 9–16 January 1968.

9. Original Russian text and German translation (Frankfurt a.M., 1967).

10. See "Behindertes russisches Kulturleben," *Neue Zürcher Zeitung*, 1 February 1967; "Untergrundliteratur in der Sowjetunion," *Neue Zürcher Zeitung*, 10 September 1967.

11. Among the protesting intellectuals were Pavel Litvinov, the grandson of the former Soviet Foreign Minister; Aleksandr Esenin-Volpin, who was once again confined to an asylum, from which he along with Tarsis and two other authors had been released after Khrushchev's downfall; Major General Pyotr Grigorenko, pensioned off in retirement, who had attracted attention earlier by his courageous stand against all attempts at restalinization; the authors Vasily Aksenov, Bella Akhmadulina, and Boris Vakhtin; Larissa Daniel, the wife of the author currently in custody; the artist Vasily Weissberg; the atomic physicist Andrei Sakharov, the mathematician Igor Shaforevich, and the biologist Yury Vakhtin.

12. *International Herald Tribune*, 9–10 March 1968.

13. With regard to the well-known underground groups whose members have been condemned in secret trials see A. Amalrik, "Will the USSR Survive Until 1984?" *Survey*, Autumn 1969, p. 50, note 6. The largest illegal organization was the All-Russian Social Christian Union for the Liberation of the People, which had its center in Leningrad. It was to have established affiliates in the Ukraine, in the Urals, and in West Siberia. Four members were given eight- to fifteen-year prison terms in December 1967, i.e., still prior to the trial of the Galanskov-Ginsburg group. Other intellectuals were brought to trial in Leningrad in March 1968. See *Der Spiegel*, 1968, no. 17, p. 135.

14. The white paper appeared in 1967 under the title, *Lykho s rozumu-portrety dvadcaty "slozhynciv"* [Understanding produces sorrow—portraits of twenty "criminals"] in the publications of the Ukrainian immigrant newspaper *Ukrainske Slavo* [Ukrainian word] in Paris. See *Neue Zürcher Zeitung*, 11 January 1968.

15. The text of the Sakharov-memorandum appears in *Die Zeit*, 9 August 1968. See also the 19 March 1970 letter of Professors Sakharov, V. F. Turchin, and R. Medvedev to the Soviet leader in *Neue Zürcher Zeitung*, 22 and 24 April 1970.

CONTRIBUTORS

OSKAR ANWEILER is Professor of Education at the University of Bochum in the Ruhr. His principal books are *Die Rätebewegung in Russland 1905–1921* and *Geschichte der Schule und Pädagogik in Russland vom Ende des Zarenreiches bis zum Beginn der Stalin-Ära.*

BORIS MEISSNER is Professor and Director of the Institute for Eastern Law at the University of Cologne. He is an executive committee member of numerous scholarly institutes, including the Board of Directors of the Seminar for Eastern Studies. Among his works are *Russland, die Westmächte und Deutschland, Russland unter Chruschtschow, Das Parteiprogram der KPdSU,* and other books on the Soviet Union.

KARL-HEINZ RUFFMANN is Professor of East European History at Erlangen-Nürnberg University and a member of the Board of Directors of the Seminar for Eastern Studies in Cologne. He is the author of "Russland (Sowjetunion) seit 1905" in *Weltgeschichte der Gegenwart,* Vol. I, and "Der Sowjetkommunismus" in *Kommunismus in Geschichte und Gegenwart,* Vol. 2.

KARL C. THALHEIM is Professor Emeritus at the Free University in Berlin. He was formerly Director of the East European Economics Department of the East European Institute. He is an executive committee member of various institutes concerned with Eastern questions, including the Seminar for Eastern Studies in Cologne. His main works are *Grundzüge des sowjetischen Wirtschaftssystem* and *Beiträge zur Wirtschaftspolitik und Wirtschaftsordnung.*

INDEX

Achminow, G. F., 149 (n. 150), 167 (n. 280)
Ahlberg, R., 154 (n. 178), 160 (n. 220), 207 (n. 2)
Akhmadulina, B., 239 (n. 11)
Aksenov, V., 70, 239 (n. 11)
Aleksinskii, M., 208 (n. 11)
Alexandrow, K., 154 (n. 181)
Amalrik, A., 240 (n. 13)
Amburger, E., 22 (nn. 11, 20)
Andreev, A., 59
Andreeva, G. M., 160 (n. 224)
Anweiler, O., 147 (nn. 82, 88), 150 (n. 116), 156 (n. 193), 208 (n. 7)
Arendt, H., 169 (n. 296)
Arsen'ev, A., 210 (n. 49)
Arzhak, N., 154 (n. 181)
Arzumanian, A., 160 (n. 221)
Auhagen, O., 146 (n. 62)

Baibakov, 235
Bauer, R. A., 159 (n. 214), 161 (n. 232), 163 (n. 251), 171 (nn. 317, 318)
Berdyaev, N., 148 (n. 94), 169 (n. 305)
Bereday, G., 207 (n. 3)
Beria, L., 60, 67, 171 (n. 323)
Berlin, I., 149 (n. 105)
Berlinius, H., 157 (n. 199), 164 (n. 256)
Bettelheim, Ch., 93
Bezkov, I., 3
Bialer, S., 152 (nn. 153, 154), 163

(n. 251), 171 (n. 323)
Bill, V., 22 (n. 19)
Black, C. E., 2, 21 (n. 6), 22 (nn. 14, 17), 143 (n. 1)
Blum, J., (n. 7)
Boettcher, E., 207 (n. 4), 220
Boiter, A., 157 (n. 200)
Brezhnev, L., 233
Brickman, W., 207 (n. 3)
Brodersen, A., 154 (n. 178)
Brunner, G., 148 (n. 97)
Brutzkus, B., 144 (n. 25), 145 (n. 28), 146 (n. 61)
Brzezinski, Z., 169 (n. 296)
Buchholz, A., 210 (n. 50)

Catherine II, 3, 4, 7, 13
Chernovil, 236, 237
Churchill, 36, 146 (n. 64)
Condorcet, 177
Croner, F., 120, 162 (nn. 245, 246)

Dahm, H., 154 (n. 176)
Dahrendorf, R., 136, 137, 139, 140, 162 (n. 244), 164 (n. 263), 165 (n. 266), 166 (n. 272), 170 (nn. 308, 309, 311, 312, 313), 171 (n. 321)
Dallin, D., 49, 68, 147 (n. 83), 150 (n. 110)
Daniel, I., 154 (n. 181), 236
Daniel, L., 239 (n. 11)
Dawydow, E., 147 (nn. 71, 72)
DeWitt, N., 147 (nn. 82, 89), 182,

243

208 (nn. 8, 16), 209 (nn. 22, 24, 27, 28), 210 (n. 39)
Djilas, M., 167 (n. 285), 169 (n. 305), 170 (nn. 307, 314)
Dobrovalskii, 236
Draht, M., 169 (n. 298)
Dreitzel, H., 125, 165 (n. 267)

Eason, 21 (n. 2)
Efimovich, A., 236
Ehrenburg, 70
Engel, 31
Esenin-Volpin, 71, 154 (n. 181), 239 (n. 11)
Evtichiev, I., 162 (n. 240)

Feldmesser, R., 21, 145 (n. 39), 152 (nn. 150, 155), 153 (n. 163), 207 (n. 4)
Fischer, 21 (n. 2)
Friedrich, C., 169 (n. 296)

Galanskov, 236, 240 (n. 13)
Geiger, Th., 171 (n. 319)
Gerschenkron, 21 (n. 2)
Ginsburg, 237, 240 (n. 13)
Glezerman, 160 (n. 225), 164 (nn. 257, 259)
Gliksman, 21 (n. 2)
Golikov, A., 146 (n. 47)
Golubeeva, N. V., 157 (n. 201), 158 (n. 203)
Granick, D., 163 (n. 250)
Grigorenko, P., 239 (n. 11)
Gronyi, I., 3

Haimson, L., 155 (n. 182)
Hans, N., 208 (nn. 5, 9)
Hayward, E., 239 (n. 7)
Hindus, M., 98, 117, 157 (n. 196), 159 (nn. 207, 214, 217), 161 (n. 237)
Hingley, R., 154 (n. 175)
Hitler, A., 132

Hofbauer, H., 162 (nn. 247, 248)
Hofmann, W., 163 (n. 249), 165 (n. 271), 169 (n. 305), 170 (n. 306)
Höhmann, H., 239 (n. 2)
Hunter, F., 171 (n. 325)

Iadov, 158 (n. 202)
Iakovlev, B., 148 (n. 98)
Ignatiev, P., 177
Inkeles, A., 149 (n. 106), 150 (nn. 111, 115), 159 (n. 214), 161 (n. 232), 163 (n. 251), 166 (n. 274), 171 (nn. 317, 318)
Iovchuk, M., 209 (n. 35), 210 (n. 38)

Jasny, N., 149 (n. 101)
Jenker, S., 157 (n. 197)
Johnson, P., 154 (n. 179)
Jugow, A., 93, 144 (nn. 19, 23, 25), 145 (nn. 27, 43, 44), 146 (n. 48)

Kasatkin, V., 208 (n. 9)
Kautsky, K., 148 (n. 93)
Kavelin, K., 6
Khrushchev, N., xiv, 59, 60, 63, 64, 65, 66, 67, 68, 70, 74, 99, 102, 103, 104, 133, 154 (n. 181), 158 (n. 204), 162 (n. 241), 171 (n. 323), 186, 194, 195, 200, 202, 213, 214, 217, 226, 229, 231 (nn. 2, 8), 233, 237, 238, 239 (n. 11)
Kim, I., 143 (n. 13)
Kornilov, A., 22 (n. 9)
Kosygin, 233, 234, 235, 239 (n. 4)
Kriwoshein, P., 22 (n. 12)
Krüger, H., 124, 165 (nn. 264, 265)
Krupskaias, N., 177
Kugel, S. A., 78, 79, 86
Kulckhohn, C., 159 (n. 214), 161 (n. 232), 163 (n. 251), 171 (nn. 317, 318)

Kurilov, F., 159 (n. 218)
Kuz'min, E. S., 157 (n. 201), 158 (n. 203)

Labedz, L., 161 (n. 232), 209 (n. 29)
Laeuen, H., 149 (nn. 107, 108), 151 (n. 127)
Lambert, H., 143 (n. 8)
Lashkova, 236
Laue, Th. von, 21 (n. 2)
Lemberg, E., 210 (n. 45)
Lenin, 16, 23, 24, 25, 28, 29, 32, 35, 45, 72, 74, 100, 136, 137, 173, 177, 228
Leonhard, W., 152 (n. 152)
Lepeletier, 177
Lewytzkij, B., 162 (n. 241)
Liashchenko, P., 21 (n. 7), 143 (n. 14), 145 (n. 26), 146 (nn. 49, 52, 60)
Liberman, J., 225, 234
Litvinov, P., 239 (n. 11)
Löwenthal, R., 133, 146 (n. 55), 151 (n. 131)
Luchenko, N., 143 (nn. 10, 12)
Ludz, P., 133, 134, 164 (n. 260), 168 (n. 295), 169 (nn. 300, 302, 303)
Lunacharskii, A., 177
Lutchenko, A., 160 (n. 223)

McClure, Th., 239 (n. 6)
Malenkov, G., 35, 60, 63, 66, 67, 146 (n. 58), 171 (n. 323)
Malia, M., 15, 16, 22 (n. 14)
Markert, W., 145 (n. 31)
Marx, K., 24, 31, 34, 72, 136, 137, 198, 204, 211, 212, 213, 218, 219, 226, 229
Mayakovsky, 30
Meder, W., 153 (n. 158)
Medvedev, R., 240 (n. 15)
Mehnert, K., 146 (nn. 59, 69), 149 (nn. 104, 106), 150 (n. 111),

163 (n. 253)
Meissner, B., xi, xii, 143 (nn. 3, 5), 145 (nn. 36, 42), 146 (nn. 53, 56), 147 (n. 87), 148 (nn. 90, 96), 149 (n. 103), 150 (n. 117), 151 (nn. 132, 133, 134, 144, 145), 152 (nn. 146, 148, 151), 153 (nn. 159, 164, 166, 167, 170), 155 (n. 186), 158 (n. 204), 164 (nn. 260, 261), 169 (n. 297), 171 (nn. 316, 324), 231 (nn. 5, 7, 9), 239 (n. 1)
Mihajlov, M., 155 (nn. 183, 188), 159 (n. 218), 168 (n. 294), 171 (n. 319)
Mills, C., 171 (n. 325)
Molotov, V. M., 107, 109
Morstein-Marx, 161 (n. 239), 162 (n. 243)

Nariza, 154 (n. 181)
Nash, E., 167 (n. 286), 168 (n. 287)
Nifontov, A., 22 (n. 9)

Oganoskii, N., 144 (n. 19)

Paustovski, 70
Peter the Great, 4, 52, 56, 176
Petroff, P., 93, 143 (n. 9)
Pfaff, D., 155 (n. 185)
Philipp, W., 14, 21 (nn. 6, 7)
Pipes, R., 15, 22 (n. 15), 208 (n. 18)
Podgorny, 236
Pod"iachikh, P. G., 79, 80, 81, 90, 91
Pollock, F., 143 (n. 9), 146 (n. 67)
Popov, M., 158 (n. 203)
Portal, R., 16, 17, 21 (n. 7), 22 (n. 16)
Prokopovich, S., 41, 144 (n. 24), 145 (n. 28), 146 (nn. 51, 63), 146 (nn. 65, 66), 147 (nn. 74,

76, 77, 79, 80, 81)
Pugachev, E., 19

Rauch, G. von, 143 (n. 2), 146 (n. 50), 148 (n. 95), 149 (n. 102), 151 (n. 128)
Raupach, H., 145 (n. 28), 151 (nn. 128, 129)
Read, G., 207 (n. 3)
Robinson, G., 22 (nn. 9, 10, 11)
Romanovich-Slavatinskii, 21 (n. 4)
Rosenberg, A., 145 (nn. 32, 37)
Rossi, P., 166 (n. 274)
Rostow, W. W., 155 (n. 187)
Rozkova, M., 21 (n. 7)
Ruffmann, K. H., 21 (n. 3), 143 (n. 1), 150 (n. 118)
Rutkevich, M., 106, 107, 116, 160 (n. 225)

Sakharov, A., 237, 238, 239 (n. 11), 240 (n. 15)
Sand, H., 239 (n. 3)
Schelsky, H., 139, 171 (n. 321)
Schiff, B., 210 (n. 46)
Schiller, O., 144 (n. 23), 145 (n. 45), 153 (nn. 161, 162, 165), 159 (nn. 208, 213)
Schmidt, H., 147 (n. 73)
Schroeder, F., 152 (n. 147), 164 (n. 258)
Schwarz, S., 93, 148 (n. 100), 149 (n. 109), 156 (n. 195), 157 (n. 199)
Semenov, V., 105, 107, 110, 111, 116, 122, 163 (nn. 252, 255)
Sering, D., 155 (n. 184)
Shaforevich, I., 239 (n. 11)
Sieger, A., 151 (nn. 135, 136)
Sik, O., 235
Simonov, K., 70
Siniavskii, A., 154 (n. 181), 236
Sokolow, 144 (n. 22)
Solzhenitzyn, A., 155 (n. 188), 168 (n. 294)

Sorin, L., 168 (n. 294)
Specovius, G., 168 (n. 291)
Ssachno, H. von, 153 (n. 175)
Stahlin, K., 21 (n. 7)
Stalin, J., 32, 34, 35, 36, 43, 44, 45, 46, 47, 48, 51, 52, 58, 59, 60, 61, 62, 63, 64, 65, 67, 70, 96, 98, 100, 106, 107, 118, 119, 120, 129, 146 (nn. 54, 57), 147 (nn. 85, 86), 148 (n. 91), 149 (n. 105), 173, 175, 183, 185, 205, 226, 228, 231 (n. 8), 233
Stokls, G., 19, 21 (n. 7), 22 (n. 12)
Stolypin, P., 6, 11, 12, 18, 22 (n. 12)
Strumilin, S., 197, 210, (n. 37)
Studenikin, S., 162 (n. 240)
Stupperich, R., 21 (n. 7)
Suslov, 236

Tarsis, V., 71, 154 (nn. 180, 181), 168 (n. 284), 239 (n. 10)
Tertz, A., 154 (n. 181)
Thalheim, K., 143 (nn. 1, 4, 7), 145 (nn. 28, 35), 146 (n. 60), 152 (n. 156), 153 (n. 159)
Treue, W., 21 (n. 6)
Trotsky, L., 23, 25, 26, 143, (n. 11)
Turchin, V., 240 (n. 15)
Tvardovskii, A., 70

Vakhtin, B., 239 (n. 11)
Vakhtin, Y., 239 (n. 11)
Vlasov, V., 162 (n. 240)
Vogt, H., 210 (n. 36)
Volin, 21 (n. 2)

Wädekin, K., 88, 131
Wagenlehner, G., 143 (n. 6)
Wagenlehner, H., 167 (n. 279), 168 (n. 290)
Weissberg, V., 239 (n. 11)
Westen, K., 154 (n. 177)
Wittram, R., 21 (n. 5)

Yevtushenko, E., 70, 72

Zaionchkovskii, P., 22 (n. 9)

Zapf, W., 171 (n. 325)
Zdravomyslov, V., 158 (n. 202)
Zlatustovskii, B., 22 (n. 9)

WITHDRAWN